Published 1980 by Galley Press
© Copyright 1972, 1973, 1975, 1980 by
The Hamlyn Publishing Group Limited
London · New York · Sydney · Toronto
Astronaut House, Feltham, England
All rights reserved. No part of this publication may be
reproduced, stored in a retrieval system, or transmitted,
in any form or by any means, electronic, mechanical, photocopying,
recording or otherwise, without the permission of The
Hamlyn Publishing Group Limited.
ISBN 0 600 37430 0
Printed in Czechoslovakia

The material in this book appeared originally in the
following titles: *Answer Book of Bible History*, by
Jeremy Miller; *Answer Book of History*, by Plantagenet
Somerset Fry; *Answer Book of Science*, by Susan Baker, and
Answer Book of Astronomy, by Iain Nicolson.
52049

BIG BOOK OF
Questions
and
ANSWERS

Written by Susan Baker, Plantagenet Somerset Fry,
Jeremy Miller and Iain Nicolson.

Galley Press

CONTENTS

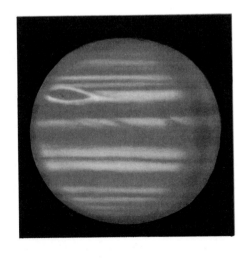

BIBLE HISTORY

What is the Old Testament?

The Old Testament is a wonderful collection of books rather like a library.

For many years, before writing was widely used, stories of the past were handed down by word of mouth. Later many of these stories were written down. Later still they were collected together. Sometimes collections of similar stories were joined together. So gradually, over a very long period of time, the books of the Old Testament were formed. Then, as writing came into use among the Hebrew people, scribes wrote down carefully the day-to-day history of their people.

When David was king a court historian wrote about the things that happened in his time. Some of the earliest pieces of writing we find in the Old Testament are poetry and songs which were easily remembered. All this took about eight hundred years, starting about 950 B.C.

What kinds of writing are found in the Old Testament?

The Old Testament is full of different kinds of books. There are books of history that tell of the great events of the past. There is a book of hymns that was used at the great religious celebrations. Much of the Old Testament is written in poetry, like the sermons preached by the prophets. Then there are stories with special meanings, written to explain what the Hebrews believed. There are books of laws too, often set out in great detail to show how God wanted the Hebrews to live together. There are laments, songs of love and victory; there are stories of people's lives and the thoughts of important men written down by their friends. All these many different kinds of writing had one thing in common – all shared a belief in God.

How did men of old learn about God?

Like all men the Hebrew people tried to find an explanation for the world around them and for the many things that happened to them. Sometimes, like Moses, they thought deeply about a problem and then grew sure that God too was thinking about that problem, and was wanting them to do something about it. When they followed their deep inner thoughts, they grew even more certain that God had helped them. They said, simply, "God spoke to me."

Others, like the prophets, grew very angry at the way rich men were cheating the poor and found God was angry too and wanted them to speak for Him. They said that God had called them.

As they learnt to look for God in all that happened to them, they found help, and said that God had guided them.

No one knows exactly when the world began, but we do know that the earth is millions of years old. The oldest rocks that have been discovered are over 3,500,000,000 years old.

The surface of the earth is constantly moving and changing. Rocks have been formed and grown old. Some have been worn down to form soil, or washed away to form new rock. Some have been compressed and become very hard and others have been changed when they became so hot that they melted. Geologists and other scientists have studied the structure of the earth and can tell what it may have been like millions of years ago.

The first forms of life were probably micro-organisms like bacteria and algae. Gradually plantlife developed, and later animals evolved slowly. Eventually the primitive ancestors of Man appeared about two million years ago.

Right Earth history begins with the birth of the Solar System with the Earth at the centre of the spiral. Numbers indicate how many millions of years ago events occurred. Geological records cover only the past two thousand million years. The history of civilized man represents a minute fraction of the history of the Earth.

When did the world begin?

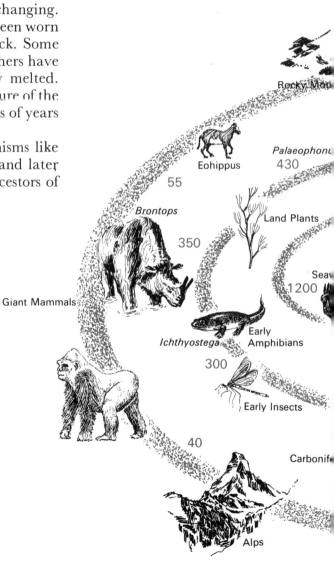

Rocky Mou

Eohippus
55

Palaeophonu
430

Brontops
350

Land Plants

Giant Mammals

Sea
1200

Ichthyostega

Early Amphibians
300

Early Insects

40

Carbonif

Alps

What is Genesis?

Genesis is the title given to the first book of the Old Testament. It means beginning, or origin, for Genesis is the book of beginnings.

Genesis starts with an explanation of the beginning of the world. We call this the creation story. It is a religious story which sets out the very deep beliefs of the Hebrew people. They were sure that the world they lived in did not start by chance but had been lovingly planned by God so that it was a good world for them to enjoy and care for.

Later in the book of Genesis we are told of the beginning of the Hebrew people in the distant land of Mesopotamia which is beside the two great rivers, Tigris and Euphrates, and was one of the great centres of the earliest civilizations. The story goes on to tell how the early ancestors of the Hebrews first came to the land of Canaan that was later to become their home.

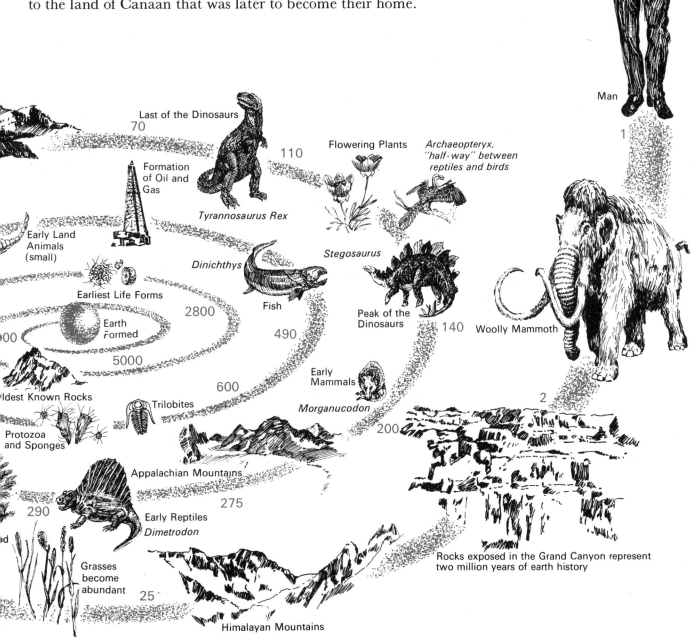

Man

Last of the Dinosaurs
70

Formation of Oil and Gas

Flowering Plants

Archaeopteryx, "half-way" between reptiles and birds

110

Tyrannosaurus Rex

Early Land Animals (small)

Dinichthys

Stegosaurus

Earliest Life Forms

2800

Fish

Earth Formed

Peak of the Dinosaurs

140   Woolly Mammoth

490

00

5000

Oldest Known Rocks

600

Early Mammals

Trilobites

Morganucodon

2

Protozoa and Sponges

200

Appalachian Mountains

275

290

Early Reptiles
Dimetrodon

Rocks exposed in the Grand Canyon represent two million years of earth history

Grasses become abundant

25

Himalayan Mountains

11

Running down through the centre of the land of Canaan is a valley. Through it flows the river Jordan which finally empties itself into a large lake called the Dead Sea. This sea is so salt that nothing lives in it or around it. About the time Abraham lived, two cities of Sodom and Gomorrah stood on its southern shore. Today these cities lie under the Dead Sea, for a great earth movement buried them. No doubt this earth movement released poisonous gases and geysers of boiling salt water. We think this happened about 1900 B.C.

Today nearby stand hills of nearly pure rock salt, worn away by rain to leave strange pillars like statues. In the Old Testament we read that Abraham's nephew, Lot, escaped from Sodom but his wife was turned to a pillar of salt.

Who was turned to salt?

Gen. 19, v. 24—28

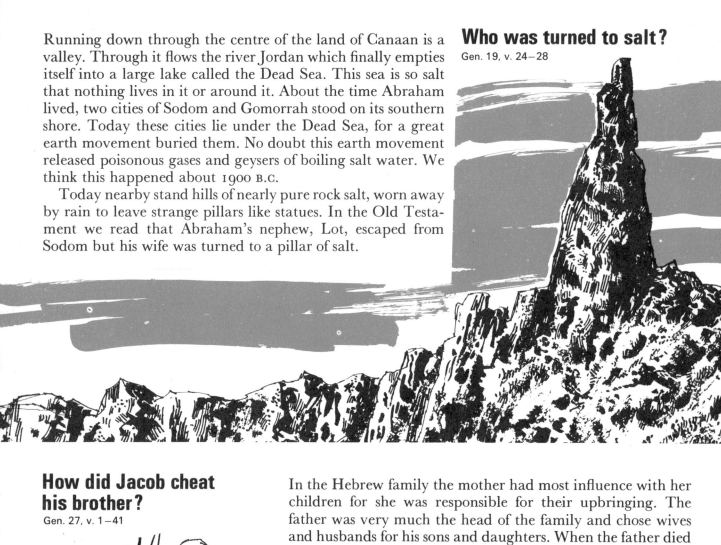

How did Jacob cheat his brother?

Gen. 27, v. 1—41

In the Hebrew family the mother had most influence with her children for she was responsible for their upbringing. The father was very much the head of the family and chose wives and husbands for his sons and daughters. When the father died his position was taken by the eldest son who also was given a double share of his possessions. This privilege was called the birthright and was greatly valued.

Now Abraham's son Isaac had twin boys, Esau and Jacob, and although Esau was a little older than Jacob, it was Jacob who gained the birthright. For when Isaac grew old the time came for him to bless his son Esau and give him the birthright. But Jacob cunningly pretended to be his brother and received the blessing instead. When Esau learnt this he was so angry that Jacob had to leave home to escape him.

Who were the Patriarchs?

Gen. 26, v. 17—22

The patriarchs were Abraham, his son Isaac and grandson Jacob, who were the ancestors of the Jewish people. All were nomads who lived in tents of goats' hair and moved from place to place seeking grass and water for their great flocks of sheep and goats. Mostly they kept to the uninhabited hills, only occasionally visiting the settlements on the fertile plains. They dug wells for water which they revisited from year to year. When water was scarce they would settle for a time on the grass lands of Egypt. Their life was very simple and they had few possessions. The patriarchs ruled over a tribe which included in its family, slaves and servants and their children.

During the day they cared for their animals, during the evening they sat around their camp fires and talked. The women cooked and weaved and cared for the children.

Below A Semitic family at the time of the Patriarchs, about 2000 B.C. This illustration is taken from a wall painting in the prince's tomb at Beni-Hasan on the river Nile.

At certain times in their lives the patriarchs felt God was very close to them. Very often, to mark the places where God had spoken to them, they raised a heap of stones or a stone pillar. Sometimes there would be a well there or a tree. Soon these places became thought of as places where God was especially found.

To show their loyalty to God they would make offerings to Him. Often they ate a sacred meal with the family and part of the meal would be offered to God at the stone pillar. Oil and wine would be poured over the stone, meat would be burnt. This helped them to feel God was there to share with them.

How did the Patriarchs worship?

Gen. 35, v. 9—15

What shape did the Hebrews believe the World to be?

Today we know much more about our wonderful world than the ancient Hebrews did. They thought the earth was flat, held up on pillars with a great pit beneath, like a bowl. The heavens above them in the sky were held up by mountains. They believed God lived in the heavens, and they called the pit beneath Sheol. In ancient times people thought everyone after they died lived a shadowy life in Sheol, but later a new belief grew, that God would rescue them from Sheol and they would live with Him.

Firmament of Heav

Earth

Sheol

In the south of Israel lies a dry barren area called the Negeb, or the dry land. This was part of the land over which Abraham and Isaac grazed their herds. Today we have re-discovered the wells that were originally dug by Abraham to water his flocks. They are wells of living water, for at the bottom of each well flows a clear fresh stream.

Thousands of small circular stone walls have also been found. Buried in them are the remains of ancient vines and olive trees. These stone walls were so marvellously made, that as the wind blew through them, the dew collected and watered the plant they protected.

So we have discovered how Abraham and Isaac were able to survive in such a dry land.

Why did the Patriarchs dig wells?

Below An Egyptian handmaid carrying water.

What were the ten plagues of Egypt?

Ex. 7, v. 11

When Moses asked Pharaoh to set the Hebrew slaves free, he first refused, but after a number of natural disasters he finally agreed. These disasters were called the ten plagues.

Egypt depended for its agriculture on the great river Nile. Every year it flooded, leaving behind rich fertile mud in which the crops were grown. That year the water became polluted, the fish died, dead frogs covered the land, flies spread disease and the cattle grew sick. There was a hailstorm which smashed the crops and a great cloud of locusts which ate all that was left. Finally there came a plague that attacked the young children, even Pharaoh's son died.

By now Pharaoh was convinced that there would not be an end to the disasters until the Hebrews left. He begged the Hebrews to go. Quickly making their preparations they left, taking gifts from the Egyptian people! It was not long however, before Pharaoh changed his mind.

The last night before the Hebrew slaves escaped from Egypt was called Passover—for that night the final plague struck. As a sign that it would "pass over" their homes, and their children would escape, they smeared lambs' blood on the door posts and the lintel.

That night they gathered in their homes and ate a hurried meal of roast lamb, unleavened bread and bitter herbs. This was the first Passover. Today, Passover is the most important Jewish religious festival. Once a year it is celebrated in every Jewish home with the same simple meal of roast lamb, unleavened bread and bitter herbs. This reminds them how God helped their people escape from Egypt long ago.

Traditionally, the youngest person present asks the head of the family, "Why is this night different from all other nights?" The answer is given, "We were slaves under Pharaoh in Egypt and God brought us forth out of Egypt." The bitter herbs remind them of the bitterness of slavery, and the unleavened bread of the haste in which they left Egypt and the hope of a better future.

What was Passover?

Ex. 12, v. 1–20

How did the Hebrews escape from the Egyptians?

Ex. 14, v. 5—31

The Hebrews escaped over the Egyptian frontier because a great disaster overcame the pursuing Egyptian army.

When the Hebrews saw the distant dust cloud, raised by the Egyptian chariots they panicked and turned on Moses, and accused him of leading them to their death for their way was blocked by water. But Moses remained confident.

It seemed that they were·trapped, but then the way opened for them to cross the water that lay ahead. They got safely over, but a great number of the Egyptian force was drowned when the shallow water they were trying to cross swept over them. They were trapped in the mud by the weight of their chariots.

Ever afterwards, with great thankfulness, the Jewish people looked back at what had happened. It gave them great confidence for the future.

Below right A tangle of papyrus reeds: taken from the tomb of Kenamon, 1600 B.C.

When the Hebrew slaves escaped from Egypt they had to cross a stretch of water called Ram Suph, which means Sea of Reeds. It was often written however, as Red Sea, not Reed Sea. The position of the Reed Sea remains a mystery.

No reeds grow by the Red Sea, but further north where to-day the Suez Canal runs, there were once shallow lakes and great reed beds. Perhaps it was here the Hebrews made their escape. Or perhaps it happened further south at the top of the Red Sea. For it has been known for strong winds to drive back the shallow waters there.

What was the Sea of Reeds?

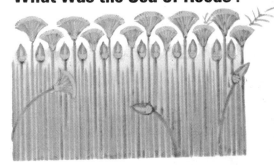

We are told that they ate manna, a white sugary substance, and quails, which are small brown birds of the partridge family.

In Spring great flocks of quails migrate from Africa to Asia and fly over the Sinai desert. After the birds have crossed the Red Sea they rest, exhausted, on the shore, and are easily caught by hand.

For water the people depended upon the small desert oasis, which Moses was skilled in finding. At Rephidim however there was no water and the people complained. Moses took his staff and struck a rock. Immediately water gushed out. Some years ago this mystery was explained. Some soldiers, of the Sinai Camel Corps, were digging under a large rock from which water trickled. When, by mistake, they broke off a piece of the hard surface of the porous limestone rock, the water was able to gush out.

What did the Hebrews eat in the Desert?
Ex. 16, v. 1−18

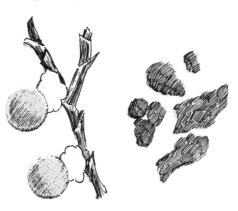

Left The Exodus of the Israelites began in the spring—the time of the great bird migrations. Even today, the Bedouin in this area catch the exhausted quails by hand as they rest on their migration flights.

Below A Bedouin camp in the desert.

What was Manna?

Ex. 16, v. 31—36

Left Manna must be collected early in the morning as ants are keen competitors for this sweet, honey-tasting food. The amount of manna available depends on favourable winter rains and varies from year to year. In good years, the Bedouin of Sinai can collect two kilos per head in a morning—a sufficient quantity to satisfy a grown man.

We have discovered that manna is a white sugary substance, which is good to eat and is formed by the plant louse. This little insect lives on the tamarisk trees in the Sinai desert and drops little sugary pieces which can be collected from the ground beneath. This manna must be collected early, for as soon as it becomes warm enough in the day, the ants come out and carry it off.

Today the Arabs gather it, for it forms a welcome addition to their food supplies. When it is first gathered it is white but it soon turns golden brown. It tastes rather like honey.

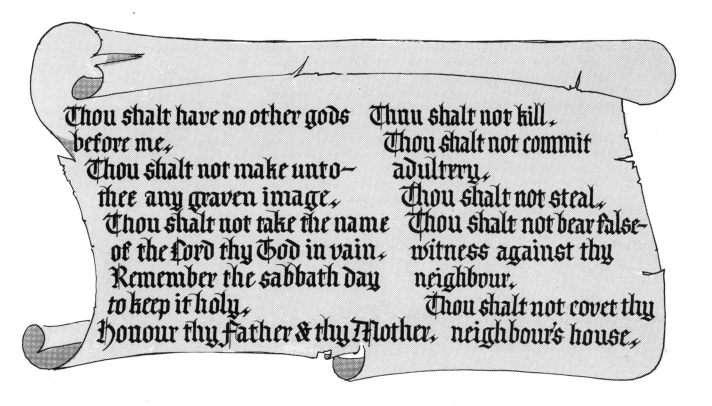

Thou shalt have no other gods before me.
Thou shalt not make unto thee any graven image.
Thou shalt not take the name of the Lord thy God in vain.
Remember the sabbath day to keep it holy.
Honour thy father & thy Mother.
Thou shalt not kill.
Thou shalt not commit adultery.
Thou shalt not steal.
Thou shalt not bear false witness against thy neighbour.
Thou shalt not covet thy neighbour's house.

What were the Ten Commandments?

Ex. 20, v. 1—17

The Ten Commandments were the ten laws or rules that Moses gave to the Hebrew people at Mount Sinai when they were wanderers in the desert. In the Hebrew language they are called the ten words or *Decalogue*. These ten laws told the Hebrew people how God wanted them to live.

They were to love God and to worship Him and no one else. They were to keep one day of the week, the Sabbath day, separate for God and they must not worship idols instead of God. The last six laws told them how they could live happily with others. Children should respect their parents. No one should kill or steal, take anyone else's wife or lie about others. No one should be greedy and envy someone else for what he owned. When Moses read these words to the people, they promised to keep the laws.

What was the Tabernacle?
Ex. 26

The tabernacle was a portable shrine where the Hebrew people worshipped God during their stay in the desert. It was often called the meeting tent. This tent was divided in two by a curtain. In the inner part, which was called the Holy of Holies, was a box which held two squares of stone. On these were written the ten commandments. In the outer part was a small table, an altar and a seven-branched candle-stick. Around the tent was a long screen of curtains to form a court 45 metres by 22 metres. In this court stood the altar for burnt offerings, and a large bowl.

What was the Ark of the Covenant?

Ex. 25, v. 10—22

The Ark of the Covenant was a box made of acacia wood. It was covered with pure gold inside and out, and four rings were fixed to its corners. Through these, two long poles were placed to carry it.

Usually it was kept in the tabernacle and on either side stood a winged figure with a human head made of gold, called a cherubim. Above the box was placed a gold throne called the mercy seat.

The Ark was thought of as the special place where God was. So when the Ark was carried into battle, God was thought to be with the warriors, fighting on their side.

What were the twelve tribes?

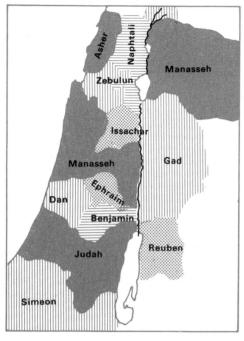

The twelve tribes were the twelve groups that made up the Hebrew nation. Each tribe takes its name from one of the twelve sons of the patriarch Jacob. The tribes were thought of as the descendants of each of Jacob's sons.

After the Hebrew people entered the land of Canaan and overcome its inhabitants, the land was divided up. Each tribe was given an area of the land for its own use. One tribe however, the tribe of Levi, became a tribe of priests and were scattered through the whole land.

Each tribe remained independent, with its own tribal ruler but when they were attacked they joined together to fight. This way of life continued for nearly two hundred years until the time came when they needed a king to rule over them and lead them into battle. Before they chose a king however, there was a time when men called the Judges became their leaders.

Who was Moses' successor?

Num. 27, v. 15—23

Joshua, with the children of Israel, before the walls of Jericho.

Joshua the son of Nun was Moses' successor. As a young man Joshua had been chosen as Moses' personal helper. On Moses' instructions he had led the people in their battle against the Amalekites, a wandering desert tribe. He had been one of the young men Moses had sent to spy out the land of Canaan. As Moses' helper, he had waited on him at the tabernacle. All this had helped train him as future leader of the people.

When Moses learnt that he was to die, he took Joshua into the tabernacle and made him the new leader. God assured Joshua that if he remained loyal to God, God would be with him as He was with Moses, but he must be strong and very courageous. Joshua's first task was to lead the people across the river Jordan and into the land of Canaan.

"Take up the ark of the covenant, and let seven priests bear seven trumpets of rams' horns before the ark of the Lord."
Joshua 6, v.6

What was "the promised land"?

Gen. 13, v. 14–18

The promised land was the land that God had promised to Abraham. God had told him that one day his descendants would inherit it. That promise had been made centuries before and it was not until many years later that the Hebrew people finally entered their new land under their leader Joshua.

The promised land was also called the land of Canaan, after the original inhabitants, the Canaanites. Moses had been told it was a land "flowing with milk and honey". This meant it was good, well-watered, land where crops would grow.

Canaan, which is called Israel today, is a small country about the size of Wales. Along the coast is rich fertile lowland. Alongside this plain, further inland, is a long range of limestone hills running from north to south. On the other side of these hills is the rich Jordan valley and beyond this are more hills and the desert.

Moses was the great leader who did more than anyone else to help the Hebrew people become a nation.

In Egypt they had been just a group of rather frightened slaves. Moses, with God's help, had rescued them. He had told them of God's promise to bring them to a land of their own. He had helped make them, though they were small in numbers, into a strong fighting force. He had given them laws to govern them. Most of all he had given them faith in God and themselves and a strong religion to hold them together. Before he died he pointed the way to their new country Canaan.

Under Joshua the land was conquered. But it was not until later that the Hebrew people finally became a nation. They were still divided in their tribes. They needed a king to unite them into a nation.

How did the Hebrews become a Nation?

Above The exact reason for the Queen of Sheba's visit to Solomon is unknown. It may have been to negotiate a trade agreement with Solomon, whose control of the trade routes jeopardized the income which the Sabaeans were accustomed to receive from the caravans which crossed their territory.

Why was Solomon called the wisest king?

1 Kings 10, v. 23—25

Just as David his father had gained a reputation for his music and poetry, Solomon, his second son, gained a reputation for writing wise sayings.

We are told that one night Solomon had a dream. In it God gave him one wish. Solomon asked for an understanding mind to help him govern the people. According to the dream, God was so pleased that He gave Solomon wealth and honour as well.

This reputation for wisdom is well illustrated in the story of the two women and the baby. Both had babies born on the same night, but one baby was accidentally suffocated. Each mother said the remaining baby was her own. So they went to Solomon to decide who should have the child. He ordered the baby to be cut in two, and half given to each! Of course, the true mother said, "No! Give the baby to the other woman rather than do that!" Solomon then gave the baby to this woman.

His reputation for wisdom spread far and wide. We are told that the Queen of Sheba, who was possibly an Arabian princess, went to visit him, taking lavish gifts.

At the very southernmost tip of Solomon's kingdom, a narrow finger of sea reaches in from the Red Sea. There Solomon built up a navy.

In about 1940 archaeologists were investigating this area, and they found the remains of copper and iron mines. They found the remains of miners' dwellings and moulds for casting the copper. They found smelting pots and the remains of a great blast furnace! It was skilfully made to funnel the desert wind through its flues to smelt the copper. Here then were the legendary mines of Solomon.

"King Solomon's Pillars" near Ezion-Geber on the gulf of Aqabah. This was the centre of the copper industry in the Ancient East.

Where were Solomon's mines?
1 Kings 9, v. 26-28

Why was Solomon so rich?
1 Kings 5, v. 13-18

Below Egypt was the chief exporter of war chariots and King Solomon had the monopoly of the trade.
1 Kings 10, v.28-29

Solomon had a great love of gold, and ceremony and display. He built magnificent palaces for himself and his wives. His three hundred-strong bodyguard carried shields covered with gold. His magnificent carved ivory throne was overlaid with gold.

Part of Solomon's great wealth came from trade with surrounding nations. He made trading agreements with Hiram, King of Tyre, and with Egypt. He exported copper by sea and took tolls from traders passing through his land. No doubt subject nations were forced to pay tribute to him. A great deal of his wealth, however, came from the taxes he forced his people to pay. He even made his people work for him without payment for one month in every three. After his death, because of the suffering he caused his people, they rebelled and the kingdom was split.

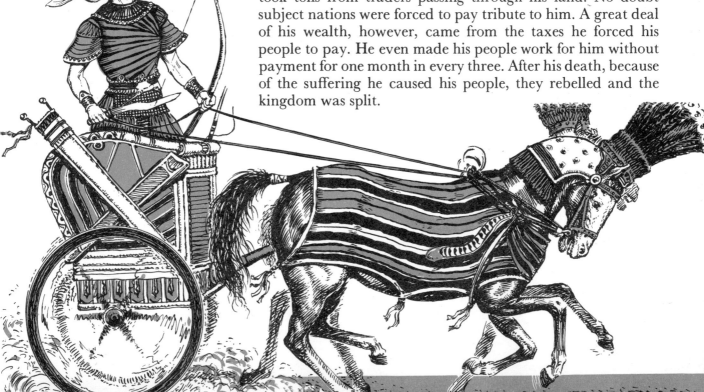

Solomon's father, David, had wanted to build a permanent home for God in Jerusalem, but it was Solomon who actually built the temple.

The congregation worshipped in the courtyard outside, where there was a great altar. Ten steps led up to the entrance hall with its huge cypress wood doors. On either side stood two ornate bronze pillars called Jachin and Boaz. Two more cypress wood doors led from the entrance hall into the main building. This was a room about 18 metres long, 10 metres wide and 14 metres high. It was panelled in cedar wood, and covered with carvings of palm trees, flowers, chains and cherubim. All was decorated with gold leaf.

In this main sanctuary was a small altar, a seven-branched candle-stick and a table. More steps led up into the Holy of Holies, a completely dark room, 10 metres square. In the centre was placed the ark of the covenant. Over it, two cherubim stood with outstretched wings – all was overlaid with gold.

What was Solomon's temple like? 1 Kings 6, v. 1–37

Solomon's practice of making his people work for him without payment had been hated. After his death, his son Rehoboam came to the throne. So the people chose Jeroboam, who had once been captain of the slave labour, to speak to the king for them. They wanted the king to ease the burden of slavery. Rehoboam consulted his father's councillors. They told him to give the people their wish, but Rehoboam took the advice of the young men of his court. "Tell the people: 'My father, Solomon, chastised you with whips, but I will chastise you with scorpions!'" So the break came. The ten northern tribes called Israel rebelled, and made Jeroboam their king.

Right **Map to show the divided kingdom of Israel in 850 B.C.**

Why was the Hebrew nation divided?

1 Kings 12, v. 1–20

Once Jeroboam became king he quickly set about building himself strongholds, one at Shechem and the other at Penuel, but there was a problem to solve.

If he allowed his people to go back to Jerusalem and worship at the temple they might transfer their loyalty to King Rehoboam—then Jeroboam would be in danger of his life! So he decided on a bold plan.

He set up new shrines at two old holy places. One at Bethel, the other at Dan. He appointed priests and held new festivals. At each of these shrines, he placed a golden calf. This was carved in wood and overlaid with gold. No doubt Jeroboam thought of them as the footstool of God—but it led the people away from their true God. For the chief god of the Canaanites had long been represented by a bull image.

Who set up the golden calves?

1 Kings 12, v. 25–29

27

Jezebel was the wife of Ahab, the king of Israel. Ahab's father, Omri, had built a new capital at Samaria and had made a treaty with the king of Sidon. This king had given his daughter Jezebel in marriage to Ahab as a sign of friendship. To please his new wife, Ahab the king had built her a temple at Samaria so that she could worship her god, Baal Melkart.

Now Jezebel was a determined woman, and she was set on making her religion the religion of Israel. First she brought in nine hundred and fifty of her own holy men, and then started to wipe out the prophets of Yaweh, the true God of Israel.

When she heard that Naboth, whose farm joined the palace gardens, had refused to sell his land to the king, she cunningly arranged his death and so gained possession of the farm.

Who was Jezebel?

1 Kings 21, v. 1–16

Who was Jehu?

2 Kings 9–10

Jehu was the military commander of Joram, the king of Israel. He became famous for the reckless way in which he drove his chariot, and for the bloodthirsty way in which he became king.

Joram had been fighting the Syrians and was recovering from a wound. Meanwhile, Jehu was told by one of the prophets that he would be king. He drove hastily to Jezreel, and when Joram came out to meet him, he shot him down with his bow. Joram's body was thrown into Naboth's vineyard, and left there. Next, Jehu murdered Ahaziah, the king of Judah, who was visiting his sick uncle, Joram. Then he caught the old queen mother Jezebel, while she was painting her face, and she too was murdered. To make sure that no one else claimed the throne, he had all Ahab's seventy sons beheaded.

Below For political reasons, Jehu was forced to pay homage to Shalmaneser III, king of Assyria (859–824 B.C.) Because of this an image of Jehu has been preserved, one of the few in existence of an Israelite king, on a four-sided commemorative stele of Shalmaneser III from his palace at Nimrud.

According to a legend, Elijah the prophet had been fed by ravens during a time of famine. No rain had fallen and the crops failed for lack of water. Jezebel the queen had led the people to believe her god, Baal, was responsible for natural happenings, but Elijah was to prove otherwise.

During the famine Elijah had lived by the brook Cherith until it dried up, and then he went to live at the house of a widow in Sidon. Another story is told of how, during this time, the widow's supply of oil and flour never failed!

After three years, God told Elijah to go and find Ahab the king and tell him that He was going to end the drought. When Elijah met Ahab he told him to arrange a contest between himself and Jezebel's Baal prophets on Mount Carmel.

A prophet was a spokesman for God. Sometimes the king would consult a prophet for advice to find out what God thought. Sometimes a prophet would stand in a public place where everyone could hear him, and tell the people how God wanted them to live. A prophet who spoke the truth was often unpopular and lonely, because people did not like to hear the truth. They much preferred to listen to the false prophets who told them only what they wanted to hear but these prophets had no true message from God.

When Ahab, king of Israel, and Jehoshaphat, king of Judah, were planning a battle against the Syrians, the false prophets gave them encouraging advice. On Jehoshaphat's insistence, Micaiah, the true prophet, was consulted. He said they would be defeated and that Ahab would be killed.

Right The wild fig tree was planted along the roadside to provide shade for travellers.

Who was fed by ravens?

1 Kings 17, v. 1–7

What was a Prophet?

When Elijah the prophet last met Ahab the king he had challenged the Baal prophets of Queen Jezebel to meet him on Mount Carmel. In the presence of the King, Elijah spoke to the people. He gave them a choice–either they must worship God, or if Baal was the real god they must follow him. The dramatic story of a contest follows.

The Baal prophets appealed to their god, with no result, but when Elijah asked Yaweh to act, the people were left in no doubt who was the true God. His sacrifice was consumed with fire.

We do not know exactly what happened, but the people were finally convinced Yaweh was the real God and it was He who provided the rain for the crops and for all living things. "Yaweh He is God–Yaweh He is God!" they chanted together.

What happened on Mount Carmel?
1 Kings 18

How was Samaria destroyed?

Samaria was the capital of Israel. In the year 721 B.C. this proud royal city of Samaria was conquered by the Assyrians. For over a hundred years the mighty empire of Assyria had been sending her armies to conquer the lands of the Fertile Cresent. Often the subject nations had to pay tribute.

When Tiglath-Pileser, king of Assyria, died, Hoshea the last king of Israel decided it was time to rebel, but the army of the new king of Assyria quickly overcame the whole land. Only Samaria, the capital, held out, until finally, after a three year siege, it too fell. The new Assyrian king, Sargon, deported many of the Israelites and put settlers in their place–so Israel disappeared as a nation. The descendants of the new settlers became the Samaritans.

30

Above A street scene in the Assyrian capital of Nineveh. It stood on the river Tigris in present-day northern Iraq.

Who were the Assyrians?

The Assyrians were a warlike race who lived along the upper reaches of the river Tigris. In the time of Israel theirs were a mighty empire, with their capital city at Nineveh. Their kings made repeated campaigns around the Fertile Crescent until they controlled all the land from the mouth of the Tigris and Euphrates rivers almost to the borders of Egypt itself. Later they were even able to conquer Egypt. Little states like Israel and Judah had no choice but to submit. Finally, however, their vast empire collapsed to the Babylonians.

Who dug a tunnel under Jerusalem?

2 Kings 20, v. 20

In 1880 a small Arab boy fell in the pool of Siloam, which was the main water supply of Jerusalem. He managed to reach the far bank but found himself in the mouth of a dark tunnel. He had rediscovered the tunnel that King Hezekiah had dug under Jerusalem to channel water from the spring of Gihon. Scratched on the wall of the tunnel was the story of how the tunnel was made.

31

What was the Exile?

After the little kingdom of Judah had fallen to the mighty Babylonian army, many of her people were transported to Babylonia where they were forced to live. It is this period in the life of the Jewish people that we call "the exile".

In exile the Jews, as they were now called, were settled in colonies and allowed to live in their own houses. One colony, or group, of Jews lived on the river Chebar, a man-made canal not far from the ancient city of Nippur. Although, at first, they mourned the loss of their temple, they were allowed to practise their religion, often meeting in each other's houses.

During this time the prophet Ezekiel lived and wrote about the future of the Jewish people. Another writer collected a book of laws that now form part of the book of Leviticus in the Old Testament.

In these ways, the Jews kept alive both their religion and the hope that one day soon they would be able to return to their own land again. This opportunity came when the Medes and Persians overran the kingdom of Babylonia.

When did the exiles return?

In 539 B.C. the short-lived Babylonian empire was overcome by Cyrus the Persian. He told all the foreign captives that they could return home and rebuild the temples of their gods. Many of the Jewish people were happily settled in Babylon and so at first few returned. The first group to return was led by the Jewish prince, Sheshbazzar. Later other groups returned, and the temple at Jerusalem was rebuilt.

Although some of the Jews had returned to Jerusalem and the temple had been rebuilt, the city was still in a sorry state. News of this reached Nehemiah, the cupbearer of the Persian king, Artaxerxes I. He begged permission to go to Jerusalem and rebuild its walls which still lay in rubble.

When he arrived there he secretly inspected the walls at night, for the neighbouring people were hostile. With his encouragement the people of Jerusalem then began to repair the walls. Each group was given its own section of the wall to complete. They worked with their swords in their hands, and a trumpeter was posted to sound the alarm. Despite the danger the walls were built in fifty-two days.

Nehemiah's enemies were led by Sanballat, the Samaritan leader, who cunningly accused Nehemiah of plotting against the Persian king. When this failed, he mocked the builders. Finally he threatened to attack but Nehemiah stood firm.

How were the walls of Jerusalem rebuilt?
Neh. 1–6

Who was Esther?
Esther 1–10

The story of Esther is a romantic one, set in the time of Nehemiah. The story tells how the king of Persia took a young Jewess, named Esther, for his wife. Her uncle, Mordecai, learnt of a plot against the king's life and was able to warn him. Later, however, because Mordecai would not bow down to Haman, the king's chief officer, Haman decided to destroy all the Jews. He did not succeed, however, for Queen Esther spoke to the king, and Mordecai was made Chief Minister, and the wicked Haman was hanged. So the Jewish people were saved. This story is remembered in the Jewish feast of Purim.

"A prudent man sees danger and hides himself; but the simple go on, and suffer for it."
Proverbs 23, v.3

What is a proverb?

The book of Proverbs is a book of wise sayings, that have been gathered from everyday life and handed down from one generation to another. It was an accepted fact that King Solomon was Israel's wisest king and so, therefore, the writer of many proverbs. The wisdom of the proverbs is a practical wisdom about how to live a good and successful life. Real wisdom, however, came from God and was found by obeying God.

The wise men, or sages, thought deeply about life and tried to find out its real meaning. Then they put their thoughts into short sayings. The sage would sometimes instruct his pupils in wisdom and begin his teaching with the words—"My son". The first chapters of the book of Proverbs start in this way. Amongst the Hebrews the wise man was as important as the priest.

We do not know exactly when the proverbs were written but we are certain that they were collected together over a very long period.

Isaiah was a young man who lived in Jerusalem. One day, when he was in the temple worshipping, he was overcome by a tremendous feeling that God was there.

We can read in the sixth chapter of his book how he described this experience, or vision. God, whose presence filled the whole world, was so great and mighty that Isaiah felt he would never live to tell about it. The whole building seemed to shake and grow dim. He felt small and worthless.

Gradually a new feeling came over him. God appeared to be asking him to tell his fellow countrymen what He wanted although often they would not understand or take any notice. So real was this to Isaiah that he spent the next forty years of his life preaching.

What was Isaiah's vision?

Isaiah 6

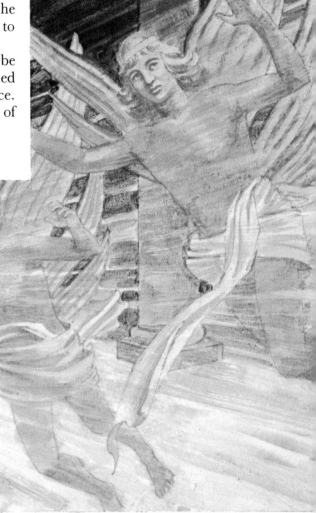

"Above
him stood the seraphim; each had six wings: with two he covered his face, and with two he covered his feet, and with two he flew. And one called to another and said:
'Holy, holy, holy is the Lord of Hosts; the whole earth is full of his glory'."
Isaiah 6, v.2-3

Who was called the Preacher?

Ecclesiastes 1, v. 1–12

The book of Ecclesiastes is rather like the book of Proverbs, since it contains wise sayings. Unlike the Proverbs which were written by many people, however, the book of Ecclesiastes was largely written by a wise man who lived about 200 B.C.

This unknown sage is often called the Preacher. He felt that although God is really in control of the world and has a plan, it is not possible to discover this plan. So it appeared to him that much that happens to people, happens by chance. He was also conscious of the short span of our lives and thought that there was nothing to look forward to after death.

How were quarrels settled?

Early in the life of the Hebrew nation family quarrels were settled by the head of the family, the father. If there was still disagreement the matter was taken to the tribal chief for his decision. We read that Moses had so many disputes to settle that he chose elders to decide the simple cases and he himself dealt with the more difficult ones.

After the Hebrews had settled down as farmers in Canaan disputes were taken to the village elders who sat in judgement by the gate of the town. If they could not reach a decision the priest at the local sanctuary was consulted. Later still, when they were ruled by a king, he automatically became the chief judge. As the king could not settle every dispute personally he chose judges who became important officials at his court.

What were the Hebrew marriage customs?

Marriages were nearly always arranged by the couple's parents. The bridegroom's father would choose a bride for his son and make a gift to the bride's parents. Sometimes the bridegroom worked for his father-in-law if he was unable to make a gift.

Betrothal, or engagement, came next and was thought as important as marriage itself. Then followed the marriage ceremony. The bridegroom's friends would bring the bride from her parents' home and everyone joined in the procession. There was singing and music, and nuts and flowers were scattered. After seven days of feasting the couple was considered married. Often the bride brought her own dowry of jewellery or gave a piece of land. For the ceremony, the bride wore a specially embroidered tunic and a veil, and the bridegroom had a garland of flowers placed on his head.

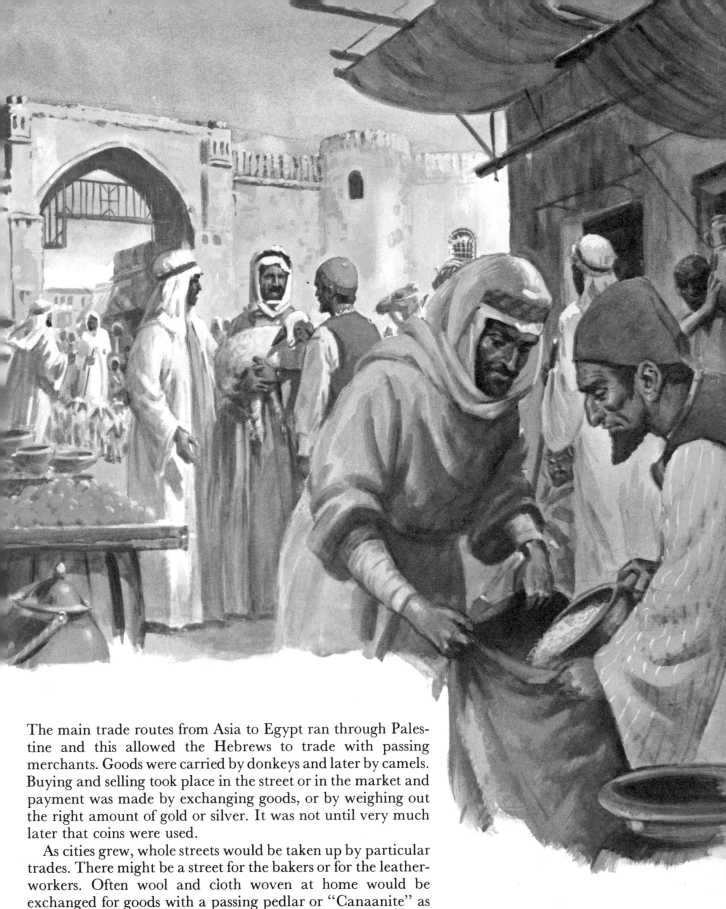

The main trade routes from Asia to Egypt ran through Palestine and this allowed the Hebrews to trade with passing merchants. Goods were carried by donkeys and later by camels. Buying and selling took place in the street or in the market and payment was made by exchanging goods, or by weighing out the right amount of gold or silver. It was not until very much later that coins were used.

As cities grew, whole streets would be taken up by particular trades. There might be a street for the bakers or for the leather-workers. Often wool and cloth woven at home would be exchanged for goods with a passing pedlar or "Canaanite" as he was often called. By the reign of Solomon great quantities of copper and iron were exported and passing merchants had to pay a toll in order to travel through the country.

How did the Jews trade?

Syrian Bear

Wolf (Middle East – India)

Jackal

Egyptian Vulture

Desert Fox

Horned Viper

What animals lived in Canaan?

The commonest animals were those tamed by man—the ass and the ox which were used for the heavy work on the farm, the merchants' camels, and the sheep and goats which provided meat. Besides tame animals, there were a great many wild ones —the cunning fox which raided the vineyards, the dangerous jackal which hunted in packs, and the pariah dogs that roamed wild.

There were also wild goats living amongst the rocky outcrops by the Dead Sea, and in the dense jungle of the Jordan Valley lions and leopards could be found. One of the most dangerous animals was the wild ox, a huge beast with great curving horns. The animal most feared by the shepherds, however, was the Syrian bear which when really hungry was known to attack and kill sheep.

What meals were eaten?

There were two main meals in the day. One eaten at midday and the other in the evening after work. Before work, first thing in the morning, a little bread was eaten and perhaps a few olives. The midday meal consisted of more bread, or parched corn, eaten with soup or goats' cheese and some wine. The evening meal, the largest of the day, was often a vegetable stew with a little meat. This was eaten with the right hand from a large bowl placed on a mat on the floor which everyone shared.

In the hot sun of Canaan the skin soon became dry, so both men and women used olive oil to keep their skin soft. The oil was often scented with a perfume made from flowers or plants. As a greeting, important visitors were welcomed by smoothing perfumed oil or ointment on their face and feet. Rich women would paint black eye shadow around their eyes and red ochre on their cheeks. We read that Queen Jezebel, Ahab's wife, painted her eyes and carefully combed her hair. Sometimes hair and even hands, nails and feet, were coloured with a red dye from the Henna leaf.

Priests also used sacred perfume or ointment. When a new king came to the throne his head was anointed with perfumed oil.

What cosmetics were used?

What were the "food laws"?

Leviticus 11, v. 1–23

The food laws were the laws about the types of food, mainly meat, that the Hebrew was allowed to eat. These foods were considered clean, but the forbidden foods were called unclean. The food laws were, in fact, religious laws, because if a person broke them he could not take part in worship with others, for he had become unclean and therefore unfit to worship God.

Animals, such as goats or sheep, which had divided or cloven feet and chewed the cud, could be eaten. But animals such as the rabbit or hare that chewed the cud and had paws, could not be eaten. Also they were not allowed to eat animals such as pigs which have cloven feet and do not chew the cud.

Fish could be eaten as well as birds, as long as they were not flesh eaters themselves, but reptiles and most insects were forbidden, except the locust and the grasshopper. Today the locust is still eaten by some desert-dwelling Arabs.

All meat, however, had to be especially prepared. This meat is called Kosher. Animals that died naturally were regarded as unclean, and as a result were unfit for food.

The main weapons used for attack were the spear, the sword, the bow, and the sling.

The Hebrew spear, like the Hebrew sword, was short and heavy. Bows were made of wood and strung with ox gut, but some powerful bows were made of strips of horn and wood bound together. The sling was the shepherd's weapon but was also used in war. For his protection the soldier carried a small round shield made of leather and wood and wore a helmet and light armour of leather or metal.

What weapons were used?

Assyrian Foot-soldier armed with sword and shield

Assyrian Archer

Assyrian Foot-soldier armed with spear

Shepherd boy with sling

How do Jewish people divide their Bible?

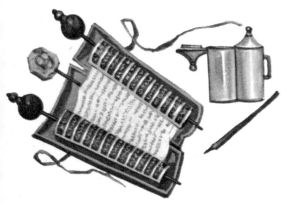

The Jewish people divide their Bible into three main sections. First come the five books of the law called Torah, or the Books of Moses. Then come the Prophets and finally, the writings or the Sacred Writings. The Prophets are again divided into two sections called the "former Prophets and the latter Prophets". The former Prophets include the books of Joshua, Judges, Samuel and Kings, whilst the latter Prophets covered Isaiah, Jeremiah, and Ezekiel and the twelve minor Prophets. The writings included all the other books in the Hebrew Bible. Sometimes the word "Torah" is used to describe the whole of the Jewish Bible.

The Jewish Bible is called the Old Testament in the Christian Bible, as the second part of the Christian Bible is called the New Testament. Some Christian churches include another section called the Apocrypha.

40

What is the Apocrypha?

The Apocrypha is a collection of fourteen or fifteen books that in some Bibles are found between the Old Testament and the New Testament. Apocrypha means "hidden" for usually these books are not read in public but are allowed to be read privately. They were sometimes thought of as books of secret knowledge. These books are included in the Roman Catholic Bible.

Some of the books in the Apocrypha, like Tobit, Bel and the Dragon, and Judith are similar to religious novels. Others, like the books of Maccabees are books of history. These two books tell how the sons of a priest, Mattathias, rebelled against the Seleucid king, Antiochus, and won freedom for their people. The eldest son, Judas, gave his name to these books for he was known as Maccabees, or "the hammer" because of his great strength in battle.

Finally, the Apocrypha includes a number of books supposedly written by famous men in the Old Testament but most probably written very much later, like the letter of Jeremiah and the book of Baruch his friend.

The story of Bel and the Dragon, dating from 100 B.C., is taken from the book of Daniel and appears in the Apocrypha.

What was the "law of hospitality"?

Gen. 18, v. 1–8

The life of the Hebrew family was governed by custom and law. There were right ways and wrong ways of doing everything. If a stranger came to the home, he was invited to stop and rest. He was greeted and offered water to drink and to wash his feet. After the greetings were over enquiries were made about his health and where he came from and where he was going. In the meantime the best food in the house was prepared and the stranger invited to eat.

Once the meal was over, the host would press the stranger to stay overnight so that he could resume his journey refreshed in the morning. Whilst a stranger was in the house he was under the protection of the owner whose duty it was to defend him and provide for him.

What was village life like?

Everyone in Israel grew up in a village, for even the towns like Jerusalem and Samaria were really only large villages. Most villages contained three hundred to five hundred people, for when it took too long to walk to your field to work, a new village grew up. There were no real streets, only spaces between the houses with their paths. In the centre of the village was the well and an open space which served as a market. Everyone spent a lot of time out of doors and so everyone knew what everyone else did. There were no secrets.

In the morning the men and the older boys went out to the fields while the girls and the younger children remained behind to help their mothers or to tend the smaller animals. Every day the women would meet around the well to gossip whilst the children listened. In the evening the men would gather together to talk and discuss the day's events. When there were disputes, the elders of the village settled them, and when there was a marriage, or a funeral, everyone joined in. Everyone shared everyone else's life.

Life in the villages revolved around the well.

When was Jesus born?

Although we do not know exactly when Jesus was born, the most likely date is in the year 6 B.C. This may seem strange, for we usually think of the birth of Jesus as the starting point of our calendar. It was in this year that the Governor of Syria held a census, probably the one that Luke mentions in his Gospel, that led Joseph and Mary to Bethlehem where Jesus was born. Certainly Herod the Great was still alive, and as he died in the year 4 B.C. the year 6 B.C. seems most likely to be the year of Jesus's birth.

While Luke, in his Gospel, tells of the shepherds who visited the baby Jesus in his humble stable, Matthew recounts a wonderful story of Eastern kings and their gifts, the jealousy of Herod and the escape to Egypt.

Jesus grew up in the little town of Nazareth which lay in the hills overlooking the fertile plain of Esdraelon, about ten miles west of the Sea of Galilee.

As a boy, he must have roamed the hills and watched the shepherds at work and seen the great variety of travellers that passed along the roads nearby. On the Sabbath he went to the Synagogue with his parents and during the week, in the mornings, he attended the Synagogue school. The rest of the day he would be at work with his father, learning the carpenter's trade and helping to make the ploughs and yokes and carts needed by the farmers. At the age of twelve he went to his first Passover in Jerusalem with his parents. Soon afterwards Joseph died and Jesus then no doubt had to work to provide for his mother. Jesus must have been an observant boy for, as a man, he was able to talk in detail about farming, the world of nature, and many things that happened in the village.

How did Jesus spend his boyhood?

Luke 2, v. 41–52

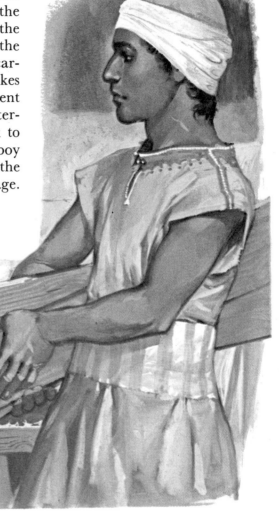

Who was John the Baptist?

Luke 3, v. 1–21

John the Baptist was the cousin of Jesus. His father, Zechariah, was a priest and was already an old man when John was born. During his youth, John spent much of his time alone, thinking, living on the edge of the desert. He wore simple, rough clothing and ate what he could find. As he grew older he became sure that God was soon to send His Messiah, or deliverer, and he felt he must go and announce his coming like one of the prophets.

At the appropriate time, he appeared by the river Jordan and started preaching to the travellers. Many stopped to listen to him. To prepare them for the coming of the Messiah, John baptized them in the river Jordan. This was a sign that they wanted God's forgiveness in readiness for the Messiah's coming.

The Gospels were written some years after Jesus died. At first there seemed no need to write about Jesus for many of his friends remembered him and his words so clearly. Besides they believed that very shortly he would come back to them, but as time went on his personal friends died and new followers wanted to know about Jesus.

Gradually, people who had known Jesus well began to write down his words and his deeds. Perhaps one person would collect together all the words of Jesus he could find and another all the parables or miracles. Soon these collections were passed around and copies made for people to treasure. So we can see that when Matthew, Mark, Luke and John came to write their Gospels they found they could collect and join together much that was already written about Jesus. The first person to write a Gospel was John Mark, a young friend of Peter's.

The everyday language of Jesus's day was Aramaic, but the language of trade that nearly everyone in the Roman empire could speak, was Greek. Greek had become the common language after the conquests of Alexander the Great. So we find that the second part of the Bible, the New Testament, was originally written in Greek, although perhaps some of the words of Jesus were first written in Aramaic before being translated into Greek.

The first part of the Bible, the Old Testament, was written in Hebrew, the original language of the Jews which was still used for worship. By the time of Jesus, a Greek translation called the Septuagint, had been made for Jews who knew no Hebrew.

Our Bibles today are, of course, all translations of the original Hebrew and Greek books.

How were the Gospels written?

In what language was the Bible written?

What are the Parables?

Luke 10, v. 25–37

Parable of the sower.
Luke 8, v.4-8

The Parables are stories that have a hidden meaning which Jesus used to teach his followers about God. Many parables tell about ordinary things that happened in everyday life, such as the following little parable of the house builders.

One man built on solid rock, the other man straight on sandy soil. When the winter rains came, the house with the sand foundation collapsed. By this, Jesus meant to warn his hearers to take care to build their lives on the strong foundation of his teaching.

The parable of the Good Samaritan, the parable of the Sower, and the parable of the Prodigal Son are perhaps the best known of all the parables. Jesus used parables to help his hearers discover what God was like and how He wanted them to live. Even if they did not discover the hidden meaning right away, they did not forget the story and as they thought about it, the meaning would become clear.

The Sermon on the Mount is a long collection of Jesus's teaching that Matthew includes in his Gospel. Matthew pictured Jesus sitting on a hillside teaching a great crowd below. He started with the Beatitudes which are sayings about happiness, for each begins with the word "blessed" which means "happy". The point of the sermon was to help the friends of Jesus to live as God wants. Jesus advised them not to hit back when they were hurt, not to criticize others, and not to become obsessed with making money, but to learn to love others, even one's enemies. He goes on to tell them not to be self-righteous but to be humble and genuine when they help others and when they pray. He gives them a prayer on which to model their own prayers—we call this "The Lord's Prayer".

What is the Sermon on the Mount?

Matt. 56—57

A miracle is the name given to the wonderful things Jesus did to help people in need. Many times Jesus used his powers to heal the sick and crippled, the deaf and the blind. We find he never selfishly used his powers for himself. When needy people came to him, he only asked for their trust so that he could help them.

In Jesus's day, illness was thought to be caused by the power of evil. People thought that they became ill because of something they had done wrong. Jesus was able to help them, for when he healed them he reassured them that their sins were forgiven and showed them that God's power was greater than the power of evil.

Today we know much more about the causes of illness and we have doctors and surgeons who are able to restore health to the sick. We should not think that the miracles were magic but rather that they were the way God used Jesus to help people of his day to show them how much He cared for them.

What were miracles?

Mark 1, v. 40—45

Why did Jesus help others?

Mark 1, v. 21—39

Many people went to Jesus for help, for news of his great healing powers soon spread and he never turned anyone away. One day, in the Synagogue at Capernaum, he helped a man with a deeply disturbed mind to find peace. That evening many more brought their sick friends to him at Peter's home where he was staying, and again Jesus cured them.

In the morning Jesus got up early to be by himself to pray to God for new strength, but Peter found him and told him the crowds were already looking for him. Often Jesus was moved with pity when he saw the sick and helpless. They were like sheep without a shepherd. Jesus cared deeply for everyone and tried to show them, by helping them, that God his Father cared just as much.

48

Why did Jesus have disciples?

Like everyone else, Jesus needed his friends to be with him and to share his life. Once he said appreciatively to his disciples, "You are those who have continued with me in my trials." Jesus must have been glad that he had friends for he would have been lonely without them. Often however, they did not understand him and he had to be very patient with them. They were a great comfort to him though, for they were loyal helpers! Sometimes they helped him in his work of teaching and healing, sometimes they helped by finding lodging for the night.

Above all, Jesus needed them to continue his work after he died. So he taught them carefully and prepared them for the task that would one day be theirs. Although they sometimes failed him and argued amongst themselves they proved loyal to him in the end.

When did Jesus break the law?

Mark 3, v. 1—6

In the time of Jesus there were very strict religious laws. One such law forbade work on the Sabbath as this was God's day. The law of the Sabbath allowed farmers to feed their cattle but did not allow people to carry anything, as this was doing work. Healing people was also forbidden on the Sabbath.

In the Synagogue one Sabbath Jesus found a man whose hand was paralysed. He asked him to stand up. The very religious Pharisees watched him critically. Jesus asked them if it was right to do good or harm on the Sabbath. When they did not answer he asked the man to hold out his hand. To his joy the man found he could use it again but the Pharisees were bitterly angry.

Why did Jesus leave his own country?

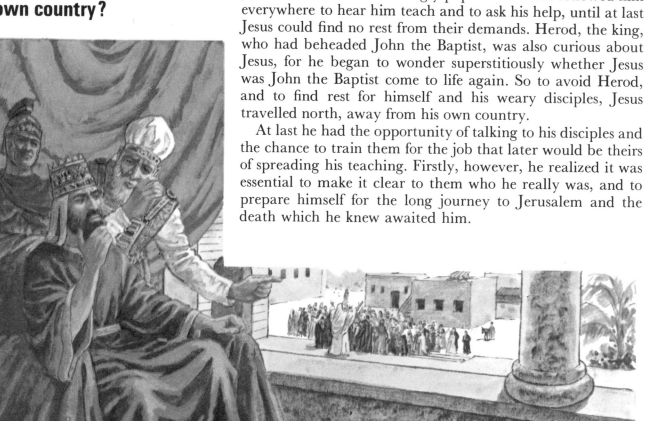

Jesus had become increasingly popular. Crowds followed him everywhere to hear him teach and to ask his help, until at last Jesus could find no rest from their demands. Herod, the king, who had beheaded John the Baptist, was also curious about Jesus, for he began to wonder superstitiously whether Jesus was John the Baptist come to life again. So to avoid Herod, and to find rest for himself and his weary disciples, Jesus travelled north, away from his own country.

At last he had the opportunity of talking to his disciples and the chance to train them for the job that later would be theirs of spreading his teaching. Firstly, however, he realized it was essential to make it clear to them who he really was, and to prepare himself for the long journey to Jerusalem and the death which he knew awaited him.

One day, during his travels in the north, Jesus asked his disciples a question while praying with them. He had wanted to ask them this for a long time but they had not been ready. First, he asked them who other people thought he was. The disciples answered that he was either a great prophet or perhaps Elijah, or even John the Baptist come to life again.

The Jesus asked the great question, "Who do you say I am?" There was a pause, then Peter answered impulsively, "You are the Christ, the Messiah of God!" At last the secret was out. Now Jesus could tell them everything he had wanted to for so long. He warned them that he would have to travel to Jerusalem and there face the religious leaders. He knew, too, that they would reject him and finally plot his death.

What was "the great question"?

Matt. 16, v. 13—26

Who were the Pharisees?

The Pharisees were a group of very pious Jews who lived strictly by the law of the Jewish religion. Besides keeping the written law in every detail they added other laws to explain the written law. In this they were helped by the scribes, a group of lawyers of religion. Although they genuinely tried to serve God, they became so intent on keeping the law that they sometimes forgot to be kind and generous to others.

What was the message of the feet washing?

John 13, v. 1–17

It was a charming Jewish custom to wash the dusty feet of visitors when they came in from the heat. When Jesus and his disciples entered a room they frequently used in Jerusalem, they were all too proud to perform this humble task.

At last Jesus took a basin of water and a towel and did the job for them. They were so ashamed that at first Peter refused to have his feet washed, but Jesus explained that he had set them an example of service. "If I wash your feet," he said, "you ought to wash one another's feet." He meant, in fact, that they should care for each other. Jesus had once said this about himself, "I came not to be served but to serve and give my life for others."

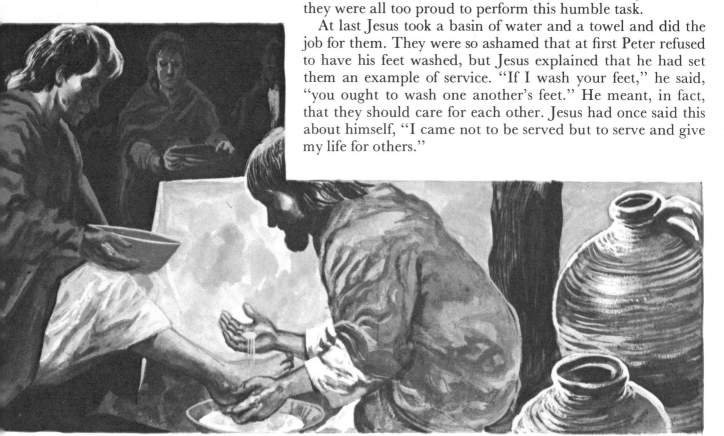

What was the Last Supper?

Luke 22, v. 1–23

The "last supper" was the last meal that Jesus ate with his close friends before he was crucified.

It was the time of Passover when the Jews were remembering how God had delivered the Hebrew slaves in Egypt. Jesus took some bread and broke it and gave it to his friends, then he took some wine and shared it with them. He explained carefully that just as he had given them bread and wine, he was soon to give his life for them and for those who came after them. They did not understand then, but afterwards they remembered his word by meeting together and sharing bread and wine. It was their way of showing how grateful they were to him.

Today nearly all Christians hold similar, special meals to show their gratitude to God for the way he has helped them by giving them Jesus. This meal is often called "Communion".

Towards the end of the meal that Jesus held, Judas Iscariot, one of his disciples, crept out to tell the priests where they could capture Jesus.

Which was the blackest hour in the life of Jesus?

Luke 22, v. 39—54

After Jesus had finished the last supper with his disciples they went out to an olive orchard, called the garden of Gethsemane, that Jesus often visited. It was late and they were tired. Jesus was overcome with great sorrow and started to pray. He knew shortly that Judas would be back with the soldiers of the High Priest. He knew also that he must die, and he prayed that God might find another way for him to help people.

He went back to his disciples and found them asleep. He asked Peter why they could not watch with him when he needed them most. They were ashamed. Jesus went back to pray, but now he realized that the only way he could truly help people was to give his life for them. With great courage he waited for Judas and the soldiers. When they arrived, the disciples ran away and Jesus was left alone. The soldiers seized Jesus and led him to the High Priest's house. There he was ill-treated by the soldiers, and interrogated by the Jewish leaders.

Why was there a plot to kill Jesus?

For a long time the Pharisees had wanted Jesus out of the way. He had told them openly how false their religion was and of course they hated him for his honesty. Besides, they felt that Jesus was teaching people beliefs contrary to the Jewish faith.

Earlier that week, Jesus had ridden into Jerusalem on a donkey, and the pilgrim crowds had gone mad with excitement. They hailed him as the Messiah. This had frightened the Sadducees who thought there might be trouble with the Roman army, which might cancel their position of power. Jesus had quite openly cleared the temple of traders who were exploiting the worshippers and this had shamed the priests. They had all tried to trap him with trick questions but had failed. So when Judas offered to betray Jesus, they were glad to plot against the man who had so often reproached them.

Judas, we are told, loved money and looked after the disciples' finances. He was also most probably a zealot, one of the freedom fighters, who longed to see the Romans driven out of his beloved country.

We do not know exactly what made Judas betray Jesus, for although the priests gave him money to betray Jesus, when Judas realized the plot had actually worked, he threw the money down at the feet of the priests and went and took his own life.

He may have hoped what he did would make Jesus rally his followers to fight the Romans and was heartbroken when it failed. He may have felt cheated by Jesus when he realized that Jesus was determined to let himself be taken, and turned traitor to save himself.

Why did Judas betray Jesus?

The Chief Priest and the Jewish Council met very early the morning after Jesus was captured and questioned him. They wanted a reason for putting him to death. Their witnesses could not agree, however. In desperation the Chief Priest asked Jesus if he was the Son of God. Jesus answered, "You say so."

This they took as a confession of guilt and said he must die. Then they took him to Pilate, the Roman Governor to get his authority for execution. When Pilate questioned Jesus, he knew him to be innocent, but the priests said Jesus claimed to be the King of the Jews, a treasonous statement since Caesar ruled the country.

By now the mob was screaming for Jesus's death and rather than have a riot, Pilate weakly gave permission for him to be executed.

Who convicted Jesus?

Luke 22–23

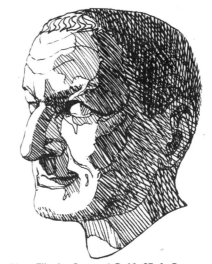

Above Tiberius Caesar. A.D. 14–37. As Roman procurator, Pontius Pilate was responsible for the administration of Judaea during the latter part of the reign of Tiberius.

How did Jesus die?

Luke 23, v. 26–46

After Pilate had given his permission, Jesus was led away for execution. The usual Roman form of execution was by crucifixion. The criminal was fastened to a wooden cross by his hands and feet and left to die. This was how Jesus was executed.

First, he was forced to carry the crossbar of his cross until, already weakened by the beatings he had received, he could carry it no further. So a passer-by, Simon, was forced to carry it for him. When he arrived at a place called the Skull he was crucified with two others, both of them thieves.

Meanwhile, the Roman soldiers who carried out the sentence, diced for his clothes. Jesus looked down at the crowd and the Jewish rulers who were mocking him and prayed for God to forgive them. One of the thieves cursed him and said, "If you are the Christ, save yourself!" But the other rebuked him, pointing out that Jesus had done nothing wrong. Finally Jesus gave his life into the care of God and died.

According to Roman law, the body of a man convicted for political reasons was given honourable burial. Joseph of Arimathea asked Pilate for Jesus's body and he and Nicodemus took it to a tomb in a garden near the place of execution which belonged to Joseph. The tomb consisted of an ante-chamber with benches, where the mourners could pray, and an inner chamber which could be sealed with a large stone wheel.

Jesus had been hastily buried in a new tomb cut into the rock in a friend's garden. As the next day was the Jewish Sabbath, Mary Magdalene, and some of the other women who were followers of Jesus, waited until Sunday to visit the tomb.

When they arrived very early in the morning they found the tomb empty and were told that Jesus had risen from the dead. This is the event known as the Resurrection. It meant a great deal to the disciples for they were convinced their beloved master was alive again! At first they had doubts, but when they saw him for themselves they were overjoyed. Jesus visited his disciples many times before finally leaving the earth, but by now they were happy and confident, for all was well.

At Easter time Christians remember this wonderful event because they are certain, too, that Jesus, whom they worship, is alive and with them all the time.

What was the Resurrection?
Luke 24, v. 1–12

Christians believe that just as God brought Jesus to life again, they will also have a new and better life when they die.

Who wrote the first history of the Church?

The book of the Acts of the Apostles is the story of what happened to the disciples after Jesus died. It is the history of the beginnings of the new Church. It was written by Luke, who though he never saw Jesus, became one of his followers. Luke was a doctor and a close friend of Paul the great missionary.

Luke also wrote the Gospel, called after him. He wanted everyone to know the truth about Jesus so that they would follow him themselves.

The book of Acts tells about the disciples, who are now called apostles, and how they and their friends told others all about Jesus and what he had done. Soon many others became followers of Jesus, both Jewish people and people of other countries who were called gentiles. However, when persecution broke out, many of the early Christians left to settle in other lands. The leading persecutor was Paul, who later became a Christian, and spent the rest of his life travelling, preaching the message of Christianity. In these ways Christianity became known throughout the Roman Empire.

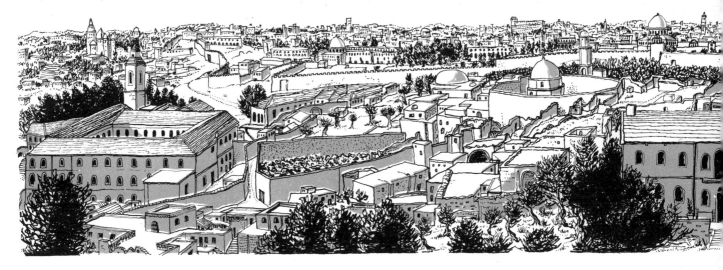

What was the Ascension?

Acts 1, v. 1–12

Above View of present-day Jerusalem from the Mount of Olives.

After Jesus rose from the dead, he appeared many times to his disciples. On the final occasion he met them at the Mount of Olives, just outside Jerusalem. He told them they must carry on his work after he had gone and that God would help them by giving them his spirit of power. In the meantime they must wait in Jerusalem until this happened. When Jesus had finished speaking to them he vanished from their sight and was never seen by them in the same form as they had seen him before.

We call this experience of the disciples, the "ascension". For the disciples, Heaven, where God lived, was above the sky. So they described Jesus ascending to Heaven to return to be with God his Father; this is why it is called ascension.

Jesus had told the disciples to wait in Jerusalem until God gave them his Spirit to help them. This they did, and then something so marvellous happened that it was difficult to find words to describe it.

They were meeting in an upstairs room with the doors locked because they were frightened. Suddenly there are all filled with such a strong feeling of God that they knew His great spirit of power had come to them. They said it was like a great wind and tongues of flame which touched their heads. This happened at the time of the Jewish feast of Pentecost.

Instantly, they were so marvellously happy that they burst out of the room and ran into the street. Soon a crowd gathered and Peter, their spokesman, told them the wonderful news.

What happened at Pentecost?

Acts 2, v. 1–17

HISTORY

What does the word civilization mean?

It is not easy to be precise about quite what is meant by the word civilization. In history, the change from barbarism to civilization came when races began to do more things for themselves than just hunt, kill and eat. Once Man discovered how to plant corn and vegetable seeds, nurture the sown earth with water and then gather the harvest, that is, when he became a farmer, then he had crossed the barrier. At this time, Man also began to think of organizing his life. He domesticated animals, traded his agricultural products with neighbours, built homes of baked mud, and made weapons and tools of bronze. He even began to organize recreation.

For some reason yet to be satisfactorily explained, the first people to become civilized were a race who occupied what is called the Fertile Crescent, a stretch of land lying between the great Euphrates and Tigris Rivers in the Near East. We call these people the Sumerians and they began to organize themselves some time about 5000 B.C. or perhaps earlier. There were, of course, many other stretches of land which lay near great rivers and which were very fertile, but the Sumerians were the first civilized men. Next were the Egyptians, and after them the Indians and the Chinese.

Left The golden head of a bull decorates this lyre from Ur.

Below The Fertile Crescent and the sites of the first civilizations.

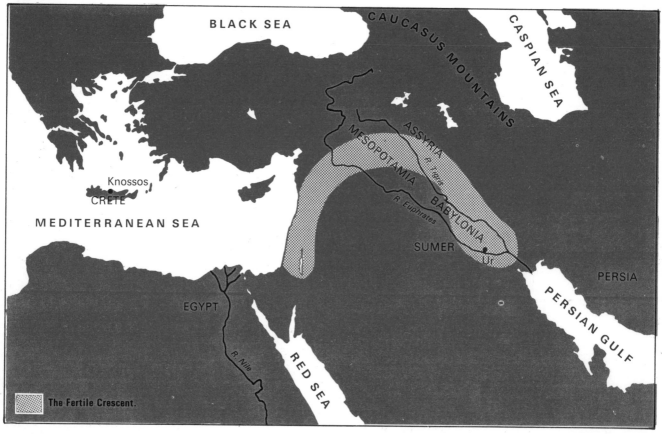

The Fertile Crescent.

The Sumerians were the first people to work out any kind of ordered language, and they devised a script to record it. This we call cuneiform script, from the Latin word *cuneus* meaning a wedge. The main characters in the language were made up of combinations of wedge shapes which were pressed into clay tablets by means of reed pens. The wedges formed what are called pictograms, that is, word pictures, which illustrated pronunciations. This script was very difficult to read, not only today for the scholars who have excavated the ruins of the old Sumerian civilization, but also for the ancient Sumerians themselves. So they devised a simpler script of some six hundred basic word symbols for everyday use.

Below The ziggurat at Ur (about 2150–2050 B.C.).

What was the Sumerians' language?

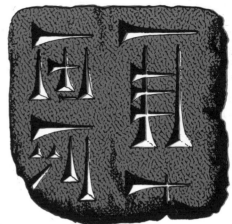

Above Cuneiform script.

Where was Ur?

Above A model of a Sumerian chariot.

Ur was a Sumerian city. Although there were many other Sumerian cities, Ur is the one which, when excavated earlier this century, yielded the most important and exciting discoveries. Its construction—and the life that the inhabitants led in it—were very much the same as in the other cities, like Lagash, Eridu and Kish.

Ur was built on the eastern bank of the Euphrates River. The city had many fine buildings. One of the largest of these was the ziggurat, that is, a large temple shaped like a tower, on the roof of which astronomers made their observations. Next door to the ziggurat was a palace for the king, and both buildings were encircled by a wall.

The Sumerians were not a people united under one king. They were a collection of city states. For some time, probably from about 2700–2300 B.C. Ur was the leading city.

The Sumerians built palaces, temples, houses and shops. They built them of brick, and were, so far as we know, the first people to do so. The bricks were made of clay dug from the banks of the Tigris or Euphrates Rivers. At first, a square or rectangular block was shaped and then left in the hot sun to bake. After a time, the Sumerians learned to bake the bricks in an oven heated by burning wood.

What did the Sumerians use as building materials?

In their earliest days the Sumerians were, apart from the Egyptians, the only civilized people in the world, if we accept the definition of civilization given in our first question. And they were separated from Egypt by many hundreds of miles of fertile land and desert. Much closer to them were many tribes to whom civilization had not yet come or was just arriving. These were peoples like the Elamites, the Semites, the Amorites, who along with many others, were to become highly cultured in time. The Semites are particularly interesting as they were the ancestors of all the Jews and Arabs.

Who were the Sumerians' neighbours?

Why did the Egyptians build pyramids?

Below The Sphinx of Chephren (about 2500 B.C.) and the pyramids of Giza.

The ancient Egyptians believed that when they died their souls continued in a life after death. To ensure that their pharaohs, or rulers, whom they treated like gods, enjoyed this new life, they embalmed the pharaohs' bodies immediately after death and placed them in tombs, which were then sealed. They also believed that the tomb had to be vast in order to stop the soul getting out before its voyage to the after-life, and also to prevent foreign, possibly evil, spirits getting in. So they built enormous structures called pyramids. These were amazing feats of engineering. They had sloping sides from a rectangular base, and contained secret passages leading to the inner tomb chambers. The huge stone blocks from which they were made were hauled up ramps by large gangs of slaves.

The largest pyramid they built was that of the pharaoh Cheops at Giza, in about 2500 B.C. It is almost five hundred feet high, and over three thousand feet round the base, that is, over half a mile. It was made of more than 2,250,000 cut blocks of stone, each weighing an average of two and a half tons.

How did the farmers on the banks of the Nile irrigate their fields?

Above Water was lifted from wells with a shaduf, a simple kind of bucket on a hoist.

In the earlier days of their civilization, when there were not many people in Egypt, farmers depended upon the flooding of the Nile to irrigate their fields which lay close to the river's banks. But when the population increased so that more fields had to be tilled and sown to produce more crops, it was found that the flooding did not provide enough water. So they cut dykes at right angles to the river bank, in rows along the Nile. When the flood water came down, it filled one dyke. This would be shut off with a wooden gate, whereupon the water filled the next dyke, and so on.

Hieroglyphics are a form of writing in pictorial symbols. These symbols were at first pictures of natural objects or events. Then later the same kinds of symbols began to express ideas. For example, the picture of an eye meant "seeing". These symbols are called ideographs.

Later still a symbol was taken to represent not only the original word but also to represent parts of other words with a similar sound. These are called phonograms.

The symbols were very complicated. Because they took a long time to carve or write, the Egyptians, like the Sumerians, developed an abbreviated script for everyday use.

What are hieroglyphics?

Below Hieroglyphics on a tomb painting, and *(below left)* on a papyrus strip.

When and where was the first civilization in India?

Indian civilization is the oldest still surviving in the world. It began more than 4,500 years ago, in a stretch of settlements along the banks of the fertile River Indus, in what is now Pakistan. Some of the settlements grew into splendid cities, two of which stand out as particularly grand. They were Harappa and Mohenjo-daro, which were about three hundred miles apart. It is likely that one or other dominated the rest. Possibly Harappa was the strongest for it was the largest.

Below The early civilizations in India and China.

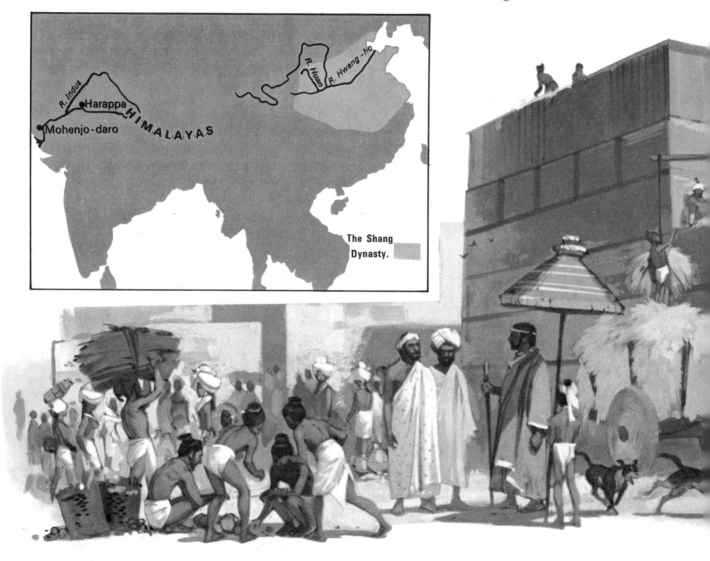

R. Indus · Harappa · Mohenjo-daro · HIMALAYAS · R. Huan · R. Hwang-ho · The Shang Dynasty.

Yes: there is a good deal of evidence that they were in touch with Sumer and Babylon. Many clay tablets with Indian scripts on them, produced in the Indus cities, have been found in excavations in Mesopotamia, the land of Sumer and later of Babylon, and these suggest that traders operated between the two areas. Likewise, relics of Sumerian-made goods have been found in Mohenjo-daro. It is likely that the Indians were also in touch with Egypt.

Did the Indians have any contact with other civilizations?

What were the houses in Harappa and Mohenjo-daro like?

Most Indian houses of those days were two-storeyed and laid out in blocks and terraces along wide streets which were set out on a grid system. They had flat roofs covered with a type of bitumen coat, which was also applied to walls to keep out the damp. Walls were made of bricks, which were made in much the same way as Sumerian bricks.

To get to the first floor they went up a narrow flight of stairs at the back. Although many of these houses, the ruins of which have been excavated, were over four thousand years old, they had plumbing and drainage, which were provided by clay piping and channelling. A first floor bath could be emptied into a channel running down the wall into a street drain. Water, which was obtained from a well, would be stored in a first floor tank and used via the pipes.

Chinese civilization began, like those of Sumer, Egypt, and India, along the banks of a great river, in this case the Hwang-ho, or Yellow, River. This river runs across central China, about two hundred miles from today's capital of China, Peking, and into the Gulf of Chihli. The earth was very fertile by the river which, like the Nile, flooded at regular intervals. But in the case of the Hwang-ho it often flooded with so much force that it broke the banks and ruined the farms and houses alongside. It has been said that the early history of Chinese civilization is the story of these floods and the efforts made to control them.

Eventually, the Chinese grasped the idea of cutting dykes from the banks into the fields to arrest the speed of the floodwaters, and to irrigate the farms.

Below left A horned dragon in bronze of the Chou dynasty, about 900–600 B.C.

Right A wine vessel of The Shang Dynasty. 12th–11th century B.C.

Where did Chinese civilization start?

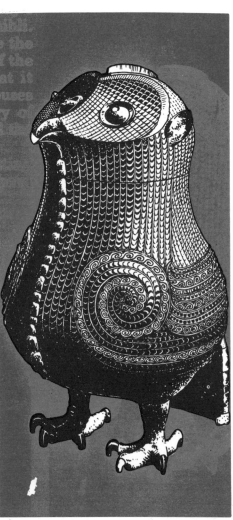

What crops did the Chinese grow?

The earliest Chinese farmers grew a crop called millet. This was a grassy plant with a head of many small seeds which were very pleasant to eat. They may also have grown a kind of wheat. Later on, when their civilization spread southwards beyond the Hwang-ho valley, the Chinese grew rice in the warmer climate. Today, thousands of years later, rice is still the main diet of the Chinese people.

Left A bronze ritual vessel for holding wine, Shang dynasty.

64

Although Chinese civilization began about five thousand years ago, it was several hundred years before they had a dynasty of rulers. Their early legends tell us of certain great men who were kings, such as Fu Hsi and Huang-ti, but the first identifiable dynasty was the Hsia family, which is said to have begun to rule in about 2200 B.C. We do not know the names of all the family, eighteen members of which were in turn emperor. One was called Yu the Great, who once saved China from a terrible flood.

The last Hsia emperor was overthrown by a northern Chinese noble, T'Ang, in about 1760 B.C. He founded a new dynasty which was to last until about 1100. This was called the Shang dynasty. T'Ang reorganized the Chinese state and ran it on feudal lines, rather in the way William of Normandy ruled England from A.D. 1066 to 1087. T'Ang became known as The Successful.

Right This is a ceremonial sceptre in jade, of the Shang dynasty.

Below left to right Two paintings on silk: Fuhsi, one of the legendary first rulers. Yao, who was the fourth ruler.

Far right The Protector against Hail and the Master of Thunder.

Who were the first Chinese emperors?

In about 1200 B.C. the Near East and its civilizations were shattered by a wave of invasions of Indo-European peoples from central Russia and south-eastern Europe. The ancient Egyptians called these peoples the "Sea Peoples" because they got as far as invading Egypt by sea as well as by land, and the name has stuck.

These "Sea Peoples" overturned the great Hittite civilization, conquered Syria, and invaded Greece. There they destroyed the Mycenaean civilization which was based on splendid cities along the coasts around the Aegean Sea. They were by no means all of the same race, but there were similarities in their languages which in time came to be grouped under the heading Indo-European.

Who were the "Sea Peoples"?

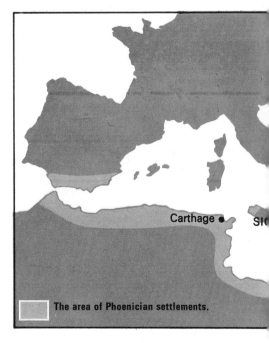

Carthage •   SIC

The area of Phoenician settlements.

What was the secret of Phoenician sea power?

The Phoenicians were Semitic people who from about 1200 B.C. occupied a stretch of land along much of what is now the west coast of Israel and Lebanon. They were sea-faring people who understood the winds and the currents of the Mediterranean, and who could handle ships with great skill. They built towns along the coast, usually on sites where there were natural harbours, and there they combined to make a strong group of cities whose wealth was the envy of the Eastern world.

They were not basically as aggressive as many other peoples of the time. They were much more interested in acquiring wealth through trade. So they explored the northern coast of Africa and the southern coasts of Spain, Sicily and Italy and set up new towns to increase their trading activities. They also became the principal conveyors of other nations' goods across the Mediterranean. For example, they took Egyptian textiles to Greece and Syrian iron to Egypt.

PHOENICIA
SYRIA
CYPRUS
CRETE
Sidon
Tyre
MEDITERRANEAN SEA
EGYPT

For about two hundred and fifty years, with one short interval, the Assyrian empire ruled a large part of the Near East, including Mesopotamia, Syria, much of Asia Minor, Palestine, and Arabia (about 870–620 B.C.). The Assyrians were a tough, warlike and stern people, but they understood the value of good farming and they were enthusiastic traders. They had mastered the techniques of iron-making introduced centuries before by the Hittites, and they put these skills to good use on the fields, in the towns and in war. They had a number of splendid kings who were not only good generals but, in some cases, also men of learning.

The Assyrian army was probably the best the world had yet seen. It was well-disciplined, equipped with fine new weapons of iron, and it was backed by a large force of charioteers who were extremely skilled in manoeuvring two-wheeled horse-driven cars. A charge by a squadron of these chariots, their crews standing upright firing arrows in quick succession, was almost impossible to resist.

How powerful was Assyria and what made it so strong?

Why was the building of Nineveh so remarkable an achievement?

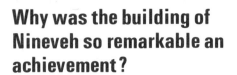

Every great emperor has always wished to have a grand city from which to rule his empire. Some have been content just to improve those they inherit. But many have preferred to start again, either on a completely new site or on the site of a small town which is in a particularly good geographical position.

Sennacherib, king of Assyria from about 705 to about 680 B.C. reconstructed the old town of Nineveh, on the great River Tigris. He made it into a wonderful new city with straight roads intersecting open parks, and he surrounded the whole place with a double wall and a series of moats. He built an aqueduct across the river about thirty miles away and this supplied water along a canal to Nineveh. It is said that the aqueduct contained more than 500,000 tons of stone.

Below King Sennacherib rides through Nineveh.

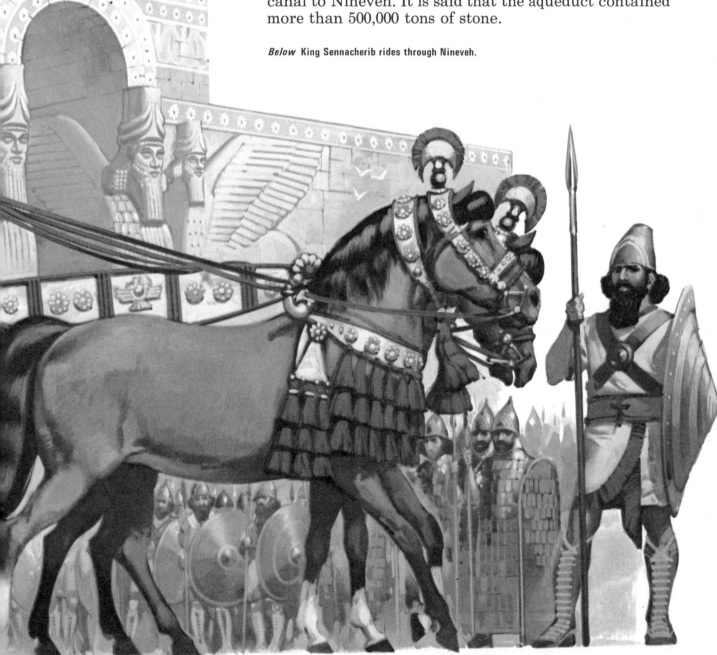

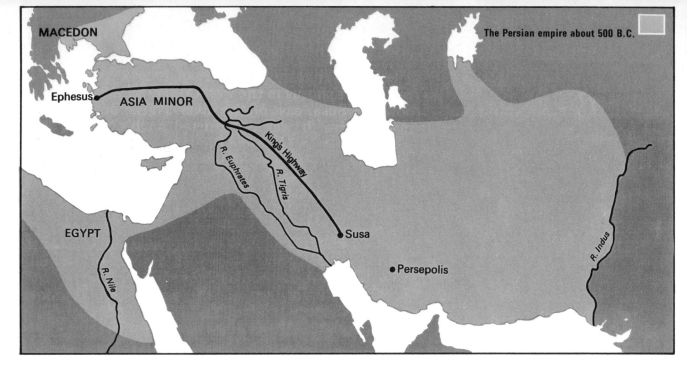

The word *satrap* is a Persian word meaning "guardian of a province". And this is what satraps were in early Persian history. They were local governors appointed by the king, responsible only to him, and given wide powers. Darius' empire was so extensive and communications were so undeveloped, that to keep it in order he had to depend on trusted officials in the regions. These satraps were usually picked from the locality which they were to govern.

What is a satrap?

Where was the King's Highway?

The King's Highway, a wide road about 1,600 miles long, ran from Ephesus in the west of Asia Minor all the way down to Susa, east of the River Tigris, one of Darius' major cities. It was constructed on his orders and it enabled him and his officials to travel about his huge domains with considerable speed. It is said that fast riders on horseback carrying urgent messages could cover the distance in less than a week. It was also a busy highway for trading caravans and other transport.

Below Xerxes' army crossed the Hellespont on a bridge made with boats.

How did Xerxes' army cross the Hellespont?

Xerxes was the son of the great Darius and he succeeded as king of Persia in 486 B.C. He was determined to avenge the defeat of the Persians by the Greeks at Marathon in 490, and after a campaign in Egypt he assembled a huge army. It gathered on the west coast of Asia Minor, and prepared to cross the Hellespont, a narrow strip of water between Turkey in Europe and Turkey in Asia, which is now known as the Dardanelles. To get this vast assemblage over to Greece, Xerxes ordered the building of a bridge of boats. Two rows of ships were lashed together with strong rope, stretching over three miles. The army was then instructed to march and the cavalry to ride, in good order across this unsteady bridge.

History does not say how many men fell into the sea and died. It was a brilliant plan, but it did not help to defeat the Greeks.

Athens was the city state where the first experiments with democratic government were tried. Democracy meant that all free citizens could elect their leaders, and if they did not like the way they governed, they could vote them out of office. Sparta, another Greek city state, had a different system. It was a military state, and elections, such as they were, did not include the votes of all free men.

There were other differences. Athenians were quite ready to fight for their city, even for Greece, as indeed they showed on many occasions, but they did not regard warfare as the highest achievement of man. But the Spartans sent their children to state military schools at the age of seven, where almost the whole time was devoted to subjects connected with war and to exercising in preparation for fighting.

How did Sparta differ from Athens?

Below The battle of Marathon.

The Greeks, under the leadership of Athens, defeated a large Persian army under the general, Mardonius, in 490 B.C. It was a turning point in history, for it was the first major defeat Persia had sustained since the founding of the empire by Cyrus the Great. It also showed the world that the Persian army was not invincible. It prevented the Persians from bringing eastern Europe into their empire.

What happened at the Battle of Marathon?

How did Athens become the leading Greek city state?

When the Athenians defeated the Persians at Marathon, they knew perfectly well that the great Darius would try again. He died, however, in 486, and his son Xerxes decided to avenge the defeat. But he, too, was defeated, at Salamis, in 480, a naval battle in which the Greek ships were mainly Athenian-built and manned.

After the Persian failures, some of the Greek cities agreed to form a league to help one another against Persia. Athens made the largest contribution and so regarded herself as leader of the league. Not all of the other member states, however, accepted her leadership without question.

Below Pericles in the market place in Athens.

Who was Pericles?

Pericles was an Athenian statesman who, from about 460 to his death in 429 B.C., was the leading man in the state. He was a successful general, a popular politician (a rare person), a lawgiver, and a man of learning and culture who encouraged the arts. He longed for all the Greek states to be united under Athens but there were too many people throughout Greece opposed to this. One thing he did was to cut down corruption among state officials who in the past had been too easily tempted to accept bribes for favours.

Legend tells us that the city of Rome was founded by two brothers, Romulus and Remus, orphans who were suckled by a she-wolf in the hills of Latium, a district in Italy. Whether either had anything to do with the creation of the city on the River Tiber or not, Romulus was the name of the first king, and he reigned from 753 to 716 B.C. It is thought that the Latin people were Indo-Europeans who went to Italy in about 1200 B.C. Romans always dated everything from 753.

Who founded Rome?

Below Legend says that Romulus and Remus both wished to be king of Rome. Romulus claimed that he was chosen by the gods. In the quarrel that followed, Remus was killed.

Why were the kings expelled from Rome?

Romulus was, according to tradition, the first of seven kings of Rome. The first six were, on the whole, able, courageous and hardworking men. The seventh, Tarquinius Superbus (Tarquin the Arrogant), was none of these things. Worse, he was treacherous, cruel and haughty. To get the throne he murdered his predecessor, Servius Tullius. Then he began to rule extremely badly.

In 510, two leading statesmen, Lucius Junius Brutus and Gaius Collatinus, persuaded the people to vote for the expulsion of Tarquin and his family. The people did not elect any more kings. Instead, they elected Brutus and Collatinus as consuls to govern Rome for one year. Thereafter, each year, two consuls were elected to run the state, and it was extremely rare for one man to hold the office more than once in his life.

Of the many qualities the Roman people had, their endurance against all odds was probably the key to their amazing success. This endurance is impossible to explain. There have been courageous and long-suffering people in all lands in all ages, but the Romans seem to have been endowed with an unequalled belief in their own greatness and in their destiny, which was to bring a practical civilization to a large part of the world.

It is interesting that Roman civilization had a wider influence on the world than any other, that the greatest man in world history, Julius Caesar, was a Roman, and that the religion with the largest number of believers, Christianity, began in a Roman province and became the official religion of the empire.

How did Rome become so great?

Above The Etruscans lived north of the Tiber, and about 650 B.C. they took control of Rome. Their rule lasted until the expulsion of Tarquinius Superbus. They left behind distinctive and beautiful bronzes, sculptures and frescoes.

Who was Camillus?

Marcus Furius Camillus was a great Roman statesman and general who in about 390 B.C. was appointed dictator in order to save the state from the invasion of the Gauls under Brennus. Although the city was sacked, Brennus was defeated in the field by Camillus who then organized the reconstruction of the city. Several times in later years Camillus was appointed Dictator in periods of national danger. He died in about 365 of plague.

When Caesar was conquering Gaul, among the tribes he was fighting were the Celts from the British Isles, who were helping their Gallic kinsmen. So he decided to invade Britain and punish the Celts. He landed in 55 B.C. and defeated them in Kent. Then he returned to Gaul. The following year he invaded again, and this time defeated them under their king, Cassivelaunus, at Wheathampstead in Hertfordshire.

Why did Julius Caesar invade Britain?

Why is Julius Caesar considered by many to have been the greatest man in history?

Most people are satisfied if they do well in one career. Some are able to excel in two. But the unique thing about Julius Caesar is that he excelled in everything he did. He was one of the great generals of history and never lost a major battle. He was the second most famous orator in Roman history (Cicero was the first). He wrote some of the finest Latin works that came out of Rome. He was a gifted scholar, lawyer and poet. As a statesman he changed the Roman system of government from being a shaky and bungling republic to an imperial state, ruled by one man through a painstaking and efficient civil service.

His work for Rome affected not only the course of Roman history, but indeed the progress of all history, and it has been said that the story of the world can be divided between the times before Caesar and those after.

Caesar made himself master of the Roman world by defeating everyone who opposed him. Among those whom he defeated were Marcus Brutus, Caius Cassius and Caius Trebonius, but instead of sentencing them to death, Caesar pardoned them. What is more, he gave them high office, titles and money.

Brutus and his friends did not agree with Caesar's reforms or his way of governing, although these were both necessary if the great Roman empire was not to break up. So they plotted with others to kill Caesar, and on 15th March 44 B.C., they stabbed him to death during a meeting of the senate in Pompey's Theatre in Rome.

Brutus probably believed that what he was doing was the best for Rome, but the others had no such honourable ideas. They were in fact very jealous and ungrateful men, and most of them were to pay for the crime with their lives.

Why did Brutus and his friends murder Caesar?

When Rome began to be ruled by an emperor, the average Roman, when he was not a soldier, craftsman, official in the government, or tradesman, was a very idle person. All his work was done by slaves, or he lived in a room or two and needed no help. He had a free issue of corn from the state at regular intervals, and he was provided with a number of entertainments like gladiatorial contests or wild beast shows. Even some of the public baths were free and there he could idle away the hours wallowing in warm water chatting to his friends.

What was life like for a Roman citizen in the time of the emperors?

Why did Rome fall to the barbarians?

Below Flavius Stilicho, a Roman general, who fought against Alaric.

In the fourth century A.D. the western Roman empire was seriously threatened by movements of barbarians along its borders. From time to time these forces broke through and ravaged far and wide. The emperors had to send armies to drive them out. After a while the Romans were forced to employ one barbarian tribe to help them defeat another. But this was a dangerous policy, for the friendly barbarians soon became so strong that they could dictate to the Roman emperors. One such chief, Alaric the Goth, served for a while as governor of a Roman province. Then he fell out with the emperor, and in 410 he besieged Rome. After a long fight, he captured and plundered the city.

It was a terrifying moment for the Romans, and it showed that the city was not as impregnable as was widely believed.

The Huns were an Asiatic tribe of warriors who were particularly skilful horsemen. They came from central Russia and they descended upon Europe in the fifth century A.D. Their greatest leader was Attila who in the 440s ravaged south-eastern Europe and, in 447, actually reached the great walls of Constantinople. Suddenly, one morning there was a terrible earthquake. Some of the towers and long stretches of wall collapsed. Attila could have taken the city then, but his men were afraid. So he turned his attentions towards Italy. There, in 452 he threatened Rome itself, but was persuaded by the Pope to spare the city.

Who was Attila the Hun?

Below Attila meets the Pope's messenger.

When did the Chinese first drink tea?

During the earliest years of the great Han dynasty it was discovered that if the leaves of a tea plant were chopped up and hot water poured on them, the result was a pleasing drink with a fragrant smell. The Chinese did not put milk into their tea.

Over the centuries the Chinese invented numerous things quite independently of other civilizations. They invented the wheel, for example, in their earliest days, and this must have been to them an original idea for they could not have had contact with Sumer in the Near East where it was also invented. They discovered how to make gunpowder for fireworks but never learned to compress it for explosive purposes. They invented ink and movable type. Their porcelain was much more attractive and much thinner than the earthenware made in many other parts of the world at the time.

What other things did the Chinese invent?

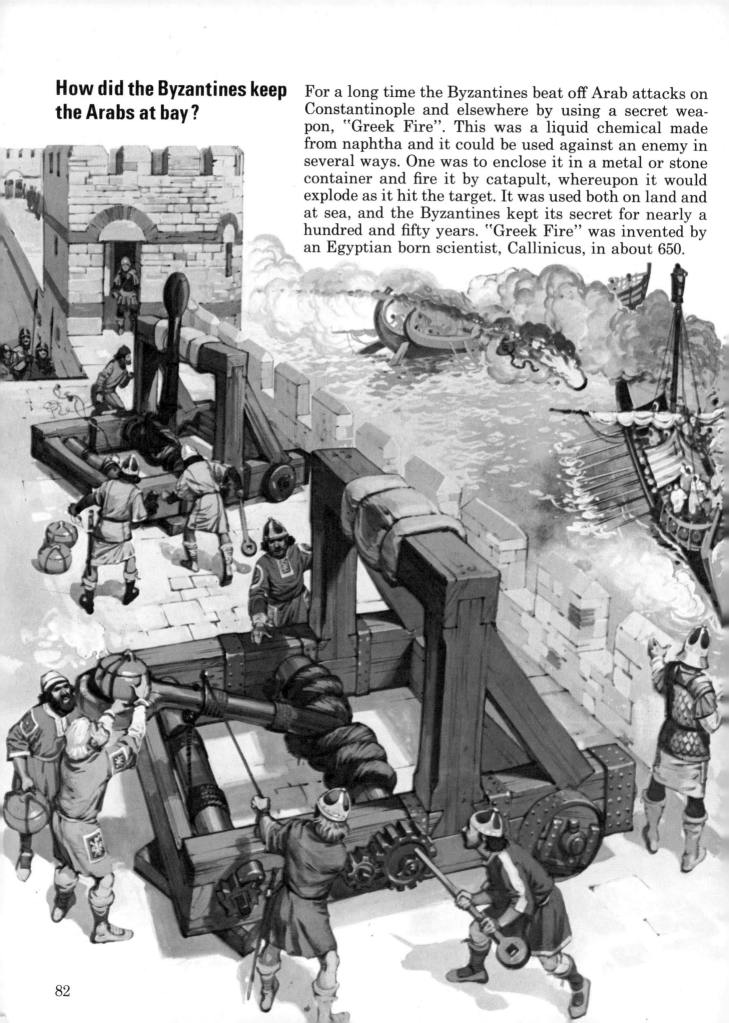

How did the Byzantines keep the Arabs at bay?

For a long time the Byzantines beat off Arab attacks on Constantinople and elsewhere by using a secret weapon, "Greek Fire". This was a liquid chemical made from naphtha and it could be used against an enemy in several ways. One was to enclose it in a metal or stone container and fire it by catapult, whereupon it would explode as it hit the target. It was used both on land and at sea, and the Byzantines kept its secret for nearly a hundred and fifty years. "Greek Fire" was invented by an Egyptian born scientist, Callinicus, in about 650.

The phrase "Dark Ages" is usually given to the centuries immediately after the fall of the western Roman Empire to the barbarians in the middle of the fifth century A.D. It is limited to western Europe because civilization continued in the East in Byzantium, and of course elsewhere in the world, for instance, the Near East, India, China, Mexico and Peru. Western Europe was broken up into various barbarian kingdoms in which surviving Christians had a hard time. Art and learning generally declined, and government such as the Romans had administered it did not exist. These bad times were shared by the peoples in Britain, but not in Ireland, and they lasted more or less up to the time of Charlemagne, in the early ninth century.

What were the "Dark Ages"?

What was life like in the "Dark Ages"?

It is difficult to imagine exactly what it was like to live in the "Dark Ages". People in western Europe had for centuries been used to ordered government and a universal system of law as administered by Rome. Now there was neither. Men used the sword to settle their differences and to obtain things that belonged to other people. The peasant farmer had to watch his land churned up, often just before harvest, by squabbling warriors fighting over who owned what property. In return for protection, some peasants gave up their freedom and became the bondsmen of these warriors who are quite often mistakenly referred to as knights.

Even supposing you wanted to learn about anything over and above farming, it was very hard to find anyone educated enough to teach you. All the great communication systems introduced by the Romans were allowed to decay and it was unsafe and laborious even to go a short journey across country.

Why was Alfred of England called "The Great"?

Very simply because he was all things to all men in England in his reign (871–900). He rallied the people of Wessex, built them into a fine army, and utterly defeated the Vikings at Ethandune, which is near Chippenham in Wiltshire, in 878. He built a new fleet of ships with which to fight off the Viking raiders along the English coasts. He founded schools and colleges and encouraged scholars and teachers. He started the Anglo-Saxon Chronicle, the first continuous history of England (it was still being kept on two hundred and fifty years after his death). He reformed the law and made it so clear and just that for generations afterwards people blessed his name.

This remarkable man was the only English king to be called "the Great". Are you surprised? No other king before or since ever did so much for England.

How did they tell the time in Anglo-Saxon England?

One of the many qualities of Alfred the Great was his inventive turn of mind. During his reign he devised the first candle clock. This was a candle made of tallow which was divided into twelve equal sections by lines or ridges, each section of which burned for an hour. The Romans had used, among other things, sundials, and many of these had been left behind in Britain.

When the barbarians broke up the western Roman empire, the survivors tended to shut themselves off in small communities. There were no more emperors to whom to pledge one's loyalty, and no government to order one's life. Gradually, out of this aimless kind of life there arose a new idea. This was the principle of a contract, or agreement, between one man and another, for the first to protect the second and the second to do something for the first in return. Strong men, usually those who could manage a horse well and use weapons skilfully while on horseback, offered such protection to weaker men. This idea developed until Europe was not much more than a collection of tiny "kingdoms" ruled by a lord who offered his protection to a number of lesser men in return for defined services. The agreement was called a *feudum,* from the Latin, and from which we get the word "feudal". In William the Conqueror's time the service in return for protection was military, a fixed number of days every year fighting for the king.

What was the Feudal System?

Who were the Vikings?

The Vikings were tough, sea-faring, barbarian raiders from Scandinavia, that is, Denmark, Norway and Sweden. In the eighth century they began their raids on the coasts of most of Europe, including the British Isles, France, the Low Countries, Italy. They also ravaged Russia and nearly laid siege to Constantinople.

Did the Vikings actually sail to America?

Under their leader, Leif Ericsson, who in the eleventh century was living in southern Greenland (a Viking colony founded by his father, Eric the Red), the Vikings sailed westwards hoping to explore the rest of Greenland. They were blown off course, spent many weeks at sea, and finally landed on a beach along which vines were growing. They called it Vinland, but it was almost certainly Labrador, part of Canada. They did not, however, realize they had discovered a new continent, and stayed there only for a few months.

Why was the Sassanid dynasty of Persian kings so famous?

The Sassanid dynasty of Persia was founded by a great warrior of Persian birth, Ardashir, who in A.D. 226 drove the Parthians out of power. The Sassanids were much more cultivated than their predecessors, and their dynasty lasted, in spite of many attempts to destroy Persia, until the coming of the Islamic Arabs in about 640. One king, Sapor II the Great, ruled for seventy years, from 309 to 379, and he defeated many Roman as well as barbarian armies who came against him. The Sassanid people were very artistic and their stone and metal work was among the best in the world.

What was China like under the T'ang dynasty?

The T'ang dynasty, which ruled the ancient Chinese empire from about A.D. 600 to about 900, introduced a new age of development in Chinese civilization. Many new ideas were born, such as the water-driven mill, and the wheelbarrow (it is strange that no one thought of this before). Other inventions of earlier years were improved, like movable type and porcelain. A piece of T'ang china today, if you could afford it, would cost thousands of pounds.

In this period, Chinese civilization spread beyond its borders, into Japan, South-east Asia and Korea.

Right A goat in jade (T'ang).

Below A T'ang dynasty horse made of procelain.

Above A statuette in terracotta of the T'ang dynasty.

If we accept the meaning of the term civilization as it has been given in the first question in this book, then civilization reached the Americas as long ago as 2000 B.C. In both Central and South America there were settlements of farmers who grew corn, which we call maize, pepper, beans and cotton. They had also begun to put up buildings in stone.

When did civilization first reach the Americas?

Who were the Mayas?

Above A clay statuette of a Maya priest, about 6th century A.D.

Below From a Maya sacred book: the Maize god *(left)* and the Rain god *(right)*.

The Mayas were the first civilized people in Central America. They were descended from races who went from Asia across the Bering Straits into Alaska and settled in the warmer climate of what is now Mexico and Guatemala. They were great builders in stone, and they put up vast temples and tombs. They were on the whole peaceful people, and much of their life was given up to religious worship and ceremony.

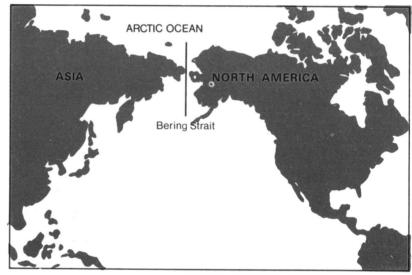

They built houses that were not unlike those in many countries in England in the seventeenth and eighteenth centuries, that is, timber-framed with thatched roofs. Their houses were probably not as large and may not have been more than one storey high. The rulers, however, lived in great stone palaces.

How did the Mayas build their houses?

The main crop of the Maya people was maize, and with it they made bread and cakes. They are also believed to have grown tobacco for smoking, which they dried out in the sun, cut into small slivers and pushed down into the bowl of a clay pipe.

What were the Mayas' main crops?

Below A reconstruction of a Maya temple, at Palenque.

What were the Peruvian civilizations?

Below left A Paraca clay vessel.
Below centre A figure of a Mochica warrior.
Below right A Paraca bowl.

We know very little about civilization in Peru before about 1300 B.C. Then we know the Chavin civilization flourished in the northern highlands from about that date to about 400 B.C. These Chavin people were skilled in the techniques of stone building.

They were followed by the Paracas, from about 400 B.C. to about A.D. 400, who were in turn followed by the Nazcas. The Nazca civilization was quite short, and then came the Mochicas, who built, among other things, a huge pyramid, called the pyramid of the Sun, which is said to contain one hundred million bricks.

The last and greatest of the Peruvian civilizations was the Inca, and this flourished from about 1200 to its collapse under the Spaniards in 1530–31.

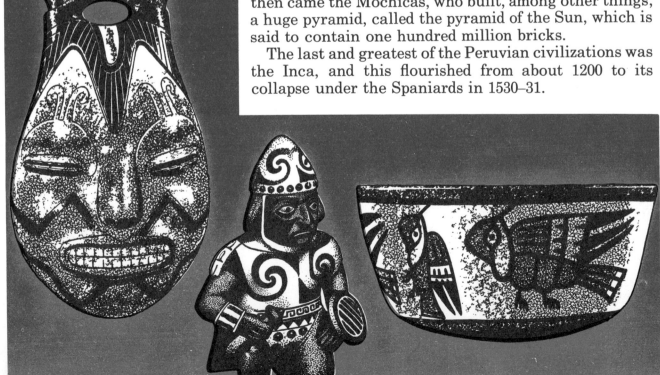

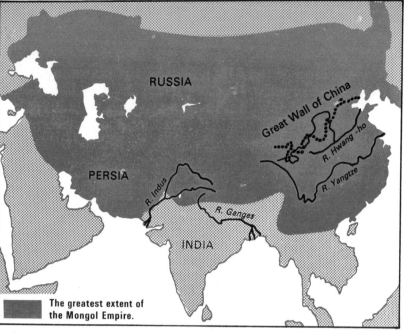

The greatest extent of the Mongol Empire.

Who were the Mongols?

The Mongols were a fierce, tough and brave race of warriors who came from central Asia, somewhere in the area between India, China and Siberia. They spent much of their lives on horseback, wandering from one place to another. They cared little about farming or town life, and had no more ambition than to raid neighbours for food. Then, at the end of the twelfth century, they found a wonderful leader, Genghiz Khan.

Who was Genghiz Khan?

Genghiz Khan was one of the greatest conquerors of history. Named Temujine at birth, and son of a Mongol chief, he was so successful as a young man fighting neighbouring tribes that when his father died he was chosen successor, and soon given the title Genghiz Khan, which means "Lord Absolute".

By the beginning of the thirteenth century he had organized the Mongols into an invincible fighting force, mounted on swift horses, inspired by his leadership, ready to conquer the world. And in less than twenty years they had overrun Persia, northern India, most of Russia and the Near East, and breached the Great Wall of China and occupied vast areas there.

When he died in 1227, Genghiz Khan's empire was so big that it took over a year to cross from one end to the other.

How did Khubilai Khan's rule affect China?

Above The Mongols sometimes built their houses on wheels.

Khubilai Khan, one of Genghiz Khan's grandsons, became king of northern China in the middle of the thirteenth century. He had all of his grandfather's leadership and military skill, and he soon overcame all China and the south-east of Asia, and made himself emperor. Then he set out to make China more advanced than it already was. Scholars and scientists were encouraged to go to Peking, his capital, to work. Fine buildings were put up, trade stimulated, and foreign visitors welcomed. One of these was Marco Polo.

Marco Polo was a Venetian merchant and traveller who in 1271 set out with his father and uncle on a journey overland through Persia, western Asia and India and finally reached Peking, the capital of Khubilai Khan's empire in China. They were brought to the emperor who showed great interest in them. Marco himself was employed by the emperor on several state matters, and soon learned Chinese and all about this remarkable civilization. He returned to Italy in 1295. Three years later when the story of his adventures was published, it made Europeans realize that thousands of miles away to the east was a civilization superior in many ways to theirs.

Why was Marco Polo's visit to Khubilai Khan so important?

Why did Columbus search for a sea route to China and the East Indies?

People in the Middle Ages in western Europe needed vast quantities of spices to disguise the taste of their often bad food, and to preserve it. The spices had to be brought overland from the East, for example from the Philippines, and so they were extremely costly. Merchants began to think about reaching these Spice Islands by sea so that the spices could be brought more cheaply.

In the fifteenth century, the Portuguese began to try to find a route round Africa and across the Indian Ocean. But in the 1480s, a Genoese navigator, Christopher Columbus, tried to persuade the Portuguese king to finance a voyage due west, across the Atlantic, rather than round Africa. The king was not interested, so Columbus turned to the king of Spain, who did give him money, and Columbus set out in 1492, landing a few weeks later in what he thought were the Indies. They were in fact the lands we now call the West Indies.

Below right Prince Henry.

If you look at a map of Europe you will see that the small country of Portugal lies on the extreme west side of Spain. More than half its entire border is lapped by the waters of the Atlantic Ocean. Naturally, a people with so much coast line would be sea-faring. They were such skilful navigators because they were encouraged to become great sea captains by Prince Henry the Navigator (1394–1460), one of the sons of the king of Portugal. He wanted the Portuguese to be the first to discover sea routes to India and the East, and he set up a school in which adventurous young men were taught all the arts of navigation and sailing.

Why were the Portuguese so famous as navigators?

Why was the Ming dynasty in China so famous?

The Ming dynasty (1368–1644) is probably best known for giving its name to some of the most beautiful porcelain ever made. But there was more to the Ming period of Chinese history than that. In about 1356 a Chinese general, Yuen Chang, led a rebellion against the emperor, who was a descendant of Khubilai Khan, and finally drove him out. Yuen was then elected emperor in 1368, and he took the name Hung Wu, which was the family name of a much older line of emperors.

Hung Wu and most of his successors devoted their reigns to preserving Chinese civilization, if possible without any influence from other civilizations. This was a pity because, advanced though China was in so many things, there were also fields in which the Chinese were behind, such as industry, and they might well have benefited by exchanges of ideas with Western nations.

Above A warrior scupltured in limestone, about 1403–24.
Right A Ming vase.

Yes, it spread throughout almost all of South-east Asia, including Indo-China, Korea, Japan, Cambodia, and parts of Indonesia and Malaya. In Burma it was mingled with Indian civilization. Many of the characteristics of these countries' culture, language, art, building, furniture and way of life are still essentially Chinese.

Did Chinese civilization spread in Asia?

Who were the Aztecs?

The Aztecs were Central American people who for many years lived as neighbours of the Mayas and their successors, the Toltecs, but they were not as advanced as either. By about A.D. 1100, however, they felt powerful enough to invade the lands of the Toltecs, and in a short time they conquered them. Like many peoples who invade the lands of more civilized people, the Aztecs soon absorbed the Toltecs' superior way of life and then improved upon it. They erected huge and magnificent buildings. They studied astronomy and mathematics. And they set up an ordered system of government with a civil service.

Their civilization was brought to a sudden end by the Spanish military adventurers led by Hernan Cortez in 1519–20, who overran their cities and countryside and treated their people with great cruelty.

In many ways the Inca empire, the last and greatest civilization in Peru, was very well organized. The country was divided into districts of about 10,000 people which were governed by high-born officials appointed by the emperor, or Inca, as he was called. These officials kept in touch with the Inca and with each other by means of relays of fast running couriers, who used a splendid system of roads built by Inca engineers.

Each of the officials would divide his area into smaller units and appoint a local man to look after each one.

The one draw-back in the system was that if the Inca died and there was no immediate successor, the government broke down through lack of leadership. The officials had for so long been used to receiving orders from the head of state. This is what happened in 1531 when Atahualpa, the last Inca, was murdered by the Spanish who had invaded Peru. The officials surrendered almost at once.

How was the Inca empire organized?

What were the Inca clothes like?

Inca society had a strict class structure: emperor, nobles, officials, merchants, craftsmen, and workers. These classes were recognized not only by the nature of their occupations, but also by their clothes. The Inca was dressed in the richest robes, with many jewels of gold and silver, metals which the Incas did not rate as very valuable. The nobles wore brightly coloured earrings with their multi-coloured robes. The workers, on the other hand, wore plain clothes, but these were made on hand looms and were hard-wearing.

What was the Reformation?

Below left Martin Luther; *(right)* John Calvin, another leader of the Reformation.

All religions from time to time need to reconsider their doctrines and clear away confused thinking. When the leaders of any faith do not do this, there is likely to be a movement among the members to reform the organization. This is what happened to Christianity in the sixteenth century.

By that time, the Church had grown rich, and bishops and senior priests had spent more time accumulating wealth than on looking after their congregations, despite the warnings they were given by a number of outspoken churchmen. The teachings and practices of the Church had become different from the simple message of Jesus Christ and his disciples. And in the sixteenth century several people began to question these teachings.

One of these was Martin Luther, a German monk who in 1517 wrote down a long list of criticisms of certain practices, and nailed it to the door of Wittenburg cathedral. This started a long struggle in the Church between those who wanted to reform the abuses to which Luther had drawn attention, and others as well, and those who would not accept reform. This conflict was called the Reformation, and it was perhaps the major talking point in Europe for nearly the whole century.

An inquisition means an enquiry, usually an official one. In the Middle Ages, the Church set up an Inquisition. This was a board of judges who listened to allegations against people who were accused of not conforming to the teachings or rules of the Church. This Inquisition had very wide powers. The accused could be kept in prison, bombarded with questions, tortured if need be, and generally ill-treated. If he was found guilty, the punishment was decided at a public meeting called an "auto-da-fé" ("act of faith") and the sentence was then carried out by the government of the country in which the Inquisition was being held. These sentences could be confiscation of property, life imprisonment, a term in the ships as a galley slave, or even death by burning or hanging.

The most famous Inquisition was the one held in Spain in the last years of the fifteenth century, in which many people, especially those of Jewish descent, suffered.

What was the Inquisition?

Below The Church of Santa Maria della Salute in Venice, begun in 1631.

Just imagine if you were grown up, had spent the best part of your life looking after a big estate and had from time to time led an army in battle—but you had never been to sea and did not know a mast from an anchor. Then, suddenly, the king sends for you and orders you to take command of the biggest armada, or fleet, of ships ever assembled and lead it against a brave and defiant island people. How do you think you would manage?

This is exactly what happened to the Duke of Medina Sidonia, in Spain. He was appointed commander of the great Spanish Armada which was detailed to sail up the Atlantic and invade England to bring the English back into the Catholic faith–and he had no knowledge of ships whatever. Is it any wonder that the operation was a disaster?

Why did the Spanish Armada fail in its attempt to invade England in 1588?

Why was Simón Bolívar called "The Liberator"?

This splendid South American soldier and statesman, who was born in Venezuela and educated in Europe, was the leader of a number of rebel movements in the South American continent against Spain, in the early years of the nineteenth century. He began by driving the Spanish out of his own land and of the next province, New Granada, and in 1819 he formed the Republic of Colombia. Then he led the rebels in Peru and in Ecuador, and in 1826 he had driven out the Spaniards from much of the western side of the continent.

His activities encouraged other movements. He longed to unite all the new republics in one federation, but he died before he could do much to carry this out, and it never happened. But he had given millions of people their freedom. That is why he was called "The Liberator".

Why did Elizabeth I never marry?

Of course we shall never know the real reason because the great queen did not tell anyone–or if she did they never recorded it. One possible reason is because she was in love with Robert Dudley, later Earl of Leicester, who was already married. When his wife, Amy, died as a result of falling down a flight of stairs at her home, gossip said her death had been arranged by Dudley. Once the queen heard this, she knew that in her position she could never marry anyone who was even suspected of murdering his wife. But it was more likely because, while she remained unmarried, she was able to play off one suitor, thus one country, against another, and gain time to make herself more secure on the throne, and the country safer from invasion.

Below King Charles I quarrels with Parliament

The two sides which fought in the great Civil War in Britain from 1642–6 were the Royalists and the Parliamentarians. The Royalists, who supported the king, Charles I, were nicknamed Cavaliers after some mounted knights were seen parading round the Houses of Parliament not very long before the war began. The Parliamentarians, who quarrelled with the king over taxation and religion among other things, were called Roundheads by their enemies because they were Puritans, that is, low-churchmen, and Puritans would not wear their hair long or sport wigs. Instead they wore close-cropped hair.

The Parliamentarians were successful, the king was executed in 1649, and the sovereignty of Parliament was established.

Who were the Cavaliers and Roundheads?

Below left King Charles I ; *(right)* Oliver Cromwell, a leader of the Parliamentarians.

What was the Industrial Revolution?

Below James Watt and one of his first steam engines.

Below John Kay, who invented a new method of weaving in 1733, was threatened by angry crowds who claimed he was taking their work away from them.

The Industrial Revolution is the phrase used to describe the period when Britain changed from an agricultural to an industrial and manufacturing country. It took place in the second half of the eighteenth and first part of the nineteenth centuries, and it was brought about by a number of things. During the period the country was not invaded and, although the navy and army were involved in several wars abroad, Britain was left alone to develop.

At this time there was a great upsurge in scientific invention, started off by the revolutionary invention of the steam engine. This meant that many other new tools, machines and gadgets were invented which could speed the rate at which work could be done. Factories were built and people moved away from the land to towns, to work in what they thought would be better conditions, with more money. Unfortunately, many factory owners made the workers work for long hours with little pay, and many grievances arose. This situation led eventually to the trade union movement.

In 1789 the French Revolution broke out. It was the most devastating revolution the world had seen, and its results, the execution of the king and queen, and the murder of many famous people, frightened the other kings and princes of Europe. By the end of the century the French were being led by a young Corsican-born general, Napoleon, who aimed to conquer Europe and unite it under French rule – with himself at the top.

The one danger to his plans was Britain, who commanded the seas. Three times Napoleon's or his allies' navies were utterly defeated by Admiral Nelson, recognized by historians as the greatest admiral in the history of the world. These victories were at the Nile, 1798, Copenhagen, 1801, and Trafalgar, 1805, when Nelson was killed.

The last victory stopped Napoleon invading Britain, and so enabled the British to begin to break his power in Europe. Napoleon was finally defeated by troops under the Duke of Wellington and Blücher at Waterloo in 1815, and after this there began a period of great change in Europe.

How did Nelson's victories change Europe?

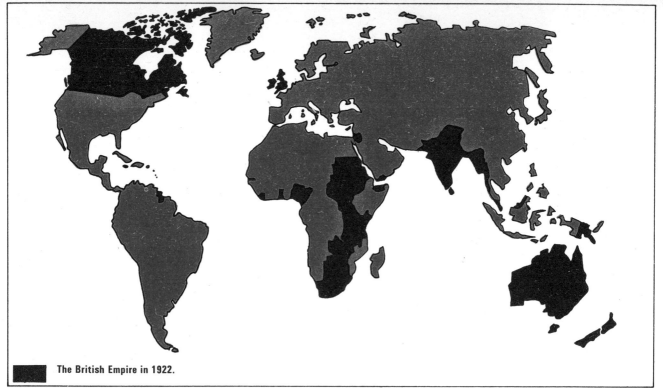

The British Empire in 1922.

How did Britain become so powerful in the nineteenth century?

Right Queen Victoria.

Britain was the one country in western Europe that did not suffer invasion or battles on her own land in the war against Napoleon. This meant that the nation was able to make progress while the others had to devote themselves to resisting Napoleon or to trying to endure his rule. Since the nation was clearly more highly indust-rialized than any other in the world, it had a head start when, after Waterloo, Europe began to rebuild itself.

Europe was upturned again in 1848 when revolutions against the ruling monarchs took place in nearly every land – except Britain. This gave Britain yet more time for industrial expansion. A third reason was that Britain produced the leading scientists and inventors of the age.

Why was Winston Churchill described as a "many-sided genius"?

This astonishing British leader, who organized the British people to fight against Hitler and the Germans in the Second World War (1939–45) was not only a statesman of the first rank. He was the author of some of the best books in the English language, which won for him the Nobel Prize for Literature. He was an accomplished painter; he had had a distinguished career as a soldier between 1894 and 1900, and again from 1915–16; and he was the greatest orator in British history. He was, as a younger man, a fine polo player and he won the Public Schools' Fencing Championships. He was also one of the most amusing conversationalists in the land.

It is easy to see why Queen Elizabeth II called him a "many-sided genius".

In the later part of the sixteenth century, France was torn by civil war between Catholics and Protestants, and one king after another had failed to do much about it. In 1589 Henry of Navarre succeeded to the throne as Henry IV. He was a Protestant, but when he saw that most of the people were Catholics, he said he would change his faith, on the understanding that if he did so the Protestants would be allowed to stay in France and continue to worship in their way. This was the occasion when he is reported to have said "Paris is well worth a Mass." He meant that it was worth his changing his beliefs to secure the French throne and end the civil war.

Right Henry IV of France.
Below The massacre of the Protestant Huguenots by the Catholics in Paris in 1572 was one of the most dreadful events of the civil war.

Why did Henry IV of France say that Paris was well worth a Mass?

What did Cardinal Richelieu do for France?

Cardinal Richelieu was the chief minister of France from 1624 to his death in 1642. In that time he had one aim—to make France the greatest nation in Europe. He ruled the country firmly, through new officials in the various regions who were directly responsible to him. In foreign affairs he intervened in wars on the sides of the nations which were fighting big powers, and so made France feared everywhere. Overseas, he encouraged French merchants to expand trade and French adventurers to found new colonies.

Right Louis XIII, who ruled France from 1610–43.

Left Cardinal Richelieu.

Who was the "Sun King"?

The "Sun King" was Louis XIV of France, who reigned from 1643 to 1715. It was a long reign and a very splendid one, too. Cardinal Richelieu had made the nation rich and strong, and Louis decided to make it the centre of art and learning in Europe. Working with a very able finance minister, Colbert, he encouraged all kinds of artistic works, especially fine buildings, and here he set an example with a great new palace at Versailles. This was the marvel of Europe, and craftsmen from many lands helped to make it beautiful.

This great king was involved in many wars in Europe, in which much of the nation's wealth was wasted and its armies defeated. But he also encouraged trade and colonial settlement in America and the East. Despite the losses in his wars with Britain and Austria, the nation was nearly as rich at the end of his time as at the beginning.

How nice it would be if one could really answer big questions of this kind properly in one or two sentences! The French Revolution was no simple rising of angry starving peasants against a cruel and greedy king and his nobles, for Louis XVI was anything but that. It was a deep-rooted revolt by many classes of people in France against the whole order of society. This feeling did not grow up overnight. It stemmed from wrongs that were generations old, and which had been talked and written about for many years. A huge gap had arisen between the royal family, with the nobility, and the middle and lower classes, and by 1789 it was quite impossible to close it. The French parliament, called the Estates General, had not met for more than a century. Feudalism, which had died out in Britain in the fifteenth century, still dominated the French country districts.

The act which started the Revolution was the storming of the Bastille, a prison in Paris, in July 1789. But conditions in the country were so bad that a vast social upheaval was inevitable.

What caused the French Revolution?

Below Louis XVI and Queen Marie Antoinette; *(right)* Maximilien Robespierre, one of the leaders of the Revolutionaries.

It has been said that more books have been written about Napoleon than any other person in history. Certainly his career was a full one, and he made an enormous impact not only upon France but also on all Europe. Whether this impact was on balance a good one or not may well be discussed for many more years yet. His legal code is still in use in France and other western European countries. But in his vain attempt to build a united states of Europe under his rule, millions of Frenchmen died, and it can be said that France has never quite recovered from that loss.

Was Napoleon as great a man as most people think?

Below Napoleon said farewell to his Guards in 1814, before he was sent to Elba.

What happened to the German people in the Thirty Years War?

The Thirty Years' War (1618–48) was perhaps the most terrible war in all history. It involved all Europe, though Britain only slightly, and the people who suffered the most were the Germans. The war was fought between Catholic and the Protestant powers, and German soil was used by the various powers for their battlegrounds.

You can imagine what it was like when you remember that in those days armies did not bother to take large supply trains with them, but instead lived off the land. And this war was fought with terrible bitterness on both sides.

The German peoples saw their fields trampled down or scorched, their towns and villages stripped of food and clothing, their buildings set on fire. Before long, plague and famine struck, in which thousands died.

Who was Frederick the Great?

Below left to right Frederick the Great, Kaiser (Emperor) William II of Germany, and Prince Otto von Bismarck.

Frederick the Great was king of Prussia, a large German-speaking state, from 1740 to 1786. He was a great military leader who won several victories in both the War of the Austrian Succession (1740–8) and the Seven Years' War (1756–63). At home he was energetic and painstaking, believing in justice for all his people. He encouraged farming, industry, the arts and building. At the same time he maintained the Prussian army in a high state of efficiency and readiness for battle.

Quite simply, by being the largest of them all, and by producing the best statesmen and military leaders in all Germany. Under the Prussian king, William I (1861–1888), and his chief minister of state, Otto von Bismarck (1815–1898), the German states were united in one great German empire. The Prussians continued to dominate the rest of the Germans right up to the end of the First World War, and indeed Hitler's principal generals were mostly Prussian-born.

How did Prussia come to dominate the German states?

Who started the First World War?

In the early days of the present century the small state of Serbia began to campaign for independence for fellow countrymen who were occupying parts of the Austro-Hungarian empire, but the Austrian government would not grant it. At the end of June 1914, a Serbian student, Gabriel Prinzip, shot dead the Archduke Franz Ferdinand, heir to the Austrian empire. The Austrians blamed the Serbian government and without further ado declared war. This brought the Russians in on the side of Serbia, which in turn made the Germans declare war on Russia.

France, meanwhile, had a treaty of alliance with Russia and so felt obliged to join in against Germany. The Germans, in order to attack France indirectly, attacked Belgium, despite the fact that the emperor, known as the Kaiser, had promised not to harm the small state. The Germans were anxious to try out a new invasion plan which would, if successful, result in the capture of most of Belgium, part of France, and the city of Paris, all in a matter of weeks.

The British, who had promised to protect Belgium, declared war on Germany on 4th August, and by their first victory over the Germans at the battle of the Marne a few weeks later, they prevented the German plan from being carried out.

When the Germans were defeated in the First World War, they were made to pay huge sums of money, called reparations, to those countries which they had harmed. The 1920s were bad years for world trade and industry, and these reparations made things worse for the Germans and a great deal of unemployment followed. Their leaders were not very helpful, either, so when the Austrian-born political leader, Adolf Hitler, started to make speeches up and down the country saying that he and his National Socialist (Nazi) party would provide work and would build an army big enough to avenge the defeat in 1918, many Germans believed him.

In 1933 Hitler was strong enough to have himself appointed Chancellor, that is, head of the government, by the president. Despite the fact that he led them into the Second World War in 1939, which they lost very badly, the Germans supported him right up to the day of his suicide in April 1945. A week later they surrendered.

Why did the Germans support Hitler and the Nazis?

Above Adolf Hitler.

Below Hitler held huge rallies where his gift for oratory had full play.

Right Joseph Goebbels, the Minister of Propaganda under Hitler.

In the second half of the sixteenth century, the Netherlands, then a collection of small states, was under the control of Spain. Some of the states were, however, largely Protestant, and they resisted the Spaniards' rule. They were led by Prince William of Orange, who was known as "The Silent" possibly because when he moved his troops to attack the enemy, he moved them so quietly they were able to take the enemy by surprise, or because of his reserved disposition. By 1579 he had won enough successes to enable the states to declare their independence, and they elected him their first Chief Stadholder, or chief head of state.

The Spaniards were not so easily defeated, however, and a few years later William was murdered.

Who was William the Silent?

Above left Prince William; *(right)* Philip II of Spain.

How did Holland become a great sea power?

Holland is a land of rivers and islands, and its coastline is washed by the choppy breakers of the North Sea. Over the centuries the people grew used to flooding and storms, and long, long ago they had learned all there was to know about ships and sailing. When at the end of the sixteenth century they won their independence from Spain, the Dutch had a new spirit of national pride. They were also great businessmen, and when they saw other nations begin to found colonies overseas, they joined in the race

Above Christiaan Huygens discovered the ring and fourth satellite of the planet Saturn. His invention of the pendulum clock was used by his clockmaker Johannes van Ceulen.

Although the great Italian scientist Galileo had shown how a pendulum worked, it was the Dutch scientist and astronomer, Christiaan Huygens (1629–1695) who first used a pendulum to regulate a clock. This brilliant man also made the first spiral balance watch.

Who invented the pendulum clock and the spiral balance watch?

Who were the Hapsburgs?

Below The Empress Maria Theresa and her husband.

The Hapsburgs were one of the most famous royal families in European history. Members of it were kings, emperors, princes and arch-dukes in many lands, chiefly German-speaking. The family began with a Count of Hapsburg in the eleventh century. Rudolph I, king of Germany (1218–91) was the first Hapsburg to be elected Emperor of the Holy Roman Empire. Among other famous members of the family were Charles V, Emperor of the Holy Roman Empire (1519–1555), in his time the most powerful monarch in Europe, Philip II (1555–98), the great king of Spain, and the Empress Maria Theresa of Austria-Hungary (1740–1780).

The Emperor Charles VI left his possessions to his daughter Maria Theresa, when he died in 1740. But soon after he died various European states claimed part of the great Austrian empire. Frederick the Great of Prussia demanded Silesia, and he invaded the country to take it by force. Maria Theresa was supported by Great Britain and Holland. The war lasted for eight years (1740–8), but at the end of it things were left much as they had been at the start.

What was the War of the Austrian Succession all about?

What was the Risorgimento?

Kingdom of Sardinia 1859.
With the kingdom of Sardinia,
formed Kingdom of Italy 1861.

MILAN
VENICE
KINGDOM OF SARDINIA
FLORENCE
ROME
NAPLES
KINGDOM OF THE 2 SICILIES

For centuries, efforts had been made to get the various kingdoms and states in Italy to unite, but they had all failed. Then, in the middle of the nineteenth century, a new movement towards this end began when King Victor Emmanuel of Sardinia and Piedmont (two of the states) appointed as his chief minister Count Camillo Cavour. This brilliant and imaginative statesman devoted his energies to bringing all the states together. He used every trick he could think of, negotiating with one king in Europe while plotting with another who was the first king's enemy. At the same time, he encouraged Italian writers, like Mazzini, to agitate for unity. The movement was called the Risorgimento.

Right Count Cavour.

Above King Victor Emmanuel.

One of the main figures in the great movement to unite Italy was a Piedmontese soldier, Giuseppe Garibaldi. In 1860 Garibaldi gathered together an army of about a thousand men in an attempt to capture southern Italy, held by the king of Naples, who was also king of Sicily, and who resisted the unification movement. He dressed his army in red shirts, trained them and took them to Sicily. In a very short campaign there he defeated the king's forces and drove them out. Then he took his "Redshirts", who had now become famous for their courage, across the mainland and defeated the king's army in Naples, driving the royal family out altogether. Two more states were now ready to join the union.

Who was Garibaldi?

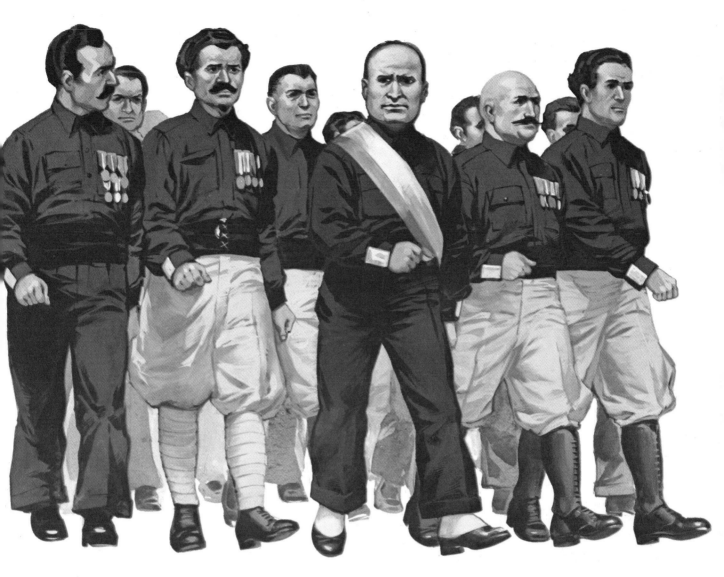

Who was Mussolini and what did his Fascist government achieve?

Benito Mussolini was an Italian journalist and political agitator who, after the First World War, formed a new party called the Fascist party. He did so because he and his associates thought there was a risk that Italy might become Communist. In 1921 his party won only thirty-one seats at the general election, but a year later he persuaded the king, Victor Emmanuel to let him form a government, and the king agreed.

For the next twenty-one years Mussolini ruled Italy as a dictator, with the silent approval of the king. His government achieved many things: good roads, new public buildings, work for everybody, but it was a hard time in which to live. There was no freedom, and opponents of the regime were sent to concentration camps or executed, just as in Hitler's Germany.

Mussolini backed Hitler in the Second World War. This was disastrous for Italy, and in 1943 he was forced to resign. Two years later he was executed by patriots.

In 1620, a number of English people, who were not allowed to worship God in their own way in England, decided to emigrate to America to set up a colony where they could have freedom of worship. In September they set sail from Plymouth in the ship "Mayflower" and after a hard crossing, beset by bad weather and sickness, in December they reached Cape Cod in Massachusetts, where they founded a settlement.

Where did the Pilgrim Fathers settle in America?

Which were the original thirteen states in America?

The settlements in America in the seventeenth century had by the eighteenth become quite extensive. More and more people had emigrated from Britain, discontented with one aspect of life or another in the home country. By about 1732 there were thirteen colonies, and they were New Hampshire, Massachusetts, Rhode Island, Connecticut, New York, New Jersey, Pennsylvania, Delaware, Maryland, Virginia, North Carolina, South Carolina, and Georgia.

The British colonists in America had in the eighteenth century grown prosperous, for it was a rich land. This wealth excited the envy of the home government in London, which saw an opportunity of raising taxes on the colonists. In the 1760s a number of taxes were imposed, for example on tea, sugar, glass, and newspapers. But the colonists were not represented in the London Parliament which imposed the taxes. Here was a serious grievance, but the home government resisted all attempts to put it right.

Eventually, when the colonists realized that they were not going to be treated fairly, they decided to fight to obtain their independence, and in 1774 the war began. Nine years later, their independence was recognized by Britain.

What caused the American War of Independence?

Below King George III.

114

Above In 1773 a group of citizens of Boston, dressed as Red Indians, boarded British ships and threw the cargo of tea overboard as a protest against the imposition of taxes.

Who was Thomas Jefferson?

Thomas Jefferson (1743–1826) was probably the greatest statesman the United States has yet produced. He was a Virginian lawyer who drafted the text of the American Declaration of Independence, issued in July 1776. This remarkable document, written in splendid English prose, has been said to be the finest statement about democracy since the times of the ancient Greeks.

Jefferson was the new republic's first ambassador to France (1784–9) and while he was there he helped the lawyers on the side of the French revolutionaries to draw up their Declaration of the Rights of Man. In 1800 he was elected third president of the United States, and was re-elected in 1804. In two terms of office he stimulated American trade and encouraged pioneers to explored westwards across the Mississippi River, and so enlarge the republic.

What was the Monroe Doctrine?

Published in 1823 by President James Monroe (1788–1831), this was in effect a declaration of "America for the Americans". Americans were by this time tired of nations in Europe interfering in their affairs. They also became impatient at Europeans founding colonies in the two continents. By issuing this declaration, the President made it clear that any such interference would be regarded as an act of war, and would be dealt with accordingly. It is a doctrine that has had to be cited on several occasions since 1823, particularly in a dispute between the United States and Britain over Venezuelan boundaries, in 1895.

The first recorded Europeans to land in Canada, if one discounts the Vikings in the eleventh century, were the Cabots who reached Cape Breton Island in 1497. In 1535 the French navigator, Jacques Cartier, sailed up the St Lawrence River but did not stay. About seventy years later, settlements were made along the St Lawrence River where Quebec now stands, under the leadership of Samuel de Champlain (1567–1635). He made several explorations in and around the Great Lakes and he set up trading stations. He was one of the explorers encouraged by Richelieu.

Who was the first European settler in Canada?

Below Jacques Cartier lands on the Gaspe Peninsula in Canada.

Below Fraser's Highlanders, one of the regiments which fought in North America.

How did Britain win Canada from the French?

Left General Wolfe.

Below General Montcalm.

In the seventeenth and eighteenth centuries, two major powers were building empires in North America, Britain and France. The French had control of much of east Canada, which bordered on British colonies in what is now the east of the United States. There were of course many clashes.

When Britain and France went to war in 1756, although the chief battlegrounds were in Europe, it was also an opportunity for the two powers to fight it out in North America, and in India where both had interests. In 1759 the British government appointed James Wolfe as commander of the expedition to drive the French out of Canada. He was a brilliant young officer, aged only 32 and already a major-general. George II, when people said that Wolfe was mad, replied "Well, I hope he bites some of my other generals!"

Wolfe led his men along the narrow defiles up the Heights of Abraham, a towering range of hills overlooking Quebec. There on top were the French, but because Wolfe had sent his men up by night, they were not detected. When dawn broke, a great battle was fought which the British won, but in which both Wolfe and the French commander, General Montcalm, were slain.

When was Australia first colonized?

Although Australia was discovered in the early 1600s it was many years before it was realized that it was a huge continent on its own. And it was not until the great discoverer Captain Cook charted its eastern coast in 1770 that anyone decided to colonize there. It was the British who settled. One of the places found by Cook was a big bay near what is now Sydney. He called it Botany Bay because of the variety of hitherto unknown plants that grew there. The British government decided to use the area as a punishment colony, that is, people found guilty of certain crimes in British courts were sent to Botany Bay instead of being sentenced to death.

Below Captain Cook lands at Botany Bay.

You will remember that on page 100 we saw how the Dutch founded colonies in the seventeenth century. One of their settlements was in South Africa. When in the nineteenth century British emigrants, too, came to settle there, it is not surprising that there were many clashes. Finally, in 1836, the Dutch settlers, called Boers from the Dutch word for farmers, *Boeren,* decided to leave and move north-eastwards where they founded new states, Transvaal and the Orange Free State. This movement was called the Great Trek.

When the Boers later asked for British help in a war with the Zulus, a powerful native tribe, the British agreed, on condition that the Boers put themselves under British sovereignty. When the war was over, the Boers expected to be given their freedom, but they were not, so they went to war.

Who were the Boers and why did they fight the British in the nineteenth century?

Gustavus Adolphus, who ruled from 1611–1632, was the greatest of the kings of Sweden. Up to his death he was also the foremost general in the Thirty Years War which involved nearly every nation in Europe. He championed the Protestant side in this terrible war, and by his brilliant military skill he won several important battles against Catholic generals, some of whom, like Count Tilly and Count Wallenstein, were very able commanders. At Lützen in 1632, he defeated Wallenstein in the field, but he was himself slain. Nonetheless he had secured the survival of Protestantism in Germany.

What did Gustavus Adolphus do during the Thirty Years War?

Below Gustavus Adolphus at Lützen.

What happened to Charles XII of Sweden?

Charles XII was another Swedish king who was also a brilliant military commander. In the years 1699 to 1708 he led armies with great success against Denmark, Poland and Russia (where he defeated Peter the Great), all of which had formed an alliance against him, and forced them to make peace. But in 1709 when he tried to march on Moscow he was defeated at Poltava and had to escape to Turkey.

He returned to Sweden in 1714 and made plans to rebuild the state which had been in decay for some time. In 1718, he invaded Norway but was killed by a stray bullet from a musket at the siege of Fredrickshald.

If you look at a map of Europe you will see how Poland is sandwiched between a number of bigger countries. It was always like that, and several times these powers decided to divide the country up between them. This was particularly sad because the Polish were–and are–a great people with tremendous national pride, courage and devotion to the Catholic faith. There had been a splendid dynasty in Poland called the Jagellons, from 1386 to 1572, and one of the most celebrated European kings, John III Sobieski, ruler from 1674-96, who saved Vienna from the Turks in 1683, was Polish.

Why was Poland so often divided up between her neighbours?

Who was the first Czar of Russia?

Russia did not become a kingdom in any true sense until about 1460. Its first ruler was Ivan the Great (1462–1505) and he did much to bring together many different peoples. It was his grandson Ivan IV (1533–84), however, who was the first king, or czar, as he called himself, from the word "Caesar". He added many dominions, encouraged trade with Europe as well as Asia, and did much to improve conditions for the country.

Towards the end of his life, however, Ivan became mad, and he committed many cruelties, so many that Europeans who formerly admired him, now shunned him, giving him the name Ivan the Terrible.

Why was Czar Peter I called "The Great"?

Peter I, ruler from 1682–1725, did more than any Russian to bring Russia into the community of European nations. In spite of the good works of Ivan III and Ivan IV, Europeans regarded Russians as savage Asians and some hesitated even to trade with them.

As a young man Peter travelled extensively in Europe. He visited England where for a while he worked in the dockyard at Deptford. He also studied in Holland and Germany.

He returned to his country in 1698 and at once put down a rebellion with such ferocity that few people thereafter dared to defy him. There was one occasion when he wanted a particular class of people to shave off their beards. They would not, so he cut some of them off himself. He rebuilt the army, created the navy, altered methods of taxation and business, education and even clothing, to bring them into line with European custom. To crown his new Russia he built a wonderful city in the north, called St Petersburg (now Leningrad) and adorned it with beautiful buildings and works of art. After his death, European powers had to accept Russia as one of the great powers.

121

Catherine was czarina (or empress) of Russia from 1762 to 1796. In many ways she was an extraordinary woman. To begin with, she was not Russian. She was a German princess who was married to Czar Peter III, but she grew to love the Russian people as if they were her own, much more so than her husband, in fact, who greatly admired the Germans. In 1762, with the help of friends, she turned Peter off the throne. She was then declared ruler of Russia.

Catherine made impressive plans to improve the life of the peasants in Russia, who were still living under feudal conditions. But this did not please the nobles who had helped her to power, since they feared their power would be undermined. So, much against her will she allowed the harshness of the peasants' existence to continue. At the same time she encouraged artists, craftsmen and writers to work in the cities of Russia, and she organized many public works.

Who was Catherine the Great?

What caused the Russian Revolution?

Above Lenin.

The Russian Revolution was another of those great movements which result from long standing and deep-rooted grievances. Even as late as 1860 there was still feudalism in Russia, and the country had no proper parliament until 1905. The gap between the rich and the poor was so wide as to be beyond belief anywhere else in Europe.

From about 1880 onwards, there were many small outbreaks of revolt, bomb attacks and so on, and in 1881 Czar Alexander II was assassinated. When the Russians were badly defeated in the Russo-Japanese War of 1905–6 things took a turn for the worse. Riots broke out in many districts and these were put down with great severity.

One of the principal leaders of the revolutionary movement was Lenin. He spent some time in Siberia as a punishment for his activities, and was then exiled. When the czar, Nicholas II, blamed for a series of crushing defeats at the hands of the Germans and Austrians in the First World War, abdicated in 1917, Lenin returned. At first he supported the moderate government of Kerensky, but in a few months lost patience for he wanted to introduce a whole new idea of government by the people through elected delegates. He drove Kerensky out and ruled what now came to be called the Union of Soviet Socialist Republics (U.S.S.R.).

How big was the Mogul Empire?

At its greatest extent, the Mogul empire was about the size of India and Pakistan today. It had been founded by a splendid Mongol chief, Babur, who was a descendant of Timurlaine and Genghiz Khan. He was the first of a line of great but generally cruel rulers, who, though of foreign birth, came to be as much a part of the Indians as the Indians themselves. One of his successors, Akbar the Great, did much to rebuild the old cities, reshape the government, and encourage trade and art.

Below Babur, the first Great Mogul in India.

The Taj Mahal at Agra in India is one of the world's most wonderful buildings. It was put up by Shah Jehan as a tomb for his wife. He was Mogul emperor of India from 1627 to 1658. This brave and violent man married a most beautiful princess, but she died young, and it broke his heart. In her memory, he had the Taj built of white marble, 130 feet square, on a marble terrace. The centre dome is about 200 feet high.

Shah Jehan built many other famous structures, and he is credited with founding the modern city of Delhi.

What is the Taj Mahal?

The biggest problem that the American people of the early nineteenth century had to deal with was slavery. This was a hideous system whereby Negro people in Africa were captured by raiding parties, forced into ships and taken across the Atlantic to the United States where they were sold by auction as servants for the household or for farms and plantations. It was chiefly the southern states which dealt in this sad human traffic, for the climate there was very sultry and white settlers did not like to work long hours in the fields. The Negroes were accustomed, of course, to working in extreme heat.

The people in the northern states, however, did not need slaves, nor did they approve of slavery. Before long there was bitter rivalry and the southern states threatened to break away from the union, that is, break up the United States. In 1860 they did break away, and a year later war was declared. It was one of the most bitter civil wars in history, and nearly three-quarters of a million people were killed. Slavery was not the only cause, but it was perhaps the main one.

What caused the American Civil War?

Above Abraham Lincoln (1809–65) President of the United States during the Civil War (1861–5). He was assassinated in April 1865.

Below General Lee surrenders to the victorious northern General Grant at the end of the Civil War.

Why did the American pioneers in the West so often fight the Indians?

The new republic of the United States was an expanding one. Beginning with thirteen states, it gradually extended westwards over the years, into the wide open spaces. Here and there were areas occupied by North American Indian tribes, some of whom had been there for many generations, and when the pioneers moved into their lands these Indians very naturally objected. Many fierce wars took place, in which tribes were supported by such famous other tribes as the Apaches and the Cherokees. The white Americans were often defeated and lost many men. What the Indians lacked in weapons they more than made up for in courage, but it did not avail them in the end, for the white men triumphed.

Theodore (Teddy) Roosevelt was president of the United States for two terms of office, from 1901 to 1909. He had had a spectacular career as a soldier and had been a vigorous governor of New York. When he became president he decided to put the United States "on the map". Although it was the most powerful nation in the world, its strength was not properly appreciated and it figured in no major international treaties. Roosevelt showed the world that the United States was a responsible nation able to make a huge contribution to the world. When he sent the U.S. Fleet on a world tour, many nations were astonished by its impressive size.

Who was Teddy Roosevelt?

SCIENCE

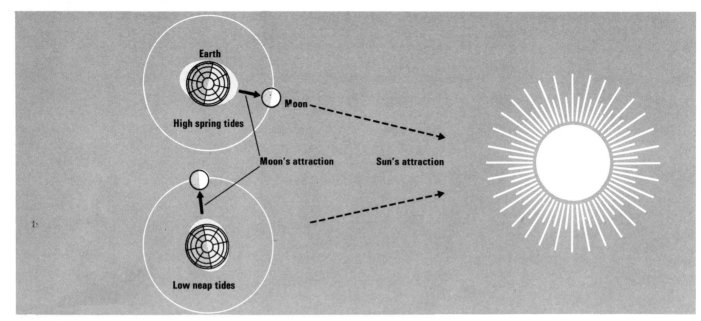

What causes the tides?

Twice every day, the surface of the sea rises and falls. This causes an ebb and flow of currents in the water. This effect is commonly known as the tide.

The tide is caused by the gravitational pull of the Moon on the Earth. All bodies exert a mutual force of attraction on each other, according to the law of gravity. For example, the Earth holds the satellite Moon in its orbit around the Earth. In its turn, the Earth is attracted towards the Moon as it moves round. Only the waters on the Earth's surface are free to actually move, and the water rises up at the point on Earth directly facing the Moon at any one time.

The waters also rise up on the opposite side of the Earth because they are effectively 'left behind'. This is because they are attracted less strongly, since they are further away from the Moon.

The distance of the Moon from the Earth varies slightly, and its path around the Earth changes.

At most places along the shores, there are two daily tides. One is when the Moon is directly overhead and the other is when it is on the opposite side of the Earth. High tide each following day is over an hour later.

Twice a year, when the Moon is closest to the Earth, there are high tides, known as spring tides.

What makes sea caves form?

Along some coastlines, the shoreline consists of rocky cliffs. These are continuously being pounded by the waves, especially in stormy winter weather, when the sea is exceptionally rough.

Near the shore, the waves tend to scoop up sand and stones and these are hurled at the cliffs, especially near their base.

Gradually the cliffs are worn away at the bottom. The overhanging part tends to fall, so the sea has managed to push the coastline back by a few metres, and the process starts again.

Where the cliffs are made of hard rock, the sea usually manages to find a few places where the rock is weaker than the rest. This is sometimes where an underground stream comes out through a crack in the rock. These wear away more quickly and the sea swirls in with extra force and scours out small caves. As the cave grows larger the force of the waves rushing into it is all the greater for being trapped in a small space.

How were the mountains made?

Early geologists often found the skeletons or fossils of millions of tiny sea creatures at the tops of some mountains. This showed that the rocks must once have lain on the seabed. This type of rock is called sedimentary rock. It is made up of millions of tonnes of sediment, or particles of rock, eroded by Sun, wind, rain and frost and washed down by the rivers from the mountains to the sea. There it settled on the bottom of the sea, becoming sandwiched between layers of the tiny skeletons, and eventually it all became compressed into rock.

It was the weight of the sediment on the seabed that disturbed the balanced forces in the Earth's crust and caused a great upheaval. The eroded mountains collapsed and folded underneath the layers of sediment, which themselves were folded and forced up into mountain folds.

Limestone and sandstone are sedimentary rocks and are eroded away relatively quickly. Mountains in limestone and sandstone regions often have queer distorted shapes because of this.

The folding and crushing that takes place during mountain building produces great heat and this changes, or metamorphoses, some of the rock. Marble and slate are metamorphic rocks. Much of the Alps in Europe are metamorphic. Their sharp, jagged appearance, caused by frost shattering and erosion show that they are relatively young, for they have not yet been worn smooth.

Some of the oldest mountains are made of hard igneous rock, such as granite, which was once molten in the Earth's interior. They usually have a smooth, rounded shape as they are worn down very slowly.

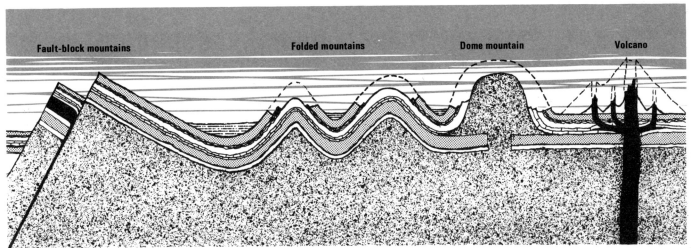

Fault-block mountains   Folded mountains   Dome mountain   Volcano

What is the inside of the Earth like?

The heart of our planet Earth is made of a very dense metallic material. Around this is a molten mass containing iron and nickel. Together these make up the *core* of the Earth, which is roughly a sphere about 7,000 kilometres in diameter.

The core of the Earth is surrounded by an extremely dense layer of partly molten rock called the *mantle*. It is about 3,000 kilometres thick.

During earthquakes, molten rock from the *sima* or *magma* escapes to the surface through cracks and fissures in the *sial* above.

The sial and the sima make up the outermost layer of the Earth called the *crust*. This is as thin as five kilometres in some places and is nowhere more than about a hundredth of the thickness of the mantle.

The crust is thinnest under the oceans where there is only a layer of sima. The sial only covers the land masses. The boundary between the surfaces of the crust and the mantle is known as the *Mohorovicic discontinuity*. There have been attempts to drill through the crust to reach the mantle and obtain samples. The drilling has taken place under the Pacific Ocean. So far it has not been very successful.

We have learnt about the composition of the crust through excavations in mines, caves and quarries. Volcanoes pour out molten material from deeper parts of the Earth and geologists are always quick to obtain samples of these for analysis.

Earthquakes cause shock waves which travel right through the Earth and provide a means for finding out more about the material inside.

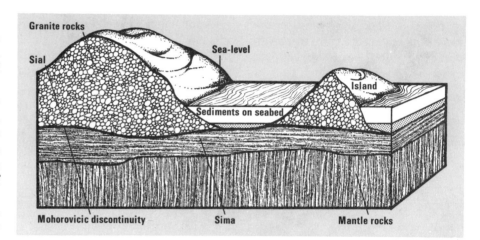

Why do volcanoes erupt?

It is the molten rock and gases that churn away under the Earth's crust until they find a weak fault or fissure through which to escape that makes volcanoes erupt. Then they force their way through, building up more pressure, until they erupt, often noisily and violently, onto the surface. Huge jets of steam rush up into the air, disturbing the atmosphere and causing storms. The jets carry mineral-laden gases and clouds of hot ash which rain down all around. Out of the crack, or vent, molten rock pours and flows downhill. We call this a *lava flow*. Successive eruptions build up a volcano cone. If the top of the volcano is blown away, the cavity is called a *caldera*.

If this molten rock, or *magma*, is a very stiff fluid, it often causes the most violent eruptions. Because it flows more slowly, more pressure is built up, and sometimes the magma at the surface solidifies to form a hard plug. Eventually the pressure becomes great enough to blow out the plug and the resulting explosion is extremely violent. Such an eruption wrecked the town of St. Pierre in Martinique, when the nearby Mont Pelée erupted in 1902.

In the Pacific there are many islands that are the tops of huge dome-shaped *shield* volcanoes. These erupt less violently, causing a gentle flow of lava. The reason for the difference in behaviour is that the magma is more liquid and contains less gas. Great pressure, therefore, does not build up.

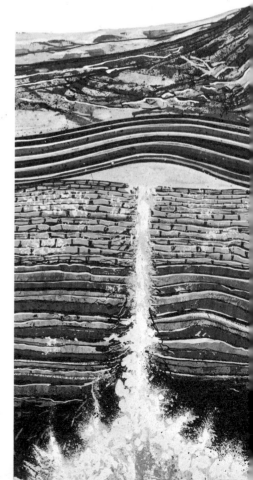

Crater

Lava

Cone

Magma

How does a glacier move?

If you are ever in the mountains, find a good viewpoint to look down the length of a valley. If the mountainsides slope down gradually to form a V shape, there is probably a stream or fast-flowing young river cutting its way downhill. But if the valley's sides are very steep, possibly even vertical, yet curved at the bottom where they join the valley floor, you are looking at a U-shaped valley, formed by a glacier. The glacier, a huge river of ice, may have long since melted away, or it may have receded back up the mountain. If it still exists, you will see a rushing river of icy, grey melt-water. The river flows out continuously from under the *snout* at the end of the glacier.

Not only the river flows down the mountain. The whole river of ice is flowing too, although it may advance only a few metres a year.

The centre part of the glacier flows fastest, while at the sides the ice drags against the valley walls, scouring them out. Over thousands of years a deep U-shaped valley is cut into the mountain.

The ice grinds the rock away to a fine powder and it is this that causes the glacier melt-water to look milky. The scouring action of the ice is increased by all the loose rocks and stones that are carried along beneath it. Where these are deposited, in great untidy heaps, they are called *moraine*.

The ice is like a solid, glassy sheet. Where it bends, on the outside corners and just before steep drops, the ice cracks and deep *crevasses* open up. These tend to close up in winter and open more in summer. Similarly, the glacier shrinks a little in summer as it melts, and grows in winter. If it shrinks more than it grows, we say it is receding. At present, most of the world's glaciers are receding.

How do small streams grow into big rivers?

A river passes through three stages in its life: youth, maturity and old age.

Particles of soil and rock gradually wear away a channel, as rain falling on mountains seeps through the soil. A little gorge may then be cut when the stream joins other streams. Zig-zag courses are made by these small rivers on hillsides when they change direction to avoid obstructions.

Over the years a river gradually cuts down the hillside, levelling off the slope. It may also cut back into the hill cutting into another little valley.

The mature river soon stops avoiding obstacles. Instead it flows past them, silting them up and eventually flowing over them.

The land alongside it may become silted up and flattened. This is a flood plain and the river is now in old age, deep, broad and full. It meanders or winds across the flood plain, depositing debris at the bends. Some bends are by-passed leaving *ox-bow lakes*, while the rest of the debris is deposited as a *delta*, where the river meets a lake or the sea.

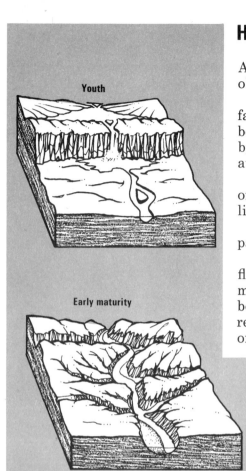

Youth

Early maturity

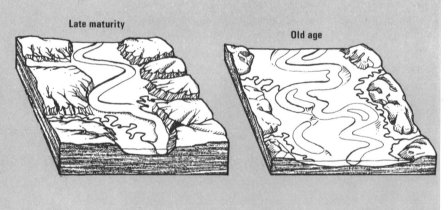

Late maturity

Old age

How are caves formed?

Most caves are the site of dried-up underground watercourses. They are usually found in hillsides of soft rock, such as limestone, which has been dissolved away by centuries of flowing water.

Caves are found where underground rivers come out at the surface. These rivers can sometimes be traced back through a whole system of caves. This may lead to a huge, deep pot-hole or shallow hole where a river has found its way underground through a fault or crack.

What are stalactites?

Stalactites are the stony 'icicles' found hanging from the roofs of limestone caves. Beneath a stalactite there may be a *stalagmite*, growing upwards from the cave floor.

They are both made of calcium carbonate. This is the mineral that is dissolved out of limestone by water flowing over it. Where the water drips slowly from the roofs of caves, it leaves the chalky particles behind. These slowly grow into the long, pointed stalactites and stalagmites. Where they are undisturbed for a great many years, these may grow to enormous lengths.

Why does frozen water make pipes burst?

Most things shrink, or *contract*, as they get colder, but water is strange, as we shall see in later pages. It contracts until its temperature falls to 4°C. Then it starts to *expand*, or get larger again as it gets still colder.

At 0°C water turns to ice. So a piece of ice takes up more space than the cold water it was made from. You can see this for yourself if you freeze some water in the refrigerator.

In frozen water pipes, the metal shrinks while the frozen water expands. The pipes then often crack under the strain. When the ice melts, water leaks from the cracks.

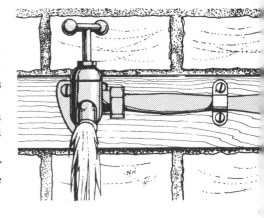

How do fish survive in frozen ponds?

Even in the hardest winters, fish and other animals living in deep ponds usually survive. This may seem surprising when there is a very thick layer of ice completely covering the surface.

They manage to survive because the water freezes from the surface downwards and in deep ponds there is unfrozen water at the bottom.

Usually, when a substance is heated, it gets larger, or expands, and grows lighter. When it cools, it shrinks or contracts, becoming heavier, or more *dense*. But water behaves in an unusual manner. If you put a pan of water on a hotplate you can see that the hot water rises to the top as it expands, and the cold water sinks to the bottom because it is heavier. But when water is cooled down, it only gets heavier until its temperature reaches four degrees above freezing point. Then, surprisingly, it begins to expand again, however far the temperature falls. So, as ice at 0°C is lighter than water at 4°C, the ice floats above the water. The thick coating of ice prevents the water from getting any colder, so the fish remain safe until the ice melts.

Why don't oil and water mix?

If you pour oil onto water, the mixture doesn't swirl into clouds like other liquids, such as fruit juice or milk. Instead the oil runs through the water in globules, rounded droplets, or ropy strands. These eventually join up again and the oil and water separate out as two distinct layers. Most cooking oils will float on the surface of water because they have a lower density than water; that is they are lighter.

Because they do not mix, oil is said to be immiscible with water. Two miscible liquids would be two that mix completely to form a homogeneous *mixture*.

A homogenous mixture is one that is of the same composition right through. Milk that is homogenized is milk that has been treated so that the cream and fats are mixed right through it so that no cream floats on 'top of the milk'.

Oil and water do not mix because the attraction of the oil molecules to each other is far greater than their attraction to water molecules. This involves the phenomenon known as surface tension.

Oils are used for water-proofing articles in such forms as varnish, polish and leather dressing. Some oils dissolve in alcohol and are used in the manufacture of perfume and flavourings.

Why are snowflakes all different?

Snowflakes look beautiful if examined through a microscope, when their hexagonal (six-sided) structures can be clearly seen.

One snowflake may be made up of fifty or more interlocked crystals, forming an intricate pattern with fern-like arms. It is unlikely that with so many possible combinations of crystals, any two snowflakes should be alike.

However, the overall form and structure may be similar for snowflakes which fall together. For they were formed under the same set of conditions, at the same temperature, from the same amount of water vapour, and so on. These conditions will determine whether the snowflakes form as needles or as plates.

What do we mean by the snow line?

In some parts of the world there are permanent snowfields. In the Arctic regions at the poles, these reach down to sea-level; in Greenland they are less than 2 kilometres above sea-level; in the Rockies they are at 3 kilometres and in the Alps at 2 kilometres above sea-level.

The height of the snow line depends on the height of the Sun, the wind, temperature and humidity. The line rises in summer and sometimes it even changes from year to year.

Did you know that there are even permanent snowfields at the equator? Some of the huge mountains, such as Kilimanjaro in Africa, rise above the permanent snowline.

How are snowflakes made?

Snow is a solid form of water that grows in the atmosphere when it is very cold and falls to Earth in the form of snowflakes.

Only one-third of the Earth's surface normally has any snow. It can come from frozen water vapour in a cloud, or even from a cloudless sky, if it contains some water vapour at a low temperature. The vapour condenses at a temperature below the freezing point.

The water forms crystals that interlock to form six-sided patterns. These may form into flat, plate-like flakes, or stack together to form needle-like flakes. Under severe conditions they may pack together into hard pellets.

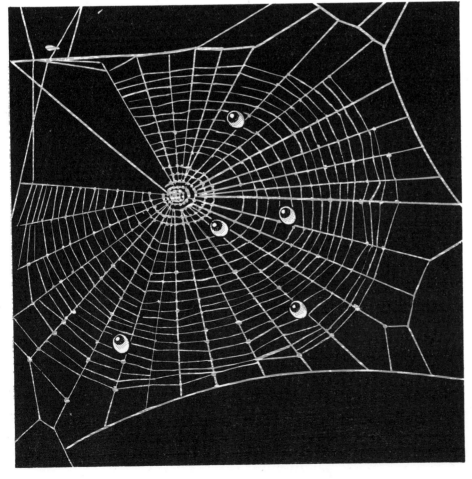

What is dew?

Dew is the name for the drops of water you see sparkling on the grass, decorating spiders' webs early in the morning.

Quite quickly, warm sunshine dries the dew off. Even if the Sun hardly shines at all, the temperature rises, and the warmth makes the water *evaporate*. But as soon as the Sun goes down, the air temperature drops and the dew falls again.

The air cannot hold all the moisture at a low temperature and the moisture, or water vapour, *condenses*, turning back into water droplets.

The amount of moisture in the atmosphere is known as the *humidity*. When the weather is very humid, it feels hot and sticky.

When it is very cold, the dew freezes. It is then called frost. The dew is often heaviest in the early autumn when the difference between the day and night temperature is greatest.

How does a siphon work?

Water always flows downhill. So how is it possible to make water flow up a pipe? You can do this yourself if you make a siphon from a piece of rubber tubing or a bent pipe.

Dip a flexible tube well under the surface of the water in a reservoir, and suck the tube carefully. After all the air is sucked out, water will come up the tube too. It will continue to flow out of the tube if the mouth of the tube is held below the level of the water surface in the reservoir.

The water flows up the pipe in the first place because by sucking out the air the pressure is reduced. It will continue to flow until the pressure at both surfaces is the same.

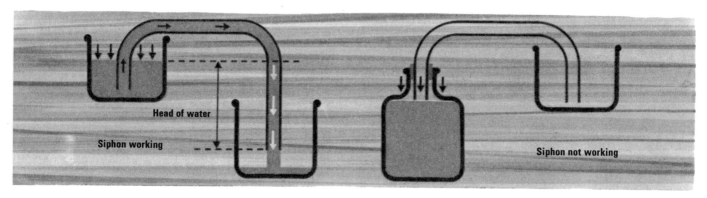

Head of water

Siphon working

Siphon not working

Where does rain come from?

Rain comes from the dark coloured clouds we call *nimbostratus* when they form in flat layers, and *cumulonimbus* if they are high banks of fluffy clouds.

The clouds contain condensed water vapour which has been evaporated by the heat of the Sun and has risen on air currents. The vapour condenses as it cools, and when the drops of water grow too big and heavy they fall, or are *precipitated*, as rain.

Rainfall often occurs where clouds blow into high land and are forced to rise into the colder air, higher in the atmosphere.

Apart from a drop in temperature, a drop in pressure can also cause rain to fall. The low pressure zone of the atmosphere, called a depression, cannot support the weight of the clouds of water droplets.

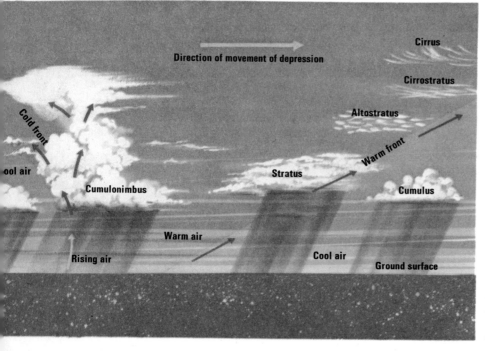

Cirrus

Cirrostratus

Direction of movement of depression

Altostratus

Cold front

Warm front

Cool air

Stratus

Cumulus

Cumulonimbus

Warm air

Rising air

Cool air

Ground surface

Left: We can learn a lot about the weather in store for us, by studying the clouds. The soft, wispy ones high in the sky are cirrus, and stratus can be seen on very grey days. The dark clouds (cumulonimbus) bring us rain and cumulus are the 'cotton wool' clouds.

Why does it rain more on high ground than on low?

The water on the Earth is being continuously recycled. The hot Sun makes the water evaporate from the sea and it rises to form clouds. These are blown inland by the wind until they reach high ground, such as a range of hills or mountains. Here, currents of air make the clouds rise higher into the atmosphere where it is colder.

The cold causes the clouds of water vapour to condense and fall as rain, often on the seaward side of mountain ranges. The rain seeps through the ground, running downhill in streams, or underground rivers. These join other streams to make rivers, which eventually flow back into the sea, or into great lakes.

There the Sun starts the evaporation process again, and rainclouds form to begin their journey to the mountains.

Rain will fall as soon as the clouds are cooled. As the air gets cooler higher up, it naturally tends to rain on high ground first.

Below: In this picture we can see how the water cycle works. Water evaporates from the sea and is carried inland by the wind in the form of clouds. Water also evaporates from rivers, the land surface and vegetation. As it rises, the vapour forms clouds. These grow cooler in the sky and then condense, and rain, sleet, snow or hail falls, finding a way back to the rivers and the sea.

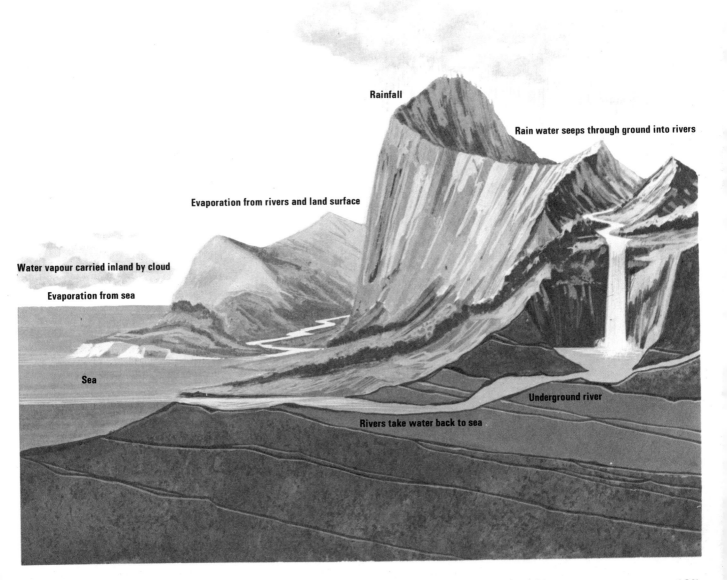

Rainfall

Rain water seeps through ground into rivers

Evaporation from rivers and land surface

Water vapour carried inland by cloud

Evaporation from sea

Sea

Underground river

Rivers take water back to sea

Why do some things float and others sink?

Whether an object will float in a liquid, or sink, depends on its *density* compared with the density of the liquid. If the density of the object is less than the density of the liquid it will float; if it is greater, it will sink.

Density is a measure of the amount of matter in a certain volume of a substance.

A volume of one cubic centimetre (c.c.) of water weighs one gram. We say that the density of water is one gram per c.c. The density of lead is 11·3 grams per c.c., which is so much greater than that of water, that almost anything made of lead will undoubtedly sink.

Cork, balsa wood and expanded polystyrene all float in water because they have a very low density. This is partly because of the large amount of air that is trapped between the fibres of these materials.

Huge ships also have a lot of air trapped in the compartments in the hull. So, although a lump of steel would sink, the overall density of a ship is low enough for it to float.

Why does cream float best on coffee with sugar in it?

If two liquids of different densities are poured together, the one with the lower density will float to the surface and form a separate layer. Light oil floats on water and cream will float on milk if it is left standing.

You may have noticed that cream will not float on hot coffee. But if you stir sugar into the coffee first, the cream will float, if you pour it carefully. You can actually see it rising to the surface. This is because, by adding sugar, the density of the coffee is increased. The density of the cream is unchanged, but it is *relatively* less dense, so it floats more easily.

You may have found that it is rather easier to swim in sea water than in fresh water, especially if it is a very salty sea like the Mediterranean. In fact, photographs have been taken of people reading as they float in the Dead Sea! This is because it is easier to float in salt water as the salt makes the sea more dense than fresh water.

Who was Archimedes?

Archimedes was a Greek who lived from about 287 to 212 B.C. He was a scientist, and studied many of the laws of physics, including the behaviour of levers. But he is probably best remembered for his study of *flotation* and for his law governing floating bodies, known as Archimedes' Principle.

This principle states that when an object is floating in a liquid, the upthrust is equal to the weight of the liquid displaced.

The *upthrust* on a body is the amount of support it receives from the liquid, or its apparent loss in weight. An object feels lighter if you hold it under water. When it floats, the upthrust is equal to its whole weight.

The weight of liquid displaced is the weight of the amount of water that is pushed aside by the object. A block of light wood may float right on the surface of a water tank, hardly displacing any water. A large, heavy block may float almost submerged. Then it will displace a volume of water equal to its own volume. A rise in the water level seen on the sides of the tank will show this.

The density of an object can be measured by using Archimedes' Principle. There is a legendary story of how Archimedes himself is supposed to have used this method to find out if the gold in the king's crown was pure, or partly fake.

Below: Archimedes discovered his theory of flotation as he was getting into his bath one day. He was so excited that he shouted *Eureka* (I have found it).

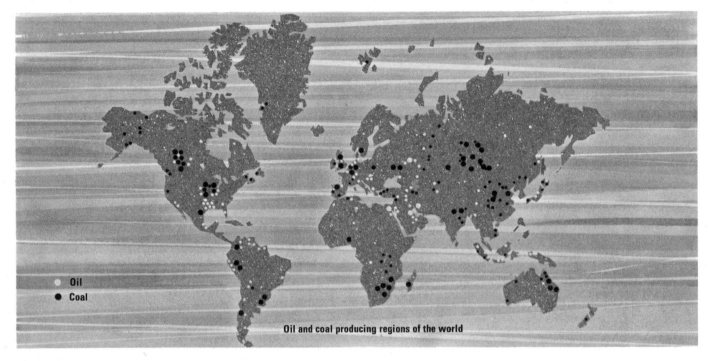

Oil
Coal

Oil and coal producing regions of the world

Where does oil come from?

Oil is a dark black liquid that comes from inside the Earth. In this form it is known as crude oil or petroleum.

The name petroleum means *rock oil*, and great pools of oil are found in traps between layers of rock, which have been folded to form anticlines, or faults. It is thought that the oil may have formed from the remains of tiny plants and animals that lived in the shallow seas in prehistoric times. The remains were probably compressed, and then later turn-ed into oil. This liquid seeped into the sedimentary rocks, such as sandstone, which were formed in the shallow seas. Later, non-porous rock, which allows no liquid to seep through, formed above them, so trapping the oil beneath it.

Geologists study rock forma-tions to find probable locations of oil fields. They drill through the surface rocks, and when they eventually strike oil, it is pumped out and carried by pipeline to oil tankers, which transport it all over the world.

After the crude oil has been purified, or *refined*, it has many important uses. It provides power, through engines and machinery, and is used as fuel to generate electricity and heat. The refining process also provides the source material for many other *by-products* such as plastics, explo-sives, paints, detergents, anti-septics, cosmetics, drugs, anaes-thetics, fertilizers, weedkillers, insect sprays, synthetic fibres and nylon.

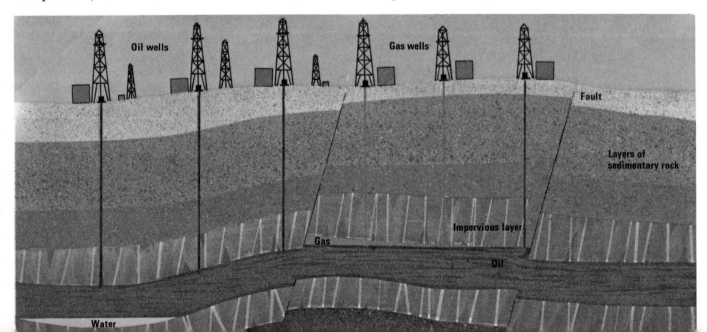

Oil wells

Gas wells

Fault

Layers of sedimentary rock

Impervious layer

Gas

Oil

Water

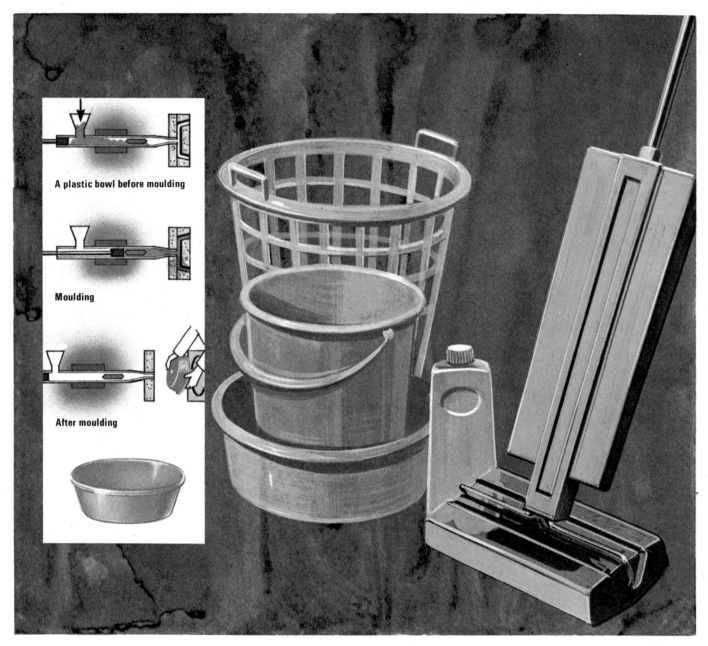

A plastic bowl before moulding

Moulding

After moulding

What are plastics?

Plastics are man-made materials. There are so many varieties that they can be moulded into any shape, made in any colour and of any strength.

Plastics are made from synthetic resins which are made up of chains of molecules. These are known as polymers. They are manufactured from coal, limestones, petroleum, salt and water.

Hard plastics, such as melamine, are used for dishes, instrument cases and hard-wearing surfaces.

Soft plastics such as polythene are used for toys, bottles and foam rubber.

Transparent plastics can be hard or soft, such as vinyl or polystyrene and are used in medicine and for packaging.

Laminated plastics, made up in layers are used decoratively. Mixed with fillers such as glass fibre, asbestos, wood or metal, they make reinforced plastics which can be very resistant to heat or corrosion.

Nylon is a type of plastic that can be used for tough work in the form of gear wheels, or woven into delicate fabric from fine fibres.

Plastic fibres such as nylon, orlon and dacron, are very light and they are also stain resistant.

The name plastic means 'able to be moulded', and plastics are shaped by many methods including moulding, casting, layering, extruding and callendering.

Are all metals shiny?

If you pick up a hard, cold, grey, evenly shaped piece of material, how can you find out what it is? Is it a bone, a stone, or a lump of wood? Or is it metal?

If you bang it and it makes a ringing sound; if you can bend it without it breaking; if it feels cold when you touch it, but it quickly warms up in your hand, then it is probably a metal. If you rub or scratch it, and it shines, then it is definitely a metal.

All the substances found on Earth are made up from basic elements. There are over a hundred different elements. Nearly three-quarters of them are metals, and all metals are lustrous, or shiny.

Metals are also sonorous; they make a ringing sound when struck. They can be cast or formed into shapes, and they are good conductors of heat and electricity.

The study of metals is called *metallurgy* and is one of the oldest branches of science.

The beautiful lustre of pure metal has made it highly valued for decorative metalwork for hundreds of years. But metals have many important practical uses. Before glass was invented, mirrors were made of shiny polished metal such as silver or bronze. Shiny metal surfaces also reflect heat as well as light.

All these properties of metals are put to good use. Because it is sonorous, bells are cast from metal. Because they are good conductors of electricity and heat, metals are used for electric cables and wires, and for cooking equipment and radiators. Because shiny metal reflects heat well, it is used for reflectors. Because metals can be shaped into such a variety of forms, making strong durable structures, they have always been immensely valuable to men.

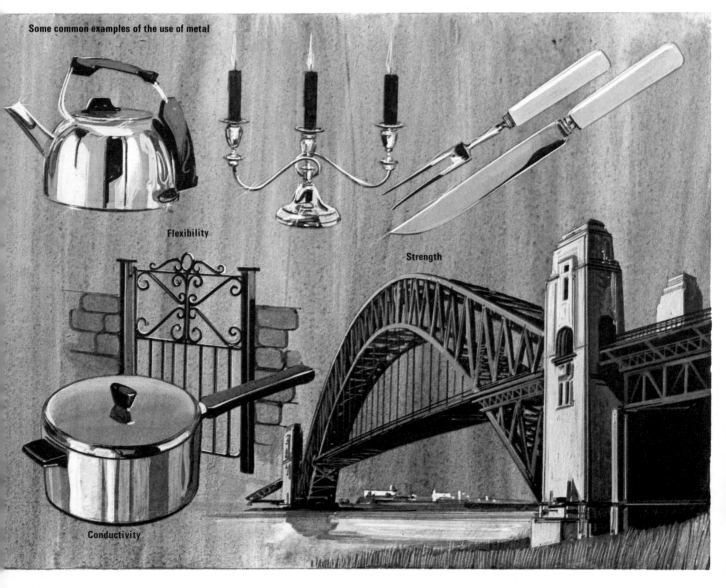

Some common examples of the use of metal

Flexibility

Strength

Conductivity

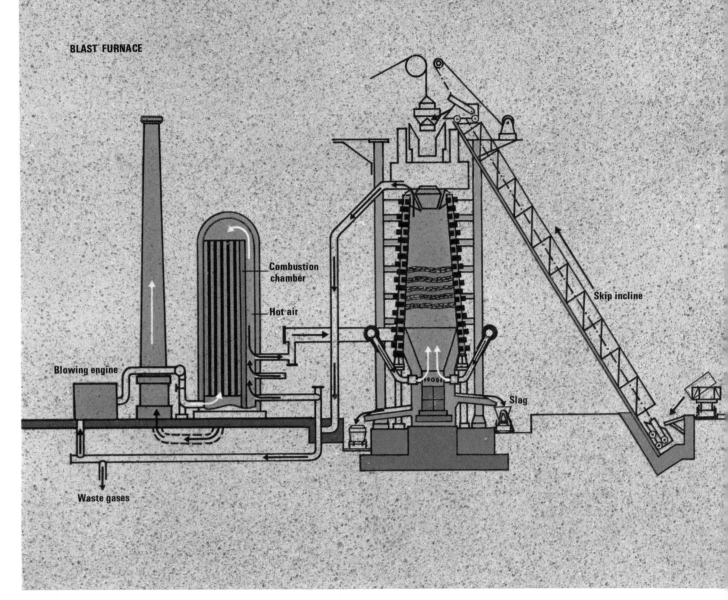

BLAST FURNACE

Combustion chamber

Hot air

Blowing engine

Waste gases

Skip incline

Slag

How is steel made?

Steel is iron from which most of the carbon has been removed. This is done by heating pig iron in a special, hot furnace.

The iron comes from iron ore which is mined from the earth. The ore is mixed with coke and limestone and is then heated in a blast furnace. The molten iron is run off and allowed to cool into slabs. It is then called pig iron.

Iron tends to be brittle, to corrode, and is not easily worked into many useful shapes. So pig iron is converted into steel, which has better properties.

Pig iron is heated by burning it in a stream of gas and air. Oxygen in the air combines with the ele-

ment *carbon* in the molten iron. They form the gas *carbon dioxide*. The metal which remains contains less than two percent of carbon.

By adding certain amounts of other elements to the melt, various types of steel are produced. Some are particularly hard, others very good for drawing into wires and so on. Another property that can be influenced is the *conductivity*. This is the ability to pass heat, or electricity along something. Steel is a good heat conductor.

It is because of this fast rate of heat conduction that metals feel hot in hot weather and cold in

cold. When you touch something metal that has been out in the Sun, it will feel hotter than your hand because it has absorbed more heat from the Sun than your body. But if you touch something metal on a cold day, it feels particularly cold. It has lost its heat more quickly than your body.

Steel is one of the most important materials of our time and we are sometimes compared with our ancestors by being described as living in the steel age.

The first industrial method for producing steel was invented in 1856 by Henry Bessemer (1813–1898). His method was known as the Bessemer process.

How big is an atom?

Atoms are the building blocks of all matter. They are so minute that a very small lump of the metal copper, weighing only a gram and being smaller than a sugar lump, would contain nearly ten thousand million million million atoms.

The countless number of different substances on Earth are made up from just over one hundred basic substances, called *elements*. These can combine or react with each other to form new substances. The smallest part of an element that can take part in a reaction, is called an atom.

For many years, men thought that atoms were solid and indestructible. Then it was discovered that the body of an atom is concentrated at its centre, called the nucleus. The nucleus is made up of two types of particles, *protons* and *neutrons*. The atom behaves as if it were ten thousand times bigger than just the nucleus because tiny particles, called *electrons*, whirl round the nucleus like planets round the Sun. But they move so fast that they seem to form a solid, outer shell.

Atoms combine or share their electrons with those of other atoms. This is how atoms of different elements combine to form *compound* substances.

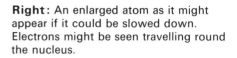

Right: An enlarged atom as it might appear if it could be slowed down. Electrons might be seen travelling round the nucleus.

Right: An atom as it might appear if greatly enlarged.

What is a molecule?

A molecule is the smallest portion of a substance that can exist on its own. A molecule of the gas hydrogen contains one atom of the element hydrogen. A molecule of the gas oxygen contains two atoms of the element oxygen. A molecule of water contains one atom of hydrogen and two atoms of oxygen. The molecules of hydrogen and oxygen have combined to form the compound water. Water is the most common compound on the Earth.

There are millions of different compounds. A great many of them contain the element carbon and these are called organic compounds.

The way the molecules are arranged in a substance affects its behaviour. In a solid, the molecules have a regular arrangement called its crystal structure. In a liquid the molecules are free to move about, although they are still attracted to each other, so a liquid flows. In a gas, the molecules are free to move about in any direction. They also vibrate very fast. So a gas tends to expand to fill its container.

Solids change to liquids because molecules have begun to break away from their positions in the crystal structure. This occurs when the substance is heated so that the molecules vibrate faster. If the liquid is heated, the molecules vibrate faster still, until some of them break out of the surface. The liquid is then boiling.

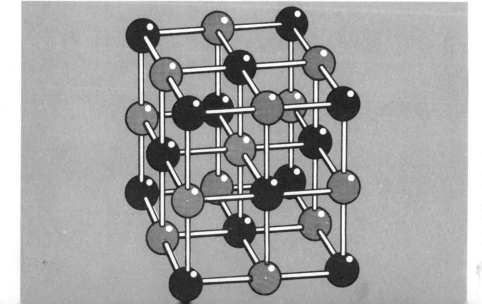

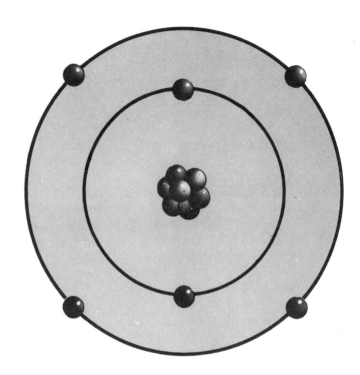

Right: An enlarged atom as it might appear if halted completely. It looks like our solar system. Protons and neutrons are in the centre (the 'sun') and electrons are seen around it (the 'planets').

What are elements?

The elements are the 103 different substances that make up all the matter on Earth. All the atoms in an element are alike. This means that an element cannot be broken down into more simple substances.

There are two kinds of elements; these are metals and non-metals. The most common metals include magnesium, aluminium, zinc, tin, iron, copper, nickel and lead.

There are only 92 different elements which occur naturally, the last one being uranium. All the others are obtained from nuclear reactions.

Some elements exist in more than one form. The different forms are known as *isotopes*. Different isotopes of an element have a different number of neutrons in the nucleus of an atom.

ELEMENTS			
Hydrogen	Wt 1	Strontian	Wt 46
Azote	5	Barytes	68
Carbon	5,4	Iron	50
Oxygen	7	Zinc	56
Phosphorus	9	Copper	56
Sulphur	13	Lead	90
Magnesia	20	Silver	190
Lime	24	Gold	190
Soda	28	Plantina	190
Potash	42	Mercury	161

Left: In 1808–1810 John Dalton, the founder of modern atomic theory, drew up this table of elements. It shows their symbols and their atomic weights.

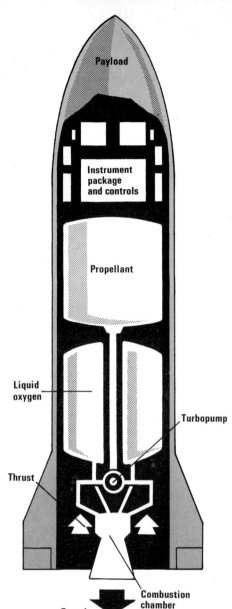

Payload

Instrument package and controls

Propellant

Liquid oxygen

Turbopump

Thrust

Combustion chamber

Reaction

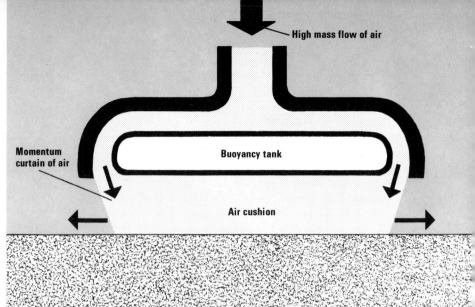

High mass flow of air

Momentum curtain of air

Buoyancy tank

Air cushion

What keeps a hovercraft afloat?

The hovercraft is an *amphibious* vehicle. It can travel on land or in water. (An *amphibian* is an animal, such as a frog, that can live on land or in water.)

The hovercraft can travel over any type of surface because it moves on top of its own cushion of air. This is produced by a large propellor or fan which blows air downwards so hard that it lifts the machine off the ground. The air escapes from under a stiff, rubber *skirt* which surrounds the edge of the base.

The air-cushion only supports the craft. It is driven forward by aircraft propellors and it is steered by rudders on the fins at the rear.

The hovercraft can move over any flat surface, but it does not need to be smooth. It has been ideal as transport in water, rough country, on building sites and over undulating ground. Some of the great rivers of Africa and South America have been explored by means of a hovercraft.

How does a space rocket fly?

A space rocket cannot fly like an ordinary aircraft, because there is no air in outer space for propellors to drive it through, nor to provide lift on the wings.

Space rockets are jet-propelled. Fuel is burnt in a combustion chamber. It produces hot gases which escape through the nozzle forcing the rocket forwards.

Unlike jet aircraft engines, the space rocket does not draw in any air from the front, or from anywhere outside. There is no air in outer space. Instead of air, the fuel has to be mixed with an *oxidant*, to make the fuel burn. It is usually liquid oxygen. The fuel

is known as the *propellant*.

In the Saturn V rocket, which was used to launch the Apollo spacecraft on their Moon missions, there are three stages. The first stage uses paraffin (kerosene) as the propellant, while the second and third stages use liquid hydrogen.

The Earth's gravitational force tends to pull everything down towards it. Rockets have to reach a speed called the *escape velocity*, to escape from the Earth's pull. This is a velocity of 11·2 kilometres per second.

Once it is out in space, side jets provide the rocket with sideways

thrust so that it can be steered on a course.

It will continue to fly onwards until it comes within the gravitational field of another body, such as the Moon or another planet.

For a rocket to travel to a distant planet, and for it to return, would require more fuel than any rocket can yet carry. The load a rocket carries is called the *payload*. This must not be too great at lift off if the rocket is to leave the ground. Scientists are developing nuclear-powered rockets that carry a small reactor aboard. This generates nuclear power to drive the rocket's engines.

How does a ship sail?

There are similarities between a ship's sails and an aircraft's wings, in that they are both curved in shape so that air flowing past creates a lifting force. A ship's sails are specially shaped so that they are not just flat sheets of fabric, but slightly belled or bagged. To get the ship to sail, the sails are held in position, or *set*, so that the wind blows across one side of the bows and fills out the sail. Wind flowing over the other side of the sail is at a reduced pressure, producing a driving force roughly in the direction of the bows. At the same time, the reaction of the wind deflected off the sail produces a forward reaction.

The ship is kept moving forward, instead of moving across the wind, by the reaction of the keel underneath the hull. This is held vertically in the stem to stern direction and makes the hull resist sideways movement. The rudder, which is positioned in the water astern of (behind) the keel, is used to steer the boat.

There are three basic sailing directions; sailing into the wind, with the wind blowing to within 45 degrees of the direction head-on to the ship, which involves sailing a zig-zag course, known as *tacking*; sailing across the wind; and sailing, or *running*, before the wind.

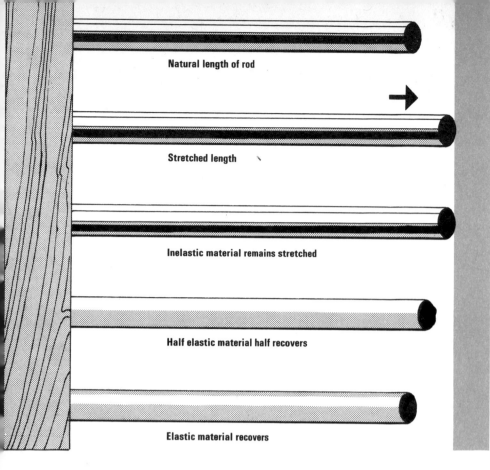

Natural length of rod

Stretched length

Inelastic material remains stretched

Half elastic material half recovers

Elastic material recovers

What is elasticity?

Most materials change their shape when put under a force that compresses or stretches them. Some do so more than others; they are said to be less *rigid*. When the pressure is removed, the changed or, deformed, object sometimes regains its original shape, depending on how much it has been deformed, and on what material it is made from.

Materials that regain their shape are *elastic*. Rubber is a well-known example. Materials, such as clay, that do not go back to their original shape at all, are inelastic.

Springs are made from elastic materials. They are designed to absorb the force of a shock and then to restore the system to its original shape and position.

Why does rubber bounce?

There are many different types of man-made rubber compounds and many of them will bounce because rubber is a highly elastic material.

When a rubber ball bounces, the rounded surface that hits the floor is flattened by the force of the impact. But because rubber is so elastic, the ball quickly starts to regain its shape and pushes itself up off the floor.

The ball never quite rises to the height it was dropped from after a bounce, because at each bounce it loses a little energy.

A round stone dropped from the same height might bounce once or twice. But it would stop sooner because it is less elastic than a rubber ball and loses more energy on each bounce.

The harder it hits the floor, the higher the ball, or stone, will bounce. The harder the floor, the more the ball will be deformed and the higher it will bounce.

146

How do you measure acceleration?

Acceleration is the rate at which the speed, or velocity, of a moving object increases.

Velocity is expressed in metres per second, or miles per hour, for example. This is the distance travelled, divided by the time it has taken to travel that distance.

Acceleration can be expressed in metres per second. This is the increase in velocity divided by the time taken to reach the new velocity.

In the box on the left in the picture above, the lines on the road are 15 metres apart. The velocity of the car does not change; it is travelling at a constant 15 metres per second. In the box on the right, the car is moving faster and faster. This is acceleration.

Below: This picture illustrates how the speed of animals varies greatly. A snail only moves at about 1 millimetre per second, while the cheetah, the fastest animal, can move at 26 metres per second.

Which is the fastest animal?

The animal that can move the fastest under its own power, of course, is the cheetah. It can move at over 60 miles per hour, that is about 26 metres per second.

Man's record running speed is so far only 11·8 metres per second, which is nearly 48 kilometres per hour. However, not many people can run even half as fast as this because they have never practised running. The average walking pace is less than 5 kilometres per hour.

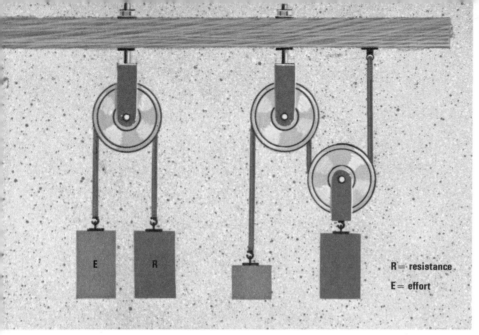

R = resistance

E = effort

Why do we use pulleys?

A pulley is another very simple machine, providing men with a mechanical advantage. By pulling down on the rope on one side of a pulley, a heavy weight can be lifted up the other side more easily than if it were being lifted straight up by hand. By using the pulley a man takes advantage of the downward pull of gravity on his body.

In a system of several pulleys, a large weight can be lifted by pulling on the rope with only a small force. But the weight will only rise a small distance compared with the distance the lifting force has to move in pulling the rope. The work done by the weight in moving up is equal to the work done by the lifting force in pulling out the rope.

In physics, the amount of work done by a force is equal to the size of the force multiplied by the distance it has moved. Pulley systems enable a small force to do enough work in moving a large distance, to move a larger force a smaller distance.

The efficiency of a machine is a measure of the amount of work put in compared to the amount of work got out. A machine is never quite one hundred percent efficient.

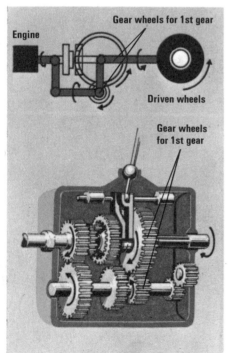

Left: The top diagram shows the gear shafts of a car, while the lower one shows a gear box, with first gear engaged.

How do gears work?

Gears are machines that can either convert a large force into a small one, or a small force into a large one.

If a force is applied to the teeth around the edge of the gear wheel, this force has a turning effect, or moment, about the centre of the gear wheel, where it rotates on a pin. The further the teeth are from the centre, the greater the effect of the force. Conversely, the gear wheel can be rotated at its centre by the axle, producing a force at the edge where the teeth strike anything.

By meshing the teeth of two gear wheels together, the force applied to one can be transferred to the other. If the teeth of the second wheel are further from its centre than those of the first wheel are from its centre, then the turning force on the second wheel will be greater than the first. If the second wheel is smaller, the effect of the force transmitted will be smaller.

What is friction?

Friction is the force that acts between two moving surfaces that are touching each other. The force of friction tends to stop the movement.

How much friction there is between two surfaces depends on how rough they are; the rougher they are, the more friction there is. This can be reduced by *lubricating* the surfaces. Oil and grease are used as lubricants for metal surfaces such as those in motor car engines. The lubricant effectively fills in all the rough parts of the surface and provides a thin, smooth film for the other surface to slide over.

The amount of friction produced also depends on the force applied to the surfaces, either by the weight of the object if the gravity acts on it in a direction perpendicular to the surface, or by an external force.

Friction can stop movement, but it can also be useful in other ways. It enables surfaces to grip together. As a wheel rotates, it

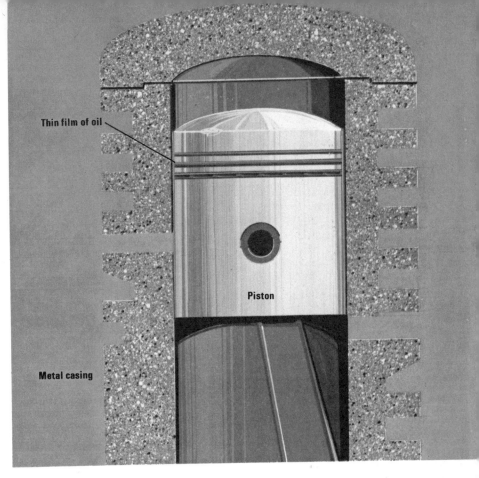

Thin film of oil

Piston

Metal casing

grips the ground at the bottom point where it touches, because of friction. If there is not enough friction, the wheel slips round and round. By placing a load on

wheels or rollers, an object that would have been difficult to slide because of too much friction, can be wheeled along because of just enough friction.

Why does hitting things make them hot?

Heat is a form of energy. It is not possible to create or destroy energy, it can only be changed from one form to another. The energy of movement, which is called kinetic energy, can be changed into heat.

The act of hitting an object, such as hammering a nail, involves using muscular energy to move the hammer. This energy is transferred suddenly to the nail at each blow. The energy given to the nail causes the molecules of iron to vibrate faster and the iron begins to heat up.

If you stop hitting the nail, the vibrations will gradually subside to their normal level.

What is an insulator?

Wool, cork, polystyrene, fibreglass, plastic and rubber always feel quite warm, even in the coldest weather. Because of this, they are called good *insulators*.

Good insulators are bad conductors. They are very slow at conducting heat through them, passing the energy from molecule to molecule much less rapidly than a metal, for example.

This property is most useful for preventing heat from being lost too rapidly.

Water pipes, for example, are lagged with insulating material such as strips of felt or fibreglass, to prevent the water from freezing in winter.

Saucepan handles are made of insulating plastic material to prevent too much heat being conducted up from the pan and burning your hand.

What is a conductor?

On a warm day, if you touch a variety of objects, some of them will feel a lot warmer than others because they have absorbed more heat. The objects that heat up quickly, also cool down quickly. On a cold day they will feel colder than other objects.

Substances that respond quickly to heat are called good conductors. Most metals are good conductors, but glass, wood, cork, polystyrene and plastic are poor conductors.

The molecules in a substance are vibrating all the time. They vibrate faster when an object is warmed up. Some substances require less energy than others to make their molecules vibrate faster. These substances are good conductors.

Good conductors of heat are often good conductors of electricity too.

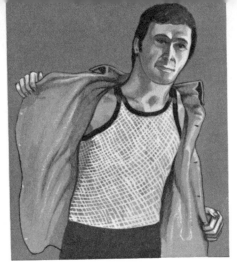

Why does a string vest keep you warm?

A string vest would certainly not keep you warm if you wore it by itself. You need to wear a shirt or sweater on top of it. The shirt traps a large amount of air next to your skin, in all the holes in the vest. Air is a good insulator. It does not conduct heat away from your body.

For the same reason, air does not allow heat to reach your body easily. So a string vest worn in hot weather will help to keep you cool.

Animals' fur and birds' feathers are both natural insulating 'clothing'. Air is trapped between the hairs of the fur or the layers of feathers. In cold weather, a bird fluffs out its feathers to trap a greater amount of air.

Why do gardeners use greenhouses?

To encourage young plants to grow quickly, they need warm, damp conditions. A greenhouse can provide this environment.

Greenhouses are made mostly of glass or transparent plastic to allow the maximum amount of sunlight to enter. It soon becomes very hot and humid inside because the heat of the Sun is trapped. The ventilation is controlled so that the moisture cannot evaporate away either, despite the heat.

Normally, hot air rises and in a house escapes out of windows, doors and chimneys. This is how heat travels by *convection*. But by keeping the door closed and only opening the windows when it gets too hot, the hot air is trapped.

The heat is not passed on to the air outside, because the glass or plastic sheets of which the walls are made, are bad conductors. So heat is not lost by *conduction*.

The only remaining way for the heat to travel is by *radiation*. The Sun's heat reaches the Earth in the form of *electromagnetic* waves which possess enormous amounts of energy. All objects *radiate* heat themselves, but they have absorbed some of the energy from the Sun's rays, to use it like fuel or food. The heat rays that plants send out have less energy than Sun rays. These heat rays do not have enough energy to pass through glass or plastic so heat is not lost by radiation.

How does double-glazing work?

Double-glazing prevents rooms with large windows from being too cold. It also helps to sound-proof a building.

Each window has two panes of glass sealed in a frame, so that air is trapped between them. Air is a bad conductor of heat, so whatever heat is conducted out of the room by the glass on the inside, is not easily transmitted to the outer pane. The air-filled space between the panes provides insulation, just as fibre-glass lagging does.

The air gap is also a poor transmitter of sound so that the double-glazing provides sound-proofing. Buildings on busy streets and near airports have double-glazing to keep out traffic noise. Recording studios have double-glazed windows so that a performance can be recorded without it being spoiled by outside noises.

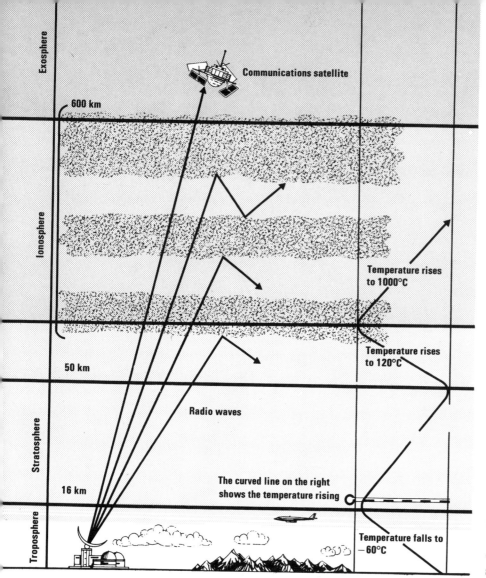

Communications satellite

600 km

Temperature rises
to 1000°C

Temperature rises
to 120°C

Radio waves

The curved line on the right
shows the temperature rising

50 km

16 km

Temperature falls to
−60°C

Exosphere
Ionosphere
Stratosphere
Troposphere

What is the atmosphere?

The atmosphere is the envelope of air that surrounds the Earth. Apart from the mixture of gases that make up air, the atmosphere also contains water vapour, some hydrocarbons, hydrogen peroxide, compounds of sulphur and dust particles, all in relatively small amounts.

There are four distinct layers in the atmosphere. Next to the Earth's surface, and stretching up to a height of about sixteen kilometres is the troposphere. The temperature in the troposphere generally falls the higher you go. Above this is the stratosphere, rising to a height of about fifty kilometres. Here the temperature rises again. Above the stratosphere is the deepest layer, the ionosphere, rising to a height of 600 kilometres. The temperature falls and rises again, sharply to over 1000°C. In the ionosphere are bands of particles that reflect radio waves back to Earth.

Beyond the ionosphere is tne exosphere. This merges into outer space.

What is pollution?

One of the most serious problems in the modern world is pollution. Man's way of life, his agriculture and his industry are spoiling this planet.

Most of our activities involve waste products and these are scattered over the land. They are polluting, or spoiling, the soil, water and air. As the population in an area increases, the problem becomes more and more serious.

By overworking the land, all the goodness is removed from the soil. In some areas the soil has changed its texture so that it is now blown away as dust. Pesticides, fungicides and chemical waste poison plant life; animals are poisoned too, or starve to death. The effluent, or waste from factories, makes river water unfit to drink. Oil slicks pollute the sea and smother the beaches. Millions of motor cars and furnaces are filling the atmosphere with poisonous fumes and dust.

Methods of reducing pollution are being used in many places. Scientific methods are applied to farming. Waste, instead of being thrown away, is being recycled. Effluent is purified before being released into the water. Smokeless fuels and filters reduce atmospheric pollution.

What is a vacuum?

A vacuum is a space which does not contain any molecules or atoms. It is impossible to obtain a perfect vacuum, but a very high vacuum can be obtained with a special machine.

The atmospheric pressure in a vacuum is very, very minute. Natural forces all work towards preventing a vacuum from forming, by filling up the space with matter. Air flows, or is sucked into a vacuum when the vacuum seal is released, until finally the air pressure is the same throughout the system.

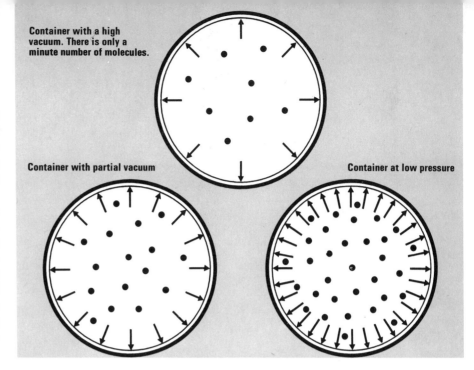

Container with a high vacuum. There is only a minute number of molecules.

Container with partial vacuum

Container at low pressure

What is a vacuum cleaner?

A vacuum cleaner is a domestic electrical appliance used to pick up small pieces of dirt and dust. It contains a powerful electric fan that sucks air into the machine quickly, blowing it through a filter and out in another direction. The sudden removal of the air at the front of the machine tends to create a vacuum. However, nature prevents this by quickly filling the space inside the machine with air from the immediate surroundings.

The suction force is so great, that small particles of dust and dirt are drawn in with the air and are collected inside the cleaner. This makes the work of extracting grit and dust from between the fibres of a carpet much easier than brushing or sweeping it up.

What is a vacuum seal?

Many of the goods we buy today are vacuum sealed. This is especially true of food packets, for the food must be kept fresh. It also applies to products that must be kept dry and to sterilize hospital equipment, too.

A vacuum seal closes the object in a partial vacuum. A small amount of air is drawn out before the container is closed. This means that the pressure on the outside of the container is greater than the pressure on the inside. The greater pressure keeps the lid or sealed edges pressed down tightly.

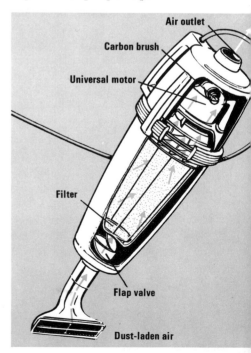

Air outlet
Carbon brush
Universal motor
Filter
Flap valve
Dust-laden air

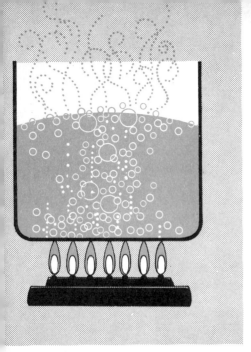

Why does boiling water bubble?

If you watch a pan of water very closely as it comes to the boil, you can see the bubbles forming. They begin as tiny specks, sparkling on the bottom of the pan, slowly growing into dome-shaped bubbles. These rise from the bottom, turning into sphere-shaped bubbles, rising quickly to the surface in a constant stream. As the bubbles rise they grow larger and larger, until they reach the surface, where they burst.

These are bubbles of air that were trapped in the water and compressed until they were too small to see. As the water is heated, the air in it expands more quickly than the liquid. Because the bubbles of air are less dense than the liquid, they rise, driven upwards by convection currents in the liquid.

As they rise to the surface, the pressure of water on the bubbles decreases and they grow larger. The bubbling becomes more intense as the water nears boiling point.

Why does it seem warmer at the sea by night than in the daytime?

A cool wind usually blows in off the sea, even on a hot, sunny day. This is the sea breeze. It is caused by *convection currents*. These are currents of hot air circulating in the atmosphere.

On the evening of the same day, after the Sun has set, it may seem surprisingly warm by the sea's edge. The sea breeze has dropped and in fact has been replaced by a breeze off the land. The convection currents are now circulating in the opposite way.

This change is caused by the different rates at which the land and the water heat up and cool down. The Sun heats land up more quickly than water, because rock and earth are better conductors of heat than water. For the same reason, the land loses its heat more quickly, after sunset.

So for most of the day, the water is cooler than the land, and the air above the sea is warmed only a little by the water. The air above the land is warmed more than the air above the sea. The hot air rises, setting up convection currents, and a current of cool air flows in from the sea to replace the rising warm air. This is the sea breeze.

At night the land cools down more quickly than the sea. So the air above the sea is warmed more than that above the land. The air above the sea rises higher, so air flows in off the land to replace it. This is the land breeze. The direction of the convection currents has been reversed.

At some stage in the morning, just after sunrise, and in the evening around sunset, the temperatures of the land and the sea are roughly equal. The air temperature is also about the same above both, so there is no flow of cool air from one place to another. The breeze ceases, the ripples on the sea die away and there is the typical calm of a fine evening or morning. Smoke drifts straight upwards and flags hang limp.

Below: The diagram on the left shows the direction of a sea breeze, and on the right is a land breeze.

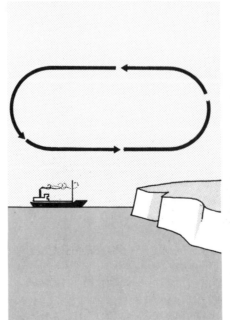
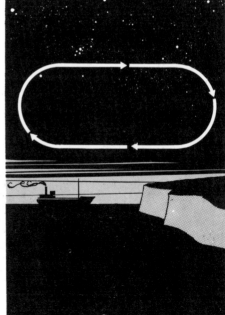

Why does hot air rise?

When a mass of air, or any gas is heated it expands, if it is not in an enclosed space. The molecules vibrate more energetically and move further apart, so there is less matter in a given volume than there is in a colder mass of gas. The hot gas is less dense than the colder gas, so it begins to rise. In fact it is the colder, more dense gas, which sinks, or is drawn in from around the sides.

A continuous upward flow of hot air is set up, called a *convection current*.

Convection currents play an important part in our weather. Convection currents keep the air in a room circulating. You can sometimes see the 'heat waves' dancing over the hot plate of a stove, or even on the road surface on a very hot day.

What causes draughts?

However hot the fire you are sitting by, you nearly always feel a draught. Normally you feel it around your feet, or down your neck.

The draught at your feet is cold air being drawn in under the door, or through gaps in the floorboards, if there are any.

The draught down your neck is probably cold air coming in from around the window.

The draughts are caused by the *convection currents* that the fire sets up. It heats the air in front of it. This rises, mainly up the chimney, and cold air is drawn in from outside the room to replace it.

To keep the air in a room fresh and well ventilated, it is important to have a top window open for the warmer, stale air to escape from. A lower window should also be open for cool fresh air to be drawn in.

How does a telescope work?

The human eye cannot see distant objects clearly. The telescope is an instrument used by sailors, marksmen, astronomers and many others, to view distant objects in detail.

There are two main types of telescope, the *refractor* and the *reflector*.

In the refractor, the light from a distant object is refracted by the glass in the objective lens. This brings it to a focus at the focal point of a second lens or eyepiece, through which the image is viewed.

One of the earliest refracting telescopes was devized by Galileo, but the poor quality of the lenses at that time did not make the image very sharp.

The reflecting telescope produces a better image. It uses a curved mirror to produce the image which is reflected from a second mirror and viewed through an eyepiece lens. Sir Isaac Newton invented the Newtonian reflecting telescope.

Above right: The boy in this picture is using a refracting telescope.

Centre: A refracting telescope, showing the objective lens and the eyepiece.

Right: The principle of both the Galilean telescope (*above*) and Kepler's astronomical telescope (*below*). In Galileo's telescope a concave lens is used, so that the image seen is the right way up. Kepler's on the other hand, uses a convex eyepiece, producing an upside down image.

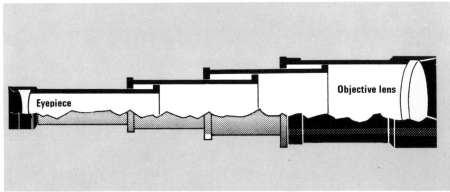

Eyepiece

Objective lens

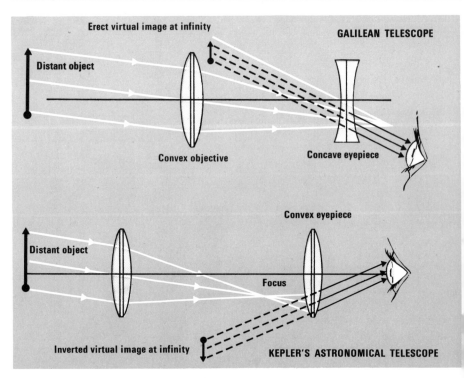

Erect virtual image at infinity

GALILEAN TELESCOPE

Distant object

Convex objective

Concave eyepiece

Convex eyepiece

Distant object

Focus

Inverted virtual image at infinity

KEPLER'S ASTRONOMICAL TELESCOPE

How do spectacles help people to see?

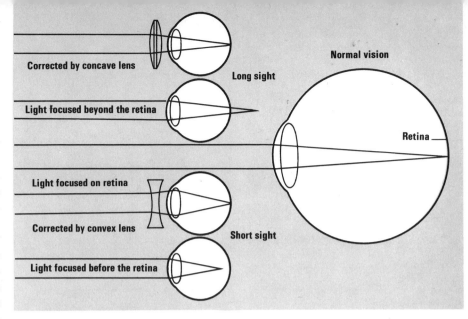

Some people cannot focus objects that are close to them. We say they are long-sighted.

Others can only see objects clearly if they are very close indeed. We say they are short-sighted, or *myopic*.

These defects of vision may happen because the lenses of the eyes cannot change shape sufficiently to focus the rays on the retina. This is the light-sensitive surface on the inside of the eyeball. The muscles may be too weak or the eyeball may be misshapen.

For short-sighted people, the image is normally brought to a focus at a point before it reaches the retina. This can be corrected by wearing spectacles with con-cave diverging lenses. These bend the rays outwards, so that the object appears to be nearer, where the short-sighted eye is able to focus as it would naturally.

For people with long sight, the point at which the lens would bring light rays from an object into focus, would be behind the eyeball if that were possible. By wearing spectacles with convex, converging lenses, this distance is reduced so that they are focused on the retina. The long-sighted person is then able to see objects at all distances quite clearly.

How does a microscope magnify?

A simple microscope has only a single lens system which will magnify objects that can already be seen with the naked eye.

Compound microscopes have two sets of lenses, the objective and the eyepiece, fixed at opposite ends of a tube. The tube is raised or lowered, above the object on the microscope slide, bringing the highly magnified image into focus. The objective, at the lower end of the tube, magnifies the image first and the eyepiece magnifies this to give an even larger image. Eyepieces and objectives of different magnifications can be used.

Below: The human eye (A) can separate dots 0·25 mm. apart. The light microscope (B) can separate dots 0·25 microns apart and the electron microscope (C) can separate dots less than 5 Angstrom units apart. (A micron is 0·001 mm. and an Angstrom unit is 0·001 microns.)

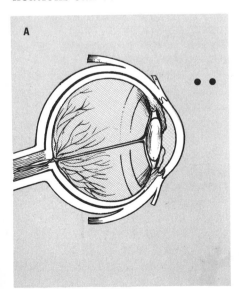

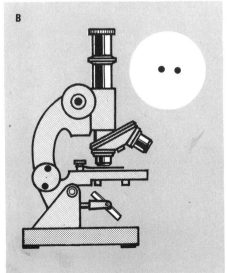

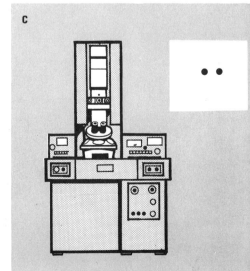

Why does a curved mirror magnify?

There are two kinds of curved mirror. *Convex* mirrors curve or bulge out towards you. *Concave* mirrors curve inwards, away from you, like a cave.

Convex mirrors reflect objects from a wide area in front of them, but make them look smaller than life size.

Concave mirrors produce a magnified reflection of an object placed close in front. The reflection of an object further away is smaller, and also upsidedown.

To obtain a magnified image, the object must be placed nearer to the mirror than its focus. The focus of a mirror is the point at which parallel rays of light, such as sunrays, are brought to a focus. When an object is closer than the focus, the reflected rays *diverge*.

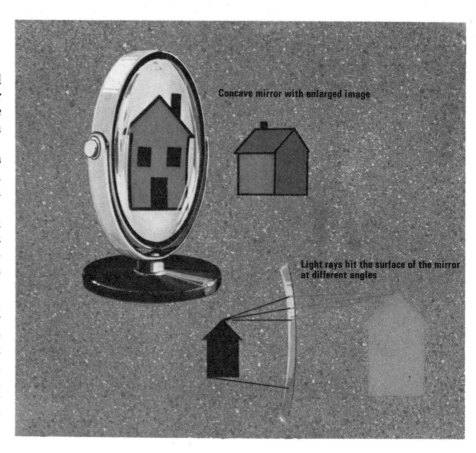

Concave mirror with enlarged image

Light rays hit the surface of the mirror at different angles

Why do mirrors invert?

All flat, or plane, mirrors obey the laws of reflection. The first law states that the reflected ray leaves the mirror at an angle equal to the angle at which the incident ray strikes it. These angles are measured between the incident and reflected rays and a line drawn perpendicular to the mirror. This particular line is called the *normal*.

The second law states that the incident ray, the reflected ray and the normal lie in the same plane. (This means that they could all be drawn on a flat piece of paper.)

The reflected ray leaves the mirror on the opposite side of the normal to the incident ray. Thus in its reflection, every point of an object appears on the opposite side of a central line. This is called mirror inversion or lateral inversion.

Why does a spoon in a glass of water look bent?

Light travels at different speeds through different materials. Its rate of travel is slowed down when it enters a more dense material.

At the surface between two materials, a ray of light changes its direction of travel. This is called *refraction*. As a ray passes into a more dense material it is bent, or refracted away from the surface. As it passes into a less dense material it is refracted towards the surface.

This is why a spoon standing partly immersed in a glass of water, looks as if it is bent at the water surface, when viewed from the side.

When viewed from above, refraction produces the effect of making water look shallower than it is. The eye sees an underwater object as if the light travelled from it to the eye in a straight line. In fact the light ray slopes down more steeply as it is refracted away from the surface. So the bottom is really further away than it appears.

What is a two-way mirror?

Two-way mirrors are popular with thriller writers. In their stories the mirrors are supposed to be used to spy on people who do not realize they are being watched. A two-way mirror looks like an ordinary mirror from one side, but you can look straight through it from the other side.

The mirror is only thinly coated with silver, on one side of the glass. Bright light is refracted through the glass and is scattered and reflected off the silver particles, producing a complete reflection on the illuminated side.

But some light passes straight through the glass. The result is that a person standing in darkness on the other side can see straight through, but he cannot be seen himself.

The same effect is produced by thick dust on a window, or sunglasses. If you look at a person wearing sunglasses, you see only your reflection in their lenses, but they can see you clearly.

Famous people who wish to travel about incognito, have smoked glass windows in their cars. This has the same result.

The person inside can see, but not be seen.

Apart from being used to produce theatrical effects, two-way mirrors have a use in optical instruments.

In the sextant, used by navigators, a half-silvered mirror is used to superimpose an image of the Sun on the instrument's scale. Using the laws of reflection, the altitude, or angle of declination of the Sun, can be measured. The ship's position can then be worked out, using a book of special tables.

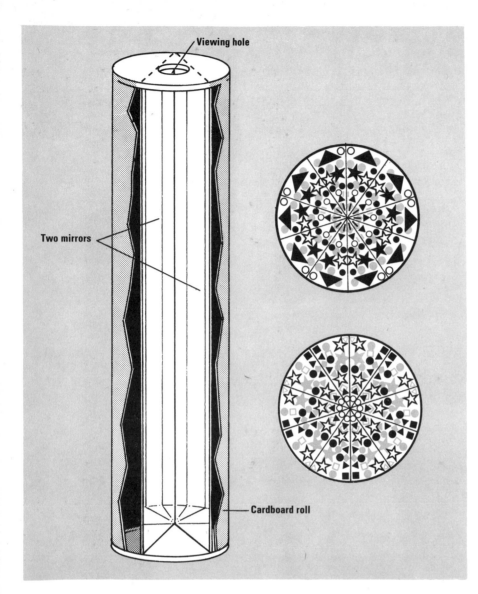

Viewing hole

Two mirrors

Cardboard roll

How does a kaleidoscope work?

A kaleidoscope is made of a tube with two mirrors in it. The mirrors are joined on one side so that they form a V down the length of the tube. Some kaleidoscopes make a pattern of what you see through the tube. Others usually have two pieces of clear material at the end you hold to the light. Pieces of different coloured plastic are fixed between them, to form the pattern.

When light enters the kaleidoscope it is bounced backwards and forwards by the mirrors so that your eye sees many images. One of these comes directly from the V made by the mirrors at the end of the kaleidoscope. All the others are reflected images of the V. The pieces of plastic in the V are therefore repeated several times, so that you see a circular pattern. To change the pattern, you simply shake the kaleidoscope.

Left: You could make your own kaleidoscope using cardboard for the outer tube and clear polythene for the material at the end that is held to the light.

How is mirror writing formed?

Ambulances often have mirror writing printed in large letters across the front. It takes a few seconds to work out what the words say; longer than it takes to read the right way round.

But the driver of a car in front of the ambulance can see the word from a glance in his rear-view mirror, and quickly gets out of the way.

Mirror writing is the mirror image of normal writing. Each part of each letter is seen in the mirror exactly opposite itself.

How does a periscope work?

A simple periscope consists of two mirrors in a long tube, both tilted at 45 degrees to the viewing holes, but parallel to each other.

The tube is held upright, so that light from an object passes horizontally through the top hole and strikes the top mirror. It strikes the mirror at 45 degrees. The ray has thus been turned through a right angle of 90 degrees, from the horizontal to the perpendicular.

The light travels downwards to the second mirror which it also strikes at 45 degrees. So it is turned through another right angle to pass out of the viewing hole horizontally again.

The viewer sees a life-size, upright reflection of the object, as if it was at eye level. In fact, the object is as far above the viewer's head as the length of the periscope tube.

Periscopes are great fun to make for yourself and play with. They are well-known, too, for their use in submarines. A marine periscope is water-tight and highly mechanized. The tube can be rotated, so that all-round vision is possible. The periscope provides the crew with a view of what is happening above the surface, while the submarine cruises along beneath the waves.

What makes a rainbow?

If it is raining, and the Sun is also shining, turn your back on the Sun and look for a rainbow. Occasionally you may even see two rainbows; a second, fainter one curving outside the other.

The rainbow is a curved band with concentric strips of colour. From the outside of the bow inwards, the order of the colours is red, orange, yellow, green, blue, indigo (which cannot be distinguished separately) and violet. These are the colours of the spectrum. The rainbow is a huge spectrum, produced by the refraction of white light through the raindrops of water.

When a ray of light passes from a less dense to a more dense material, it is bent, or refracted, because light travels more slowly in the dense material. White light is a mixture of all the colours of the spectrum. Each colour has a different wavelength.

Shorter wavelengths are refracted or bent, more than the longer ones, because they have a higher frequency and travel faster. The different wavelengths become separated and we see the colours individually.

What is the spectrum?

The spectrum is the group of electromagnetic waves with wavelengths to which our eyes are sensitive. Each is registered by the brain as a different *colour*. The colours are red, orange, yellow, green, blue, indigo and violet. Colours at the red end of the spectrum have the longest wavelengths and at the lowest frequency. Those at the blue end have the shortest wavelengths and the highest frequency.

Radiation of wavelengths just longer than red light is known as infra-red. Radiation of wavelengths just shorter than violet is known as ultraviolet.

The normal white light that we see is a mixture of all the different wavelengths in the spectrum. Added together, the colours produce the effect our brains register as white. If the white light is split up, so that we can see all the wavelengths separately, we can see the colours of the spectrum.

One way of doing this is to pass white light through a transparent substance which refracts or bends it, such as a glass prism. Radiation of different wavelengths travels at different speeds. The shorter the wavelength, the faster it travels. Consequently longer wavelengths are refracted through a smaller angle when they enter a new material, such as the glass prism. Each wavelength or colour passes out of the prism in a different place.

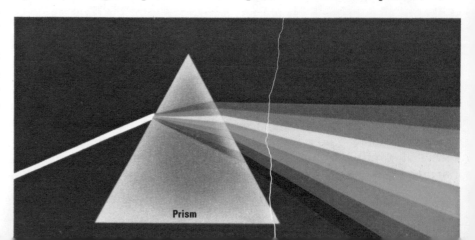

Prism

What are primary colours?

White light is a mixture of radiation at different wavelengths. Coloured light is radiation of a particular wavelength. As we have seen, if a beam of white light is split or refracted, it can be shown to contain all the colours of the spectrum.

But not all the colours of the spectrum are needed if we want to produce white light. It can be made by mixing the three *primary colours* as can be seen in the picture; there are red, green and blue. Any colour can be produced by mixing certain proportions of the primary colours together.

The colours of lights are altered by using colour filters. These block out certain wavelengths. This is because mixing colours in light is an *additive* process; different wavelengths are added together.

Mixing coloured paint is a quite different process. Once again, there are three primary colours. But these are red, yellow and blue. When all three are mixed together, they effectively produce black, or at least a very dark, muddy brown.

We see paint, and all normal solid objects, as having a colour because their surface *reflects* light of a particular wavelength. At the same time the surface absorbs

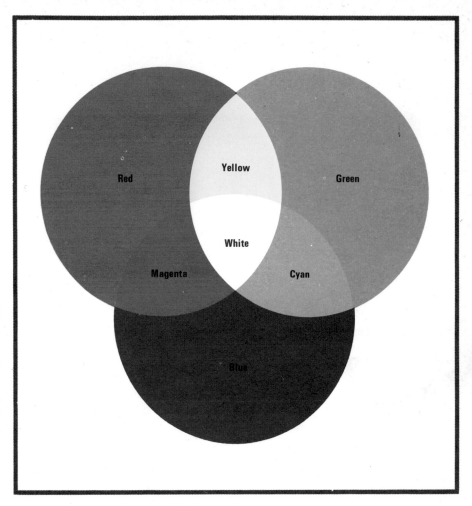

wavelengths of all the other colours.

When white light, which is a mixture of all wavelengths, falls on, say, a red object, all the wavelengths except that of red light are absorbed. Only red light is reflected in this case.

Each primary colour reflects only its particular wavelength; all others are absorbed. When all three primary colours are mixed together, all the wavelengths are absorbed, so the mixture appears black. Because mixing paint involves the absorption, or taking away of wavelengths, it is called a *subtractive* process.

What are complementary colours?

The three primary colours in coloured light are red, green and blue. Any colour can be obtained by mixing them in certain proportions. All three mixed together in equal proportions make white light.

When only two primary colours are mixed together they produce a *complementary colour*. Red and green mixed, produce *yellow*. Red

and blue mixed produce a pinkish-purple colour called *magenta*. Blue and green mixed produce *cyan*, which is a greenish-blue peacock colour.

If the complementary colours are added together they produce white light. They are effectively another set of three primary colours.

In coloured paints or pigments,

the three primary colours are red, yellow and blue.

Their corresponding complementary colours are orange, made from red and yellow, green made from blue and yellow, and purple made from red and blue.

In colour photography, a colour negative shows all the complementary colours to the real colours in the picture.

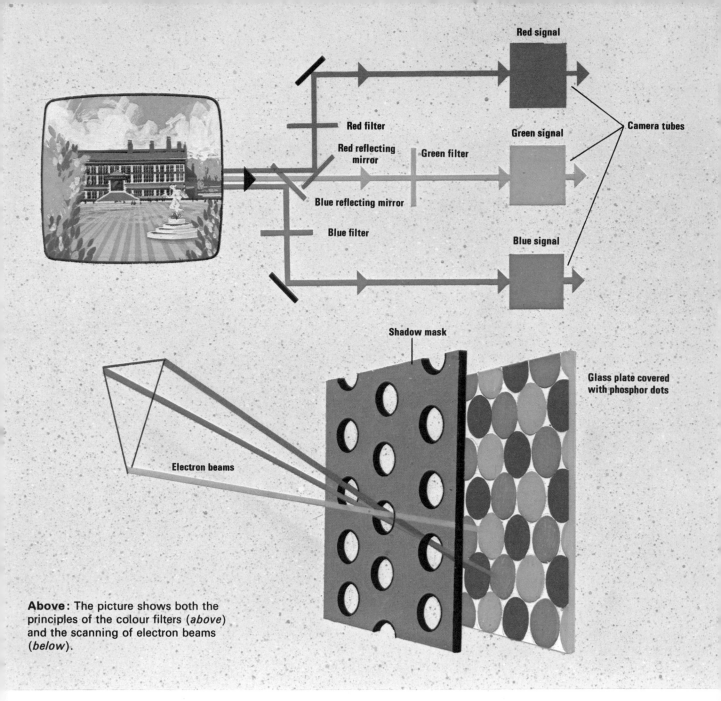

Red signal

Red filter

Red reflecting mirror

Green filter

Green signal

Camera tubes

Blue reflecting mirror

Blue filter

Blue signal

Shadow mask

Glass plate covered with phosphor dots

Electron beams

Above: The picture shows both the principles of the colour filters (*above*) and the scanning of electron beams (*below*).

How does colour TV work?

Colour television pictures are transmitted on three separate signals, as can be seen in the picture above. These are red, green and blue. In coloured light, all colour can be produced by adding together certain proportions of red, green and blue light, according to the laws of colour addition.

The colours are split by using mirrors and filters. The three coloured signals are then converted into electrical signals by the camera tube so that they can be transmitted from the television transmitter.

The colour television receiver, or set, has a special screen, coated with tiny phosphor dots. These are arranged in clusters or groups of three.

Each one of the phosphor dots in a group emits a different primary colour when it receives a signal. Each cluster can therefore produce a mixture of red, green and blue. This varies according to the signals received.

The television receiver receives the three separate signals from the transmitter and converts them into three scanning electron beams. These scan the screen at a fixed rate and excite the phosphor dots of the corresponding colour in each of the clusters.

Our eyes and brains finally see the combination of this array of dots as an image exactly like the scene being televized by the camera.

How do colour filters work?

Filters are made of transparent material which only allows light of a certain colour to pass through. This is the colour that the filter appears to be when looked at in white light. White light is made up of equal quantities of the three primary colours, red, green and blue. A yellow filter, for example, allows only red and green light to pass through. It filters out blue. Red and green light make yellow, so the beam of white light looks yellow when seen through the filter. A blue filter allows only blue light to pass through it and so on.

If a red light is shone through a green filter it produces a black beam, that is, no light at all. The green filter allows only green to pass through; as all red light is stopped, no light passes through at all.

Red filter

Yellow filter

Green filter

Why are sunsets red?

The sky overhead looks blue, especially when the Sun is high overhead. This is because there is more short-wave (blue) radiation in the light that reaches us, due to scattering by molecular particles in the upper atmosphere.

When the Sun is on the horizon the sky often appears orange or red because there is more long-wave (red) radiation in the light that reaches us. The short-wave (blue) light radiation has been lost because of collisions with dust particles in the lower atmosphere.

Light from the Sun on the horizon travels through the atmosphere close to the Earth's surface. When the Sun is overhead, the light has to travel a very much shorter distance through the atmosphere.

This part of the atmosphere is dense and laden with particles of dust and dirt. When light radiation strikes these particles it is absorbed and re-emitted at a longer wavelength. The longer the light's path through a dirt laden atmosphere, the greater the proportion of long-wave radiation in it.

Another factor is the frequency of the light radiation. The short-wave radiation waves vibrate at a much higher frequency than the long-wave radiation. This increases the chances of them striking a dust particle and being absorbed. If the light's path lies mainly through the lower atmosphere, much of the short-wave (blue) radiation is lost, so the sunset appears red.

The reddest sunsets are seen where the air is heavily polluted by smoke and fumes from industrial areas.

What is an electron microscope?

A microscope is an optical instrument used to produce an enlarged image of a minute object. This is done so that it can be studied in detail by the human eye.

In an ordinary microscope the object is illuminated by a beam of light and the image is then enlarged by means of glass lenses.

In an electron microscope, the object is bombarded by a stream of electrons, instead of a light beam. The electron stream is focused by means of magnetic lenses. These are powerful magnetic fields that can bend the electron beam and change its direction.

The image is focused onto a screen and is produced in a similar way to the image on a television screen.

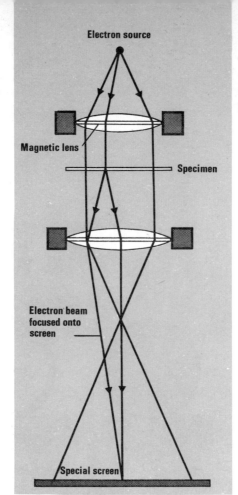

Why do sodium lights sometimes glow red?

In some towns the street lights are an orangy-yellow colour. These are sodium vapour lamps. The light is produced by passing an electric current through sodium vapour at low pressure. The vapour molecules vibrate at a certain frequency and emit a yellow light.

When the lamp is switched on, the flow of electrons is slow at first, until all the vapour molecules become fully excited. While only a few of them are vibrating, at a low frequency, light of a longer wavelength is emitted. This is the pink or red colour that is sometimes seen when the street lighting first comes on, or when a lamp is not working properly.

Yellow sodium lights are used because the yellow light is not absorbed by fog or mist as much as white light is.

What does fluorescent mean?

A substance that is fluorescent is one that is capable of absorbing light of one wavelength, or colour and then re-emitting light of a different wavelength, or colour.

Road signs are sometimes made of fluorescent fabric or coated with fluorescent paint. They can then glow brightly when a light is shone on them.

Theatrical effects and decorations also make use of some fluorescent paints and materials.

Fluorescence is a form of luminescence; that is, the emission of light from an object which is not the result of the object being heated up.

A fluorescent lamp is one that consists of a glass tube thinly coated inside with a fluorescent substance. The tube contains a gas which emits ultra-violet (UV) light radiation when a voltage is applied to the lamp. The UV radiation is converted to visible light radiation by the fluorescent walls of the tube. This type of lighting is commonly known as strip lighting.

How do neon lights work?

Neon is a gas which glows when electricity is passed through it, if it is enclosed in a glass tube at a low pressure.

The tube contains two electrodes, the cathode and the anode, one at each end of the tube. An electric current is supplied to the lamp and the gas acts as a conductor between the two electrodes. The current is said to flow from the positive anode to the negative cathode. In fact there is an actual flow of electrons, which carry a negative charge, from the cathode to the anode.

The electrons are passed from atom to atom and during the exchange, light radiation is given off. This produces the intense coloured glow all along the tube.

Neon lights are used extensively in the brightly coloured illuminated signs that are used for street advertising at night.

Neon is one of the inert, or inactive gases that occurs naturally in the atmosphere in very small quantities. It is obtained by distilling liquid air.

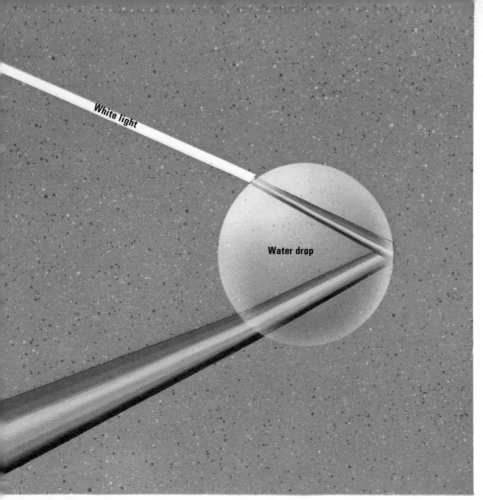

White light

Water drop

What makes rainbows in drops of water?

White light, such as sunlight, is made up of all the wavelengths in the visible spectrum. The shorter the wavelength, the higher the frequency of the vibrations; and the more vibrations there are, the more chances there are for collisions with the atoms of the substance they are travelling through.

The light rays are bent as soon as they strike a new substance, such as glass or water. The shorter wavelengths are bent more than the longer ones. Some of the rays are also reflected from the inside surface of a raindrop before they are refracted again as they pass out of it. Different wavelengths leave the raindrop at different points and these are seen as the separate colours of the rainbow.

What makes rainbows in bubbles?

In soap bubbles, the rainbow effect is produced by the phenomenon known as *interference*. The thin, filmy wall of a soap bubble is in fact only a few molecules thick.

Very thin films cause light waves of certain wavelengths to be cancelled out. The colour that is cancelled out depends on the wavelength of that colour in relation to the thickness of the film.

Where a colour has been cancelled out of a beam of white light, its complementary colour is seen. This gives the soap bubble its colour. The colour will change as the film changes in thickness, usually by evaporating until the bubble bursts. Different colours will be seen on different parts of the bubble because the soap film is of varying thickness.

What makes the coloured rings on puddles?

The coloured rings on puddles are usually caused by a thin film of oil spread over the surface. Different colours are seen where the oil film is of different thickness.

Thin films produce coloured, rainbow effects because of the interference of light waves. Light travels in waves which have crests and troughs just like those in water. When two waves cross each other, where the crest of one meets the trough of another, their effect is zero.

In water waves, this means the water is flat at that particular point. In light waves, it means that wavelengths are cancelled out of the light beam. The light beam then takes on the complementary colour to the colour of the wavelength cancelled out.

What are moiré patterns?

A moiré pattern is the effect produced when light shines through two gratings which are moving over each other. The gratings could be formed by two pieces of net curtain moving in the wind, or two sets of railings which are stationary, but appear to move as you walk or travel past, or two pieces of gauze which you can move separately. All sorts of patterns appear in different shapes. They may produce a series of wavy lines, or rings.

Moiré patterns have always been particularly popular for the effect they produce in water silks.

Moiré patterns are caused by the interference of trains of light waves. Interference occurs when separate trains of light travel to your eye along paths which are slightly different in length. Some of the trains of light waves cancel each other out.

Why does thunder follow lightning?

The sound of lightning travels at a speed of $\frac{1}{3}$ kilometre per second. The light reaches us almost instantaneously. To work out how far away the heart of a storm is, count the number of seconds between the flash and the crash. Then divide by three to work out its distance in kilometres. As the storm travels nearer, the time between the two will grow less.

Lightning is caused by an electric discharge across air molecules. The atmospheric conditions cause parts of the clouds to become positively charged, air molecules in another part to become positively charged and air molecules in yet another part to become negatively charged. When a potential difference builds up, a current flashes from the positive to the negative part of the cloud. In fact, there are up to ten flashes along the same path, in quick succession. The eye sees them as one continuous streak.

The current heats the air up and causes it to expand. Because there are several strokes in quick succession, the rapid expansion and contraction of the air causes huge sound waves to build up. These produce the thunderclap.

The electrical discharge can take place from cloud to cloud, or from a cloud to the ground. A tree or high building which is struck by lightning can be badly burnt. To safeguard against this, high buildings have lightning conductors. These are conductors with an insulated casing that project above the highest point of the building, such as the tip of a church spire. The lightning strikes the conductor and is conducted safely down the side of the building into the earth.

How does radar work?

Radar is an abbreviation of the name for RAdio Detecting And Ranging systems.

A radar aerial is dish-shaped. It transmits short-wave radio signals that are reflected off objects in their path and travel back to the aerial which also acts as a receiver. The incoming signal is passed to a cathode-ray tube so that it can be seen on a screen like a television screen.

As the direction of the signal and the time it takes to travel to the object and back can both be measured, the exact position of the object can be calculated.

The strength of the returning signal indicates what type of material it has been reflected off. The metal in vehicles produces a much stronger signal than the dense cloud at the centre of a hurricane, for example.

What makes some music loud?

The loudness, or volume, of a sound depends on the amount of energy that goes into making the sound.

The sound is produced by the vibration of air molecules. The rate at which the molecules vibrate determines the pitch of the sound, that is, whether it sounds high or low. The amplitude of the vibrations determines the volume or loudness of the sound. The amplitude of the vibration is the height, or depth of a wave.

The molecules use up energy as they vibrate. Sound waves therefore tend to decrease in amplitude and the sound grows quieter and dies away, unless more energy is supplied.

In many musical instruments, the energy is supplied by human muscles. They may be used to pluck a string, blow into a pipe or strike a drum, for example.

The loudest sounds are produced by the greatest movement of the air. This can be seen in a roll of drums, plucking, striking or bowing a string very hard, or blowing a lot of air into a pipe.

When sound is reproduced by electrical means, such as in radio, the volume can be increased by an amplifier. This is an electronic device that increases the amplitude of the sound output by putting in more energy. The extra energy is drawn from a power supply. Amplifiers are used with electric guitars.

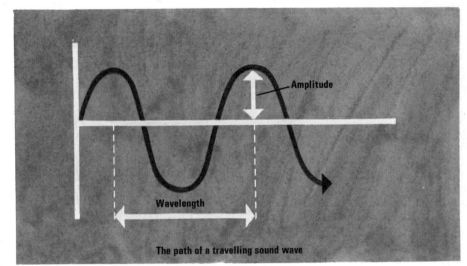

The path of a travelling sound wave

What is radar used for?

Radar is used for navigation and tracking systems. Ships and aircraft can locate their positions by directing a radar beam at known points on land. They can also avoid collision courses by keeping track of other moving vehicles.

Radar tracking systems keep a check on the movements of all aircraft or ships within their range. They are also used for missile detection.

Automatic control systems for guiding vehicles and missiles have been developed. This involves feeding the incoming signal into a computer.

Radar is useful for studying weather conditions and is invaluable for overcoming them. Unlike all tracking and navigation by sight, radar is unaffected by darkness, fog or clouds.

The 250-foot radio telescope at Jodrell Bank

How does a recorder make music?

A recorder is a wind instrument consisting of a pipe with an open end. At specific intervals along the pipe there are holes. These can be closed by covering them with the fingers.

When the column of air inside the pipe vibrates, it produces a musical note. It can be made to vibrate by blowing through the mouthpiece. As the air passes the sharp edge of the opening in front of the mouthpiece, it sets up eddies. These pass down the pipe in waves.

The length of the air column is varied by placing the fingers over the holes in the stem. The shorter the air column, the more vibrations the air makes.

How does a guitar make music?

A guitar is a stringed instrument. It produces a musical sound when the strings are plucked. This sets up vibrations in the strings, which are stretched across an opening in the hollow body of the guitar. The vibrations in the strings cause the air inside the guitar to vibrate or *resonate*.

The note produced by a string depends on its tautness and its length.

The strings can be wound tighter before playing to produce higher notes while playing. The effective length of a string is reduced by pressing down onto one of the metal ridges, or frets, on the neck. This also produces a higher note.

How do we get a sound from a record disc?

The surface of a record has a continuous spiral groove in it, leading from the edge to the centre. In the groove are minute waves and bumps, which cause the needle travelling along it to vibrate. These vibrations are converted into a variable electric current by a small component in the pick-up known as the cartridge. The current passes to the amplifier, which magnifies it

many times. This amplified current is then fed to the speaker.

The speaker consists of an electromagnet and a cone. In this the electrical energy of the current is converted into mechanical energy, making the cone vibrate. The vibrations set up sound waves and the listener hears a reproduction of the sound that was originally recorded on the record.

You can tell which parts of a

record will sound loud and which will be quieter, by looking carefully at the disc. The quiet passages are those where the grooves are very fine and closely spaced. The loud passages are where the grooves are wider apart.

Below: This picture shows how a record is made from the time when the music is first recorded, to the finished product on the record player.

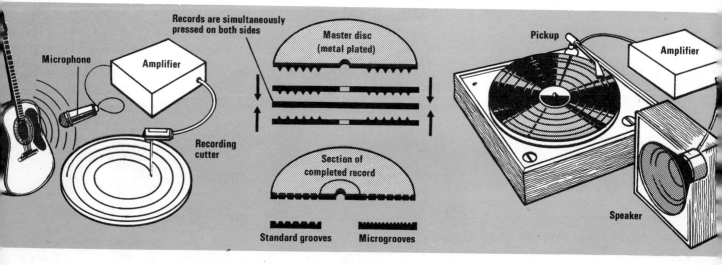

What is quadrophonic sound?

At a live performance of music, the sound travels to you from all the individual players and singers in their different positions. If you play a record on an ordinary record player, all the sound comes to you from one speaker, so you hear it as if it all came from a single point.

Quadrophonic sound is an attempt to reproduce the sounds you hear from all directions at a live performance. In the mid-1950s, stereophonic sound equipment was marketed. This system involves two speakers which reproduce the sound as if it came from a position on a straight line drawn between the two speakers. Stereophonic sound is more realistic than sound from one speaker, because the sound is heard as if it was coming from the correct position, from left to right, in front of the listener.

Quadrophonic sound is an improvement on stereophonic sound in two ways. It adds depth, so that the players are heard as if they were positioned before or behind each other. It also reproduces the sound which would be reflected off the side and back walls, as it would be at a live performance.

To produce these effects, four speakers are used, two placed in front of the listener, and two behind him. But it cannot be produced from an ordinary record just by using four speakers. A stereophonic record is specially made to send different sounds to the two speakers and with a quadrophonic record a slightly different sound is sent to each of the four speakers. A special amplifier is also needed to select and distribute the signals picked up from the record.

Right: The top picture represents stereophonic sound. Quadrophonic sound is shown below with the sound waves coming from four speakers.

173

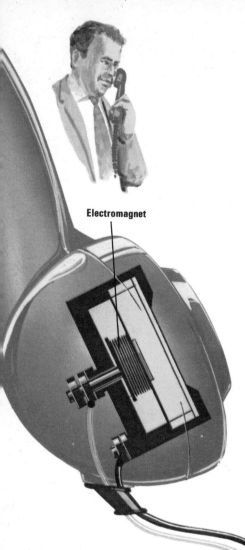

Electromagnet

How does a telephone work?

A telephone converts sounds into electric currents, so that they can be transmitted to a place that is out of normal hearing range. A second instrument receives the current and reconverts it to the original audible sounds. The telephone was invented by Alexander Graham Bell in 1876.

Each telephone handset contains an earphone receiver and a microphone transmitter. In both of these, there is a movable diaphragm and an electromagnet.

In the transmitter, the sound waves produced by the speaker's voice cause the diaphragm to vibrate. This movement produces changes in the strength of the magnetism of the electromagnet behind it. The magnetism of varying strength produces a correspondingly variable electric current.

At the receiver, another electromagnet uses the varying current to reproduce movements in the receiver diaphragm. These are exactly the same as those produced in the first diaphragm by the voice. These movements in the receiver diaphragm produce the sound waves heard by the listener, who hears an almost perfect reproduction of the speaker's voice.

Telephones are connected to telephone exchanges by wires, where they can be linked to another telephone through the switching mechanism. The exchange may be manual, where the operator has to plug the call into the socket with the right number, or they can be automatic, where relays select the position mechanically.

For long distance calls the current is amplified. This can be relayed along co-axial cables. As many as 3600 calls can be relayed along the same cable at the same time and are sorted out, electronically, at the other end.

Why does a magnet pick up a string of pins?

Dip a magnet into a pile of loose pins and it will come out bristling with them; some of them sticking to the magnet, some sticking to other pins.

The magnet exerts a force over the space around it which is known as the *magnetic field*. The way in which the space is magnetized follows a definite pattern, dependent on the shape of the magnet. This pattern can be represented by a series of lines, known as *lines of force*. When a metal object is placed near a magnet, these lines of force flow into it, turning the object into a weaker magnet that can attract other objects.

This is what happens to the chain of pins. Each pin becomes a very small, individual magnet itself, attracting another pin. The pins are not permanent magnets. When the main magnet is removed, the chain collapses as lines of magnetic force no longer flow through the pins.

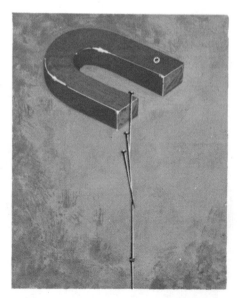

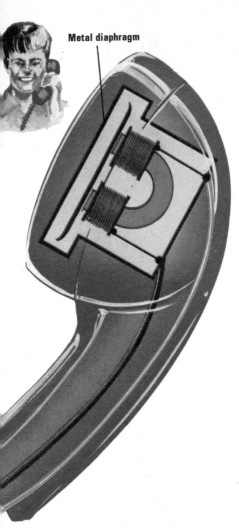

Metal diaphragm

How can you magnetize something?

The simplest way to magnetize a piece of iron, such as a nail, is to stroke it with another magnet. Use the end of a bar magnet, holding it like a pencil. Stroke the nail firmly, making each stroke in the same direction and keeping the magnet well away from the nail when returning it to the beginning.

After a few strokes, the nail should have become a strong enough magnet to attract other pieces of metal.

Another way to magnetize the nail is to wrap a coil of wire around it, laying the coils along its length. Attach the ends of the wire to a battery. After a current has passed through the wire, the nail will be magnetized.

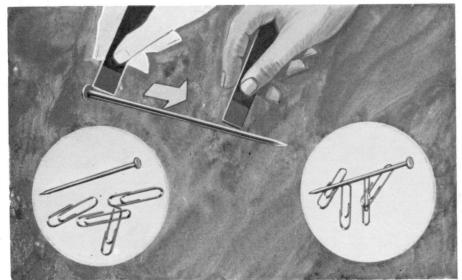

How can you tell if a piece of metal is a magnet?

Two nails will be attracted and stick together if one of them has been magnetized. They may also stick together if they are both magnetized, and the north pole of one is brought up to the south pole of the other. However, if two north poles or two south poles are brought together, they will repel each other because *like* poles of the same sign (north or south) always repel each other. *Unlike* poles of the opposite sign always attract each other. These are two of the basic laws of magnetism. Repulsion is necessary to prove that a piece of metal is a magnet.

Every particle in a nail is like a miniature bar magnet. Before it is magnetized these lie at random in all directions and their total magnetic effect is zero because they cancel each other out.

Stroking the piece of iron with the pole of a magnet attracts all the poles of opposite sign in the particles. The *orientation* of their magnetism is changed, so that they all lie in the same direction, producing a north pole at one end of the piece of iron, and a south pole at the other.

An electric current passed through a coil which is also wrapped around a piece of iron also brings the magnetism of all the particles into alignment.

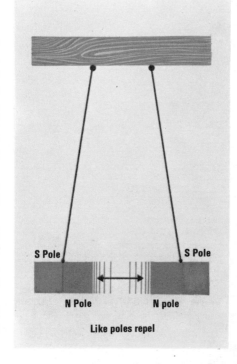

S Pole S Pole

N Pole N pole

Like poles repel

Where does electricity come from?

Electricity is vital to our modern way of life. We need it for lighting, heating, cooking, air-conditioning, refrigeration, transport, machinery, entertainment and communications. Without it we could certainly not live our lives in the way most of us do today.

Electricity exists in many forms. It can be transformed into light in a light bulb, heat in an electric fire, or sound in a telephone.

Where does electricity come from in the first place? We receive it in our homes down wires, from the power transmission lines. It has come from the power station where it was generated and changed to a suitable voltage by transformers.

The electricity is generated by means of electromagnetic induction. Huge electromagnets are rotated inside coils of wire. This induces a current in the wire. The

power to rotate the generator is obtained from turbines operated by steam power. This in turn is obtained from burning coal, or from a nuclear reactor, or from water power in a hydroelectric power station.

Electricity also reaches our homes in the form of electromagnetic waves. They are picked up by an aerial and converted into sound on a radio, or a picture on a television screen.

Electricity occurs in nature in the form of lightning and also in the electrical discharge that causes the phenomenon known as St Elmo's fire. This is the ghostly halo seen around the tips of ships' masts and aircrafts' wings during storms.

Another form of natural electricity is static electricity. It causes a piece of amber which has been rubbed hard, to attract small pieces of fluff or paper. Nowa-

days, it is more common to see it shown by a gramophone record attracting dust and fluff. It was, in fact, the ancient Greeks who gave electricity the name *elektron*, which is the Greek name for amber. The records of the Greek philosopher Thales who lived about 600 B.C. show that he carried out such experiments with amber.

Electricity can be produced chemically by the process known as electrolysis.

Small electric currents are also produced by the interaction of certain metals when they are both heated. This is known as thermoelectricity.

All electricity is associated with the movement of electrons, which exist in every atom of matter. These electrons carry an electric charge and it is the flow of electrons which produces an electric current.

176

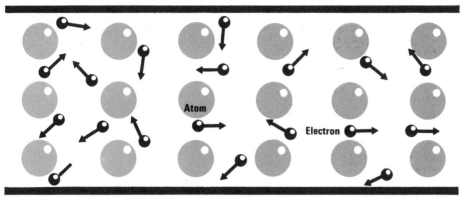

When electrons move at random there is no current

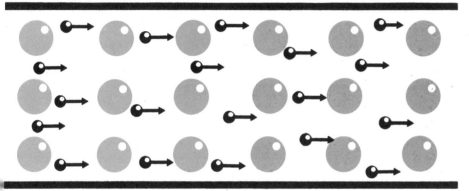

When electrons move in the same direction the current flows

What is an electric current?

An electric current is a flow of electrons through a conductor.

An electron is a part of an atom. All atoms consist of a central part, or nucleus, which has a positive charge, and one or more electrons. These are tiny, negatively charged particles that travel in orbit round the nucleus like planets round a sun.

Each element has a different number of electrons in its atoms. Some elements have electrons that are free to move from atom to atom. Many of these are metals. Normally, the electrons are moving about among the atoms in all directions at random. But the electrons can all be made to flow in the same direction. This continuous flow of electrons is called an electric current.

Electric current is measured in units called *amps*.

Who discovered how to make electricity?

A famous English physicist and chemist, Michael Faraday, who was born in 1791, made many important discoveries concerning electricity, magnetism and electrolysis. These included his experiments in which he found that, if a wire moves through a magnetic field, a current is induced in the wire. This is called *electromagnetic induction*. In fact, Faraday used a stationary coil of wire, known as a solenoid. He attached this to a galvanometer, which indicated that a current flowed in the wire when a magnet was moved in and out of the solenoid. The direction in which the current flowed depended on which way the magnet was moving.

This discovery led to the development of the generator.

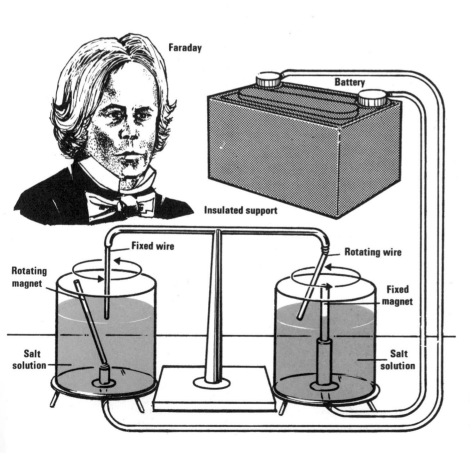

Faraday

Battery

Insulated support

Fixed wire

Rotating wire

Rotating magnet

Fixed magnet

Salt solution

Salt solution

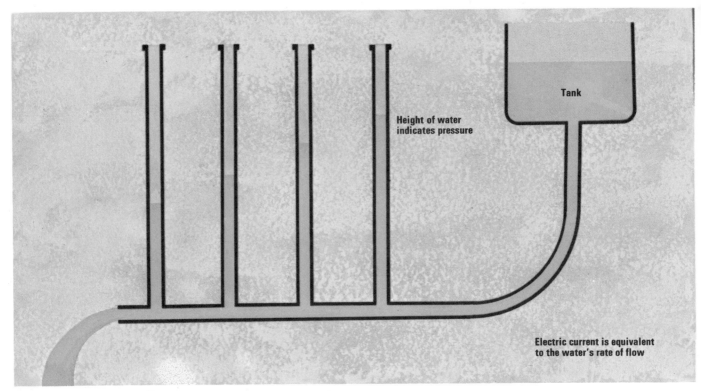

Height of water indicates pressure

Tank

Electric current is equivalent to the water's rate of flow

What is voltage?

Voltage is a measure of potential difference.

The size or strength of the potential difference that will cause a current to flow through a conductor is measured in *volts*.

The unit is named after the Italian scientist, Count Alessandro Volta, who lived from 1745 to 1827. He studied electricity and built the first battery, or *voltaic pile*. This provided a source of *electromotive force* (e.m.f.) or potential, that could be used to make a current flow through a conductor.

One volt is defined as the potential difference that exists between two points in a conductor that is carrying a current of one amp and using one watt of power.

Voltage is measured with an instrument known as a voltmeter. It contains a very high resistance so that the current continues to flow mainly through the conductor across which the voltage is to be measured.

Voltage can be increased or decreased by *transformers*.

Throughout the U.K. electricity is transmitted on power lines, in which the voltage may be as high as 400,000 volts. Very high voltages are dangerous and the power lines have to be very well insulated. To be used in homes, the voltage has to be reduced by transformers to about 240 volts.

What is potential difference?

An electric current flows through a conductor because there is a *potential difference* between the two ends. If you compare the electric current to water flowing along a pipe, the potential difference is equivalent to the difference in water pressure at the ends of the pipe. The water will only flow when there is a difference in pressure between the two ends of the pipe. And the greater the pressure, the more swiftly it will flow. The current is equivalent to the water's rate of flow.

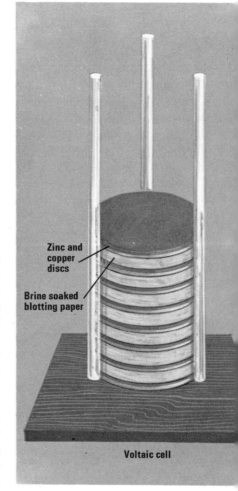

Zinc and copper discs

Brine soaked blotting paper

Voltaic cell

How is electricity measured?

All modern homes use power supplied by the mains electricity supply. The amount that is used is measured by a meter (a picture of one is shown on the right). This contains a digital counter or clock, showing the number of units that have been consumed.

The units are kilowatt-hours. The meter registers how many kilowatts of power have been used up each hour.

The watt is the unit of power which is named after Sir James Watt. One watt is the amount of power, or energy, used per second, when a current of one amp flows through a conductor which has a potential difference of one volt across it.

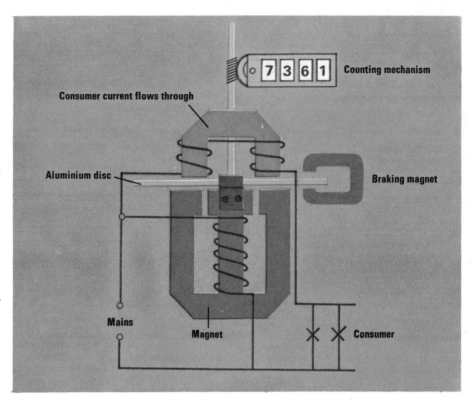

Counting mechanism

Consumer current flows through

Aluminium disc

Braking magnet

Mains

Magnet

Consumer

What are fuses for?

Fuses are intended to make an electric circuit safe from the danger of overheating. If the current does rise towards danger level, it causes heating in the thin fuse wire. This will melt, breaking the circuit and stopping the current from flowing.

What causes electric shocks?

A person may receive an electric shock if he touches a badly insulated, *live* electrical appliance; that is, an appliance that has a voltage across it.

If the appliance is at a positive potential a current will try to flow through the body to a place at a lower potential, such as the earth, or a metal object. A person wearing rubber boots is safer than one without, because with them he is insulated from the ground. This means that he does not provide a conducting path for the electricity. But if he touches say, a car battery terminal while he holds onto the metal bodywork of the car with his other hand, he will receive a shock from the battery.

People receive shocks from appliances plugged into the mains if the insulation on them breaks down. Handheld appliances usually have rubber or plastic covered handles, as do many tools such as screwdrivers and pliers intended for touching electrical fittings.

What is a transformer?

If a magnet is moved through a coil or wire, it can produce a current in the wire. This is called *electromagnetic induction*. Transformers work by electromagnetic induction.

They contain a soft iron core which is wrapped with a few turns of wire that form the *primary coil*. An alternating current flows through this wire. The core is also wrapped with a *secondary coil* of wire that has a different number of turns. If the secondary coil contains more turns than the primary coil, it will have a greater output voltage than that of the primary input. The current in the secondary coil is induced by the constantly fluctuating magnetism of the soft iron core, induced by the alternating current in the primary coil.

The ratio of input to output voltages is roughly equal to the ratio of the number of turns of wire in the primary and secondary coils.

A transformer that changes current at one voltage to current at a higher voltage is called a step-up transformer. One that changes the voltage down is called a step-down transformer.

Step-down transformers are used to reduce the voltage of 400,000 volts, at which the mains supply is transmitted across the country, to the voltage at which it is used in our homes, about 240 volts.

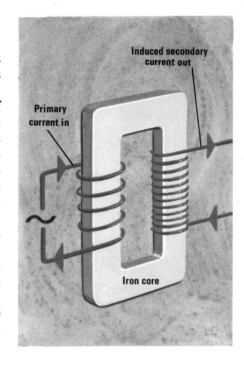

What is a generator?

A generator is a machine that uses mechanical energy to produce electrical energy. Small generators are also called dynamos. The principle they work on is that of electromagnetic induction.

If a permanent magnet is moved in and out of a coil of wire, it induces, or generates an electric current in the wire. Conversely, if a coil of wire is rotated in a magnetic field, a current is induced in the wire.

The magnetic field around a magnet is made up of invisible lines of force which are rather similar to the ridges in a ploughed field. The pattern these lines make up depends on the shape of the magnet. When a coil is rotated in a magnetic field, it cuts across the invisible lines of force. The faster these lines are cut by the coil, the greater the current induced in it. The number of turns of wire in the coil also affects the size of the current; the more turns there are, the greater the current.

Above: A hydroelectric power station, showing the difference in water level. This difference is caused by the dam.

In a power station, the magnetic field is rotated inside the coils. The field is produced by huge electromagnets. Current has to be fed to these by wires, but these cannot be connected directly or they would become tangled as the electromagnet rotated. The electrical connection is made by slip rings and carbon brushes. The brushes are fixed, and slide over the rotating slip rings, so that there is a permanent conducting path.

Mechanical energy is used to turn the electromagnets and it may be produced by a variety of means. In *turbo-generators* the shaft is rotated by a huge turbine. The turbine is rotated by water in a hydroelectric power station, or by steam produced by burning coal, oil or nuclear fuel.

Electric generators are vital to our way of life. They provide the power we use for transport, heating, lighting, factory machinery and all the electrical appliances we use in our homes every day.

What is hydroelectricity?

Hydroelectricity is electrical power obtained as a result of using water-power to drive a dynamo.

A dynamo converts mechanical energy into electrical energy. The mechanical energy provides the turning force required to rotate the armature, or rotor coil in the field of the electromagnet. This induces an alternating current, that is, one that builds up, then drops back to zero, builds up in the opposite direction and returns to zero, in a continuous cycle. The mechanical energy provides the turning force required to rotate the shaft in the generator.

In the case of a hydroelectric generator, the mechanical energy is produced by water turbines. These derive their energy from the enormous force of water flowing into them. This is regulated by sluice gates at the foot of the dam. The dam causes the water to build up behind it to a tremendous depth, thereby increasing its potential energy.

Turbogenerators are also driven by the force of waterfalls. Hydroelectricity is generated in vast quantities in mountainous countries where there are plenty of fast flowing rivers.

What is a transistor?

A transistor is a semiconductor device. It can be used to perform the same functions as a thermionic valve.

Semiconductors are a particular group of elements. They include carbon, silicon and germanium. Normally they are not good conductors, but it has been found that by adding a minute quantity of certain other elements, the conductivity of the semiconductors can be increased. In some, the addition of the impurities allows some of the electrons to move freely as in a metal. These are called n-type (negative) semiconductors. In others, the impurity creates a lack of free electrons so that positively charged particles appear to move through it. This is called a p-type (positive) semiconductor.

When a metallic conductor is heated its resistance increases as its temperature rises. In a semiconductor, however, the resistance decreases as its temperature rises; its conductivity rises and the electrons flow more freely. Semiconductors also differ from metallic conductors in that their conductivity is not the same in both directions.

Because of this ability to conduct freely in one direction only, semiconductor devices are used as rectifiers, in the place of thermionic valves.

A transistor is such a device. It consists of a sandwich of n-type and p-type semiconductors. It may be an n-p-n transistor or a p-n-p transistor. The three semiconductors are equivalent to the three connections in a triode valve, one being the cathode, one the anode and the middle of the sandwich is equivalent to the grid.

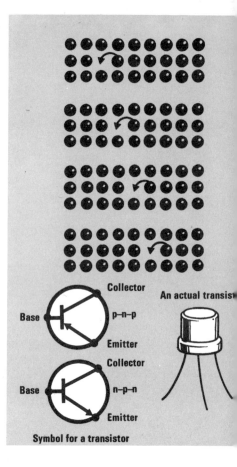

An actual transistor

Symbol for a transistor

What does 'solid state' mean?

Solid state physics is the study of matter in the solid state. The term solid state is also commonly used to refer to solid state devices. These are electronic devices such as transistors, semi-conductors and integrated circuits, that do not involve any moving parts, heated filaments or gases as valves do.

Solid state devices are very small and strong and can be mass produced cheaply. They are used in many items of modern equipment, from transistor radios to computers. Their small size has made it practical to build highly complex circuits which otherwise would have taken up an enormous amount of space.

Right: Modern electrical components can be made very small indeed.

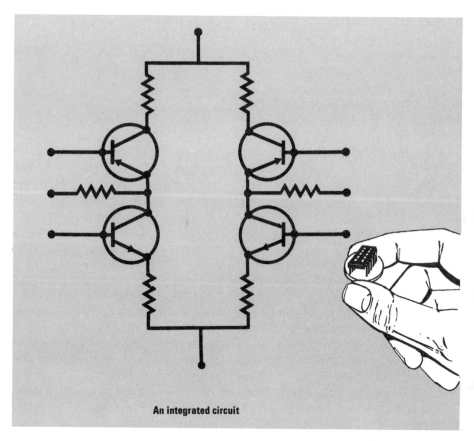

An integrated circuit

What is electrolysis?

A chemical reaction can produce an electric current by means of electrolysis. The solution in which such a reaction takes place is called an electrolyte. The current passes between two electrodes, from the positive anode to the negative cathode. Conversely, if an electric current is passed through an electrolyte by applying a voltage to the electrodes, it can cause a chemical reaction to take place.

This happens in the car battery. The chemical reaction between the lead plates and the sulphuric acid in the battery produces the electric current a car requires for its lights. By passing a current produced by the dynamo, in the opposite direction, the reverse of this chemical reaction takes place. This restores the electrolyte and the electrodes to their original chemical composition so that they can continue to react and produce a current.

Electrolysis is used for electroplating metal objects. To copperplate an object, for example, it is suspended in copper sulphate solution, connected to the negative side of a battery. A second electrode is also connected, to the positive side of the battery, so that it acts as the anode, and is also suspended in the electrolyte. The current from the battery causes a chemical reaction to take place in which copper from the electrolyte is deposited on the cathode. The object becomes brightly coated with a layer of copper. If you look on the back of a piece of silver cutlery, you may see EPNS engraved in it. This stands for Electro Plated Nickel Silver. This type of silver is known as *plate* to distinguish it from solid silver.

What is a diode?

A diode is a thermionic valve (a radio valve containing a heated cathode). When a filament is heated it gives off, or emits, electrons, just as boiling water will give off steam. The hotter the filament, the more electrons are given off. These electrons have a negative charge and will be attracted to anything that has a positive charge. This behaviour is known as thermionic emission.

In a thermionic valve the air is removed. In this way a vacuum is left which allows the electrons to move freely. The valve contains a heated electrode, the cathode, and this emits electrons.

A voltage is applied to the valve so that there is a potential difference across it. Another electrode, the anode, is held at a higher potential than the cathode.

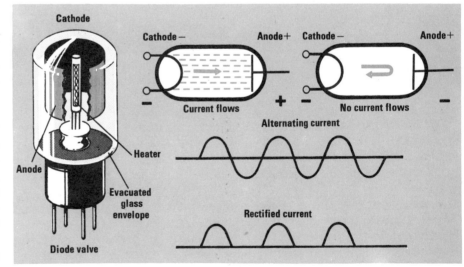

The negatively charged electrons are attracted to the positive anode.

Because the current only flows in one direction in a diode, it can be used to *rectify* an alternating current to direct current. It only conducts during one half of the current cycle.

Above: A diode can act as a rectifier, changing alternating current to direct current.

What does 'radioactive' mean?

Something that is radioactive gives off electromagnetic radiation of a very high frequency and short wavelength. This is because it contains certain types of atoms with unstable nuclei.

The nucleus of an atom is made up of protons and neutrons. All the atoms of a particular element contain the same number of protons, but they can contain different numbers of neutrons. Atoms of an element containing different numbers of neutrons are known as isotopes of an element. Certain isotopes are *unstable*; they emit radiation. These are known as radioactive isotopes or *radioisotopes*.

The most common form of radiation is called *beta particle emission*. A beta particle is an electron, but it is not one of the orbiting electrons from an atom. It is emitted from the nucleus where it is produced as a result of the disintegration of a neutron. The other products of this disintegration are a proton and a neutrino. The addition of another proton to an isotope changes it into the isotope of another element, since atoms of all elements always contain the same number of protons. This isotope may also be unstable and may disintegrate, or decay, further, to become another element. The decay continues until a stable isotope is formed. Throughout these changes beta particles are emitted.

Another common form of radiation is *alpha particle emission*. An alpha particle contains two protons and two neutrons. So the emission of an alpha particle changes a radioisotope to the isotope of an element with two fewer protons in its nucleus. Only the heavier elements emit alpha particles.

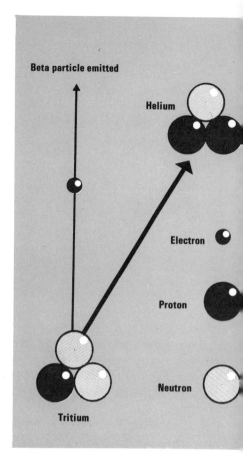

What is a geiger counter?

A geiger counter is an instrument for detecting radiation. It contains a gas which is held at low pressure. The gas surrounds a metal cathode cylinder, which has a thin wire anode running down its centre. There is a potential difference of about 1,000 volts across the electrodes. If any particles of ionizing radiation, such as alpha, beta or gamma rays, enter, the gas is ionized and there is a momentary current through the tube. This action produces a change in voltage which is amplified electronically to provide a digital read-out, or, in some instruments, it even lights a neon lamp or activates a loudspeaker.

Instruments that indicate levels of radiation are vital for people's safety. Radioisotopes are used in medicine to treat certain diseases, but the amount of radiation, the *dose*, has to be extremely carefully controlled. In some types of cancer, radiation is used to kill off the overactive cells. But an overdose of radiation could lead to vital organs being damaged.

People who work in radiation areas have to be screened from the radioactive source. Isotopes are handled by remote control and are stored in rooms and cases lined with lead. The streams of alpha and beta particles are absorbed by the lead, where they would pass straight through normal brickwork.

Portable geiger counters are taken to suspected areas where a radiation leak may have occurred, or where a source of radioactive material is discovered.

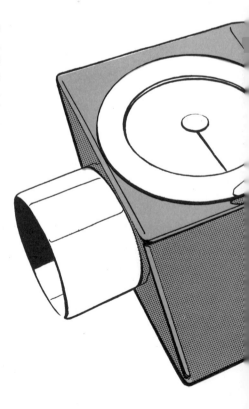

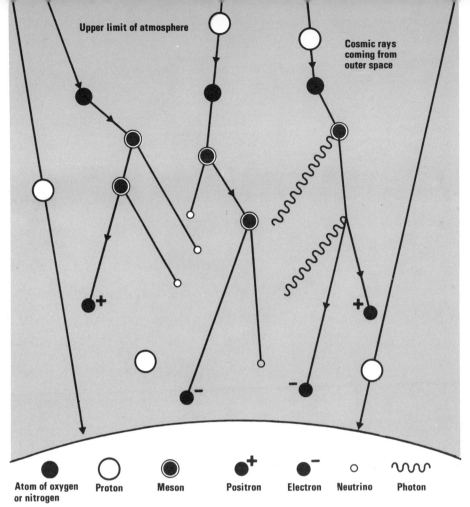

Upper limit of atmosphere

Cosmic rays coming from outer space

| ● Atom of oxygen or nitrogen | ○ Proton | ◉ Meson | ●⁺ Positron | ●⁻ Electron | ○ Neutrino | ∿ Photon |

What are cosmic rays?

Cosmic rays are very high energy radiation coming from outer space. Some come from the Sun, which is itself like a gigantic nuclear explosion, emitting high energy radiation all the time.

Cosmic rays strike the Earth continually from all directions, but fortunately the atmosphere prevents most of it from reaching the surface. The cosmic rays consist mainly of very high energy protons and alpha particles. Some of these collide with molecules of gas in the atmosphere, producing secondary cosmic rays and cosmic ray showers of *elementary particles*.

Cosmic rays have extraordinary penetrating power. They pass through not only the atmosphere, which is equivalent to passing through one metre of lead, but they also penetrate into the sea and underground.

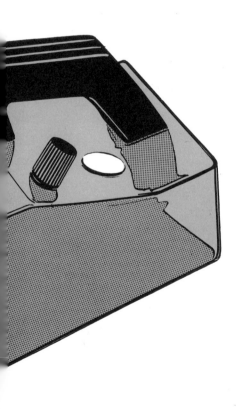

What is fall-out?

Fall-out is the radioactive matter which is deposited on the surface of the Earth from the atmosphere, after a nuclear explosion. There are three different types. *Local* fall-out consists of the large particles landing within 160 kilometres of the explosion. This takes place within the first few hours after the explosion.

Tropospheric fall-out is the deposition of fine particles which were carried up in the troposphere. It takes place all around the world, mainly in places at the same latitude as the scene of the explosion, and occurs within a few weeks.

Stratospheric fall-out continues for years. It is the deposition of fine particles of radioactive matter, blown up and carried in the stratosphere. It takes place all over the globe.

What is uranium?

Uranium is one of the Earth's most valuable, naturally occurring elements. It is a hard, white metal and is both the heaviest metal and the heaviest naturally occurring substance. Its great value is due to the fact that it is radioactive. Natural uranium contains 0·71 percent of the isotope uranium-235. This isotope can produce a nuclear chain reaction. It is used in nuclear reactors and nuclear weapons.

Uranium was the source of the first effects of radioactivity to be investigated. In 1896 the French physicist, Becquerel, found that some kind of emission from a lump of uranium produced an image on a photographic plate.

In 1940, scientists discovered that by bombarding uranium with neutrons, it could be transformed into heavier elements as it absorbed the neutrons. These elements are known as the *transuranic elements*. They include plutonium, thorium and curium. Curium was named in honour of Pierre and Marie Curie, who were the great pioneers of radioactive research.

How do we get nuclear energy?

Nuclear energy, or atomic energy, is released in nuclear reactors and nuclear weapons. It is released during a nuclear reaction where *mass* has been converted into energy.

Einstein's theory of relativity explains how mass and energy are really two different forms of the same thing. When the nucleus of an atom breaks up an enormous amount of *kinetic energy* is released. This is the energy of motion, and it is released because the particles in the nucleus move at tremendously high speeds when the atom is 'split'.

We obtain a useful amount of nuclear energy from a chain reaction. This is a continuous process in which the neutrons, emitted by the nucleus of one atom breaking up, cause the destruction of several neighbouring nuclei. This also leads to the release of more neutrons, and hence a continuous chain or *fission reaction*.

The initial reaction can be brought about by bombarding radioactive material with elementary particles. Some materials have to be enriched to keep a chain reaction going. The energy obtained from nuclear reactions has many uses. It can be converted into heat and used in power stations; several ships and submarines are already in service, powered by nuclear reactors, and it is also used in nuclear weapons.

What is nuclear fission?

Nuclear fission is a type of nuclear reaction during which the nucleus of an atom splits into two, releasing a vast amount of nuclear energy. Particles from the nucleus, known as neutrons, are also emitted. These will bombard the nuclei of neighbouring atoms causing them to split, starting a *chain reaction*.

Only fissile atoms will split when struck by a neutron. These atoms are relatively rare. The isotope uranium-235 is such a substance. It is found in very small quantities in natural uranium.

The enormous amounts of energy that are released during nuclear fission can be converted into heat and used as a source of power to drive engines and generators. The energy can also be put to a destructive use in nuclear weapons. In the atom bomb, all the energy of a fission reaction is released at once. The great dangers in this are not only the destructive force of the shock of the explosion. The contamination of the land and the atmosphere by the release of radioactive particles, known as fallout, also needs careful control.

The fission reaction in a nuclear reactor also has to be carefully controlled.

Fissile radioactive material is stored in small quantities of less than a certain amount, known as the *critical mass*. Below the critical mass, neutrons escape from the surface of the body of material, so there are not sufficient moving within the material to set up a chain reaction.

How does a nuclear reactor work?

Fissile material, such as uranium containing the isotope uranium-235, is used in a controlled nuclear fission reaction. It produces nuclear energy in a nuclear reactor, or creates more fissile material.

The atoms of the radio-active isotope split, releasing vast amounts of energy and emitting neutrons which bombard other fissile atoms, causing them to split. The rate of this chain reaction has to be very carefully regulated. To slow it down, a *moderator* is used.

In some reactors the fuel has to be *enriched* to make sufficient fissile atoms available. The great heat produced by the nuclear reaction has to be controlled by using a coolant.

In a *fast reactor* the fuel is enriched by increasing the proportion of the uranium-235 isotope in the fuel, or by adding another fissile element such as plutonium. Little or no moderator is used and the fast neutrons reach very high energy levels.

The *convertor reactor* converts fertile material into fissile material. Fertile material contains isotopes which can absorb neutrons and change into fissile isotopes.

In a *thermal reactor*, a moderator consisting of a neutral substance such as carbon is used to slow down some of the fast neutrons. As fast neutrons they would tend to be absorbed by uranium-238. As slow neutrons they are available to cause fission of the uranium-235 isotopes. This type of reactor generates heat which is extracted by a coolant and used to heat water. It can then provide steam to drive the turbines for electrical generators.

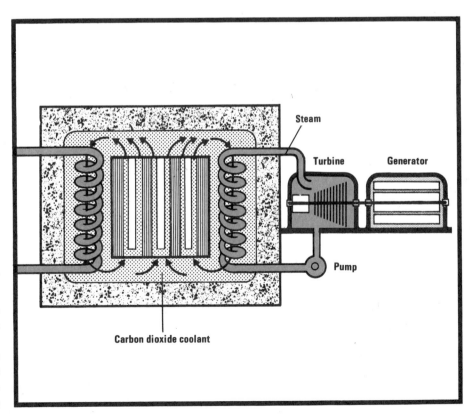

Steam

Turbine

Generator

Pump

Carbon dioxide coolant

What drives electric trains?

There are three main types of modern electric trains. Very powerful, diesel-electric locomotives pull the fast expresses in many countries. In these a diesel engine, run by oil, drives a generator which produces the electricity needed for the electric motors. These in turn drive the train and supply power to the train for heating and lighting.

The record for the fastest railway locomotive is held by a French electric one. It draws its power from an overhead wire through a strangely shaped frame called a *pantograph*. On some railways, a similar type of locomotive draws its power from a *live rail*, which is a third rail placed alongside the track.

Multiple unit coaches have motors at the ends of each coach. This train is used on suburban and local services because the number of coaches which can be coupled together is flexible.

How does an electric motor work?

The principle of the electric generator is based on the fact that, if a conductor is moved through a magnetic field, a current is induced in the conductor.

The electric motor works on the converse principle. If a current is passed through a conductor which is situated in a magnetic field, the conductor will be made to move. In a simple motor, the conductor is a coil, the *armature*, which rotates between the poles of a magnet. This produces a direct rotational movement to the drive shaft.

Current is supplied to the coil through a *commutator*, which reverses the direction of the current. In this way the shaft is kept turning in the same direction.

Some motors run on direct current (d.c.); others run on alternating current (a.c.).

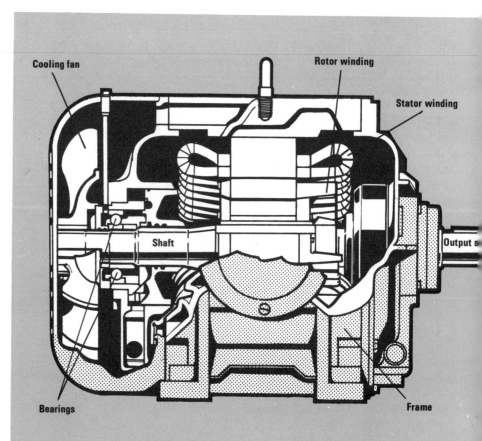

Cooling fan

Rotor winding

Stator winding

Shaft

Output s

Bearings

Frame

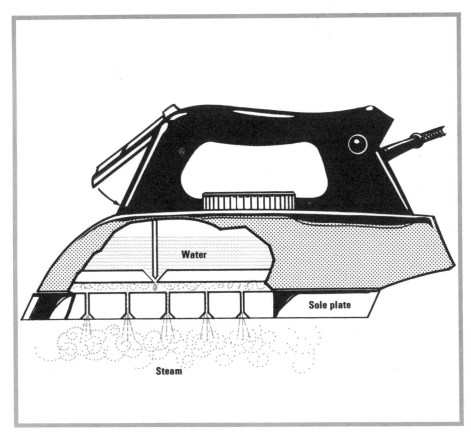

Water

Sole plate

Steam

How does a steam iron work?

It is easier to iron the creases out of cloth which is damp than when it is 'bone dry'. The steam iron is designed to dampen the cloth and iron out the creases all with one stroke.

The flat base, or sole-plate of the iron is made of heavy, highly conductive metal and is heated by an electric element immediately behind it. Next to the element are tubes containing the water which is heated to boiling point at the same time.

A switch makes it easy for you to release the steam when it is required.

The steam rises and comes out through several holes in the sole-plate. The sole-plate is also grooved, so that the steam flows along and dampens more of the cloth.

How does an electric convector heater work?

Convector heaters make use of natural convection currents to heat a room. Hot air rises because as the air is heated, it expands and grows less dense as the gas molecules move further apart. The lighter and less dense hot air rises and heavier, more dense, cool air is drawn beneath to replace it. These currents of air, called *convection currents*, are set up wherever the air is heated in one spot.

A convector heater contains an electrically heated filament enclosed in a case. It allows cool air to be drawn in underneath and heated air to rush out through the grill at the top.

A forced *convector heater* also contains an electric fan. This sucks cold air in and blows it across the elements to speed up the circulation of the air.

Hot air

Heating elements

Cold air

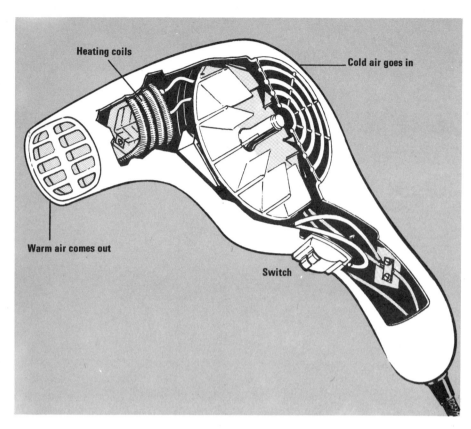

Heating coils

Cold air goes in

Warm air comes out

Switch

How does a hair drier work?

A hand-held hair drier gives out a jet of hot, dry air from a nozzle. This will very quickly make water evaporate from wet hair.

The air is sucked in by a small electric fan and is blown across the electrically heated elements. These elements then heat the air, which dries the hair.

Hair driers contain a thermostat, so that the air does not get too hot and singe the hair or damage the drier. The thermostat automatically cuts off the current from the elements if they overheat, if the air intake is blocked or if the fan stops. This is why it is so important not to lay the hair drier down and block the air intake. This intake is easy to find; usually it is the gridded section on the side.

Who invented radio?

Radio is a system in which electrical signals are sent from one place to another as electromagnetic radiation, instead of sending a current along wires—hence the name 'wireless'. Wireless telegraphy was invented by Marconi. In 1896 he sent a wireless message nearly 15 kilometres, and in 1901 he succeeded in transmitting a signal across the Atlantic, from England to Newfoundland.

Radio involves the transmission of electromagnetic energy in the form of *ground waves*. These follow the curve of the Earth's surface. The energy may also be in the form of *sky waves*, that are reflected off the electrically charged layer in the atmosphere, known as the *ionosphere*. The signal is sent out from a transmitting aerial and is picked up by a receiving aerial. Early radio signals were sent in *Morse Code*, by tapping a transmitting key.

Since the invention of the microphone and the electronic valve, it has been possible to convert sound into radio signals, providing us with the radio broadcasting systems of today.

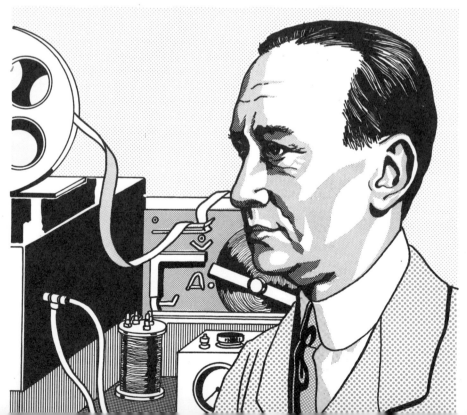

When was television invented?

The history of television is a long and controversial one. Over fifty years of research by scientists in many countries were involved in making it.

The cathode ray tube, which is the screen on which we receive a picture on our television receiving sets, was invented by Sir William Crookes in 1878.

The picture is built up on the screen, bit by bit, by the process known as *scanning*. The first mechanical scanning system was invented by Nipkow in 1884.

In 1923 Zworykin patented the iconoscope, which was the forerunner of the television camera. Later, he also demonstrated how a receiver works. Regular television broadcasts began in New York in the 1930s.

Meanwhile, other television systems had been worked on. In Britain, Logie Baird demonstrated his system, which worked by infra-red rays. He made successful transmissions in black-and-white and colour, and also across the Atlantic.

How is a TV picture produced?

The screen of a television receiver is coated with a fluorescent chemical which glows for a short time after being struck by an electron beam. This screen is at the end of a cathode ray tube, down which the beam is sent. The beam is made to flash across the screen from side to side, moving down slightly each time, covering the whole screen, or frame, in 625 lines. This process is known as scanning.

Each line forms part of the picture. The beam makes 30 frames per second. (The eye sees continuous movement after 12 pictures per second.) The electron beam is produced, after amplification, from the signal received from the broadcasting transmitter. At the same time a sound signal is received and the two are synchronized so that they are presented simultaneously.

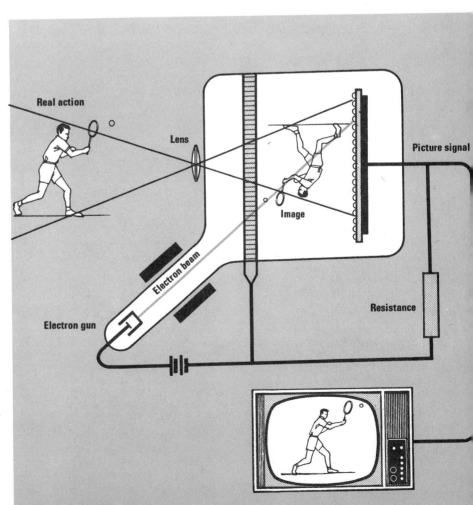

Real action

Lens

Picture signal

Image

Electron beam

Resistance

Electron gun

How is a TV picture transmitted?

The signal plate of a television camera is covered with thousands of light-sensitive dots. Light from the scene which is being transmitted falls on these dots and produces a signal which is picked up by an electron beam scanning the plate. The signal from the beam is amplified and is broadcast from the transmitter as *modulated radio frequency electromagnetic radiations*.

The signal is carried on a very high frequency carrier wave which travels in straight lines, unlike radio signals which can follow the curvature of the Earth. So the directional aerials that pick up the signal have to be placed high up, on housetops. A *relay transmitter* picks up the signal from the broadcasting transmitter and sends out, or relays, a stronger signal to places further away, where the original signal would have been too weak to pick up.

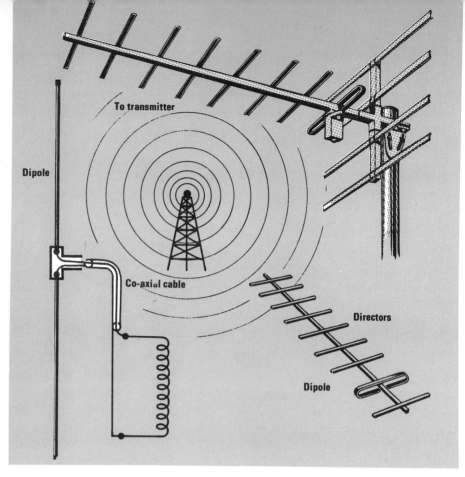

The sound and vision signals travel along co-axial cable, into the receiver set. Here they are amplified and changed into sound from a speaker and a scanning electron beam produces the picture that we finally see on the screen.

What is video tape?

Some television broadcasts are of live performances in which the signal from the camera is sent out immediately by the transmitter. Filmed recordings are also broadcast. A more direct method of recording television programmes, for transmission at another time, is on video tape. This is magnetic tape which contains information for both the audio (sound) and video (picture) signals, which are recorded on the same tape.

Video tape does not have to be processed like film, so is immediately available for playing back. It is used for action replay, and slow motion shots, which are especially popular in broadcasts of sporting events.

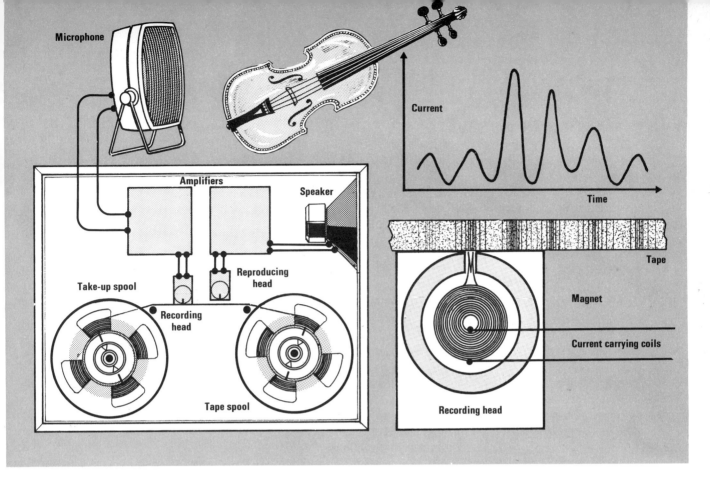

Labels in figure: Microphone · Amplifiers · Speaker · Current · Time · Take-up spool · Reproducing head · Recording head · Tape spool · Tape · Magnet · Current carrying coils · Recording head

How does a tape recorder work?

Sound recordings are usually stored either on record discs, or magnetic tape. Magnetic tape is plastic tape, coated on one side with the metallic powder, iron oxide, which is magnetic.

When the magnetic tape is passed in front of an electromagnet, the iron oxide becomes magnetized, strongly or weakly, depending on the strength of the current in the electromagnet. The magnetized tape is then used to induce a current in another electromagnet.

The sounds to be recorded are picked up by a microphone which converts them into an electric current that varies with time. This current is amplified, which makes it stronger and shows up the variations more clearly. It is then fed to the recording head.

The recording head consists of an electromagnet made from a coil of wire, which carries the current, wound onto a curved iron core.

The magnetic tape is wound onto a spool and connected to a second, take-up spool. This is rotated by an electric motor, which can be driven at several constant speeds. As it is wound onto the take-up spool, the tape passes the recording head at a constant speed. The varying current in the recording head produces correspondingly varied magnetized sections on the tape.

To replay the recording, the direction of the tape is reversed and it is rewound onto the original spool. Then the tape recorder is switched to *play* and the tape moves past the heads once again. But this time the reproducing head is in operation. It is very close to the recording head and is similarly constructed. The moving magnetized tape induces a current in the reproducing head, which is the same as the original current produced by the microphone. This current is amplified and fed to a loudspeaker.

ASTRONOMY

What can we see in the sky?

The appearance of the sky is always changing and there are many astronomical bodies to be seen, except, of course, when it is cloudy! In the daytime sky, we can usually only see the Sun as it is by far the brightest thing in the heavens. The Sun supplies the Earth with all its light and heat, and so is of the utmost importance to us living on Earth. Small, wonder, then, that ancient civilizations thought of the Sun as a powerful god.

In the night sky, there are many things to look at. The brightest object is the Moon, which looks like a luminous disc and almost exactly the same size in the sky as the Sun. Like the Sun, the Moon rises in the east (that is, if you live in the northern hemisphere of the Earth). It then climbs higher in the sky until it reaches its highest, when due south. Thereafter, it sinks lower, until it sets in the west. In addition, over a month the Moon changes shape from a thin crescent to 'full moon' and then back to a thin crescent again.

There are many stars to be seen; about two thousand can be seen by an average person on a clear night, and even a small telescope will show tens of thousands more. Although the stars appear to be dotted at random on the sky, a closer look will show that they tend to form patterns, called constellations. If you watch the sky carefully throughout the year, you will see that different constellations are visible at different times.

There are also some 'stars' which change their positions (ordinary stars stay in the same patterns) from day to day. These are the planets (a word meaning 'wandering star'), of which five can be seen from time to time without a telescope.

Often you may be able to see a tiny, bright meteor flash across the sky, and occasionally, the ghostly shape of a comet.

Above: Here is a diagram showing how the Moon works like a mirror. The Sun's light is reflected off the Moon's surface, back to Earth.

How does the Moon shine?

Although the Moon seems quite bright at night, it does not shine by its own light. It simply reflects light from the Sun back to the Earth like a giant mirror. Surprisingly, too, the Moon does not reflect sunlight very well; in fact it only reflects about seven per cent of the light that falls on it (astronomers say it has an *albedo* of 0·07). This is because of the nature of the rocks and dust which makes up the Moon's surface. The Earth, on the other hand, is a good reflector of sunlight. If you were to stand on the Moon and look up at the Earth, then the Earth would seem about four times bigger, and nearly a hundred times brighter than the Moon seems to us. Sometimes when the Moon is a thin bright crescent, we can see the dark side faintly illuminated by this light reflected from the Earth. This is known as earthshine.

What is the difference between a star and a planet?

The basic difference between a star and a planet is that a star is a hot, luminous body, producing its own light, whereas a planet is a body like the Earth, or the Moon, which shines only by reflecting light from the Sun. Stars are mostly giant bodies made of hot gas, just like the Sun. In fact, the Sun itself is a very ordinary star, neither particularly large nor particularly hot. The stars seem like faint points of light in the sky simply because they are so very far away. Even the nearest star is more than forty million million kilometres away, while the Sun is a mere 150 million kilometres from the Earth.

The planets which we see in the sky are bodies travelling round the Sun. There are nine planets known, and in order of distance from the Sun, they are, Mercury, Venus, the Earth, Mars, Jupiter, Saturn, Uranus, Neptune, and Pluto. The three most distant ones are too faint to be seen without a telescope, but the others may be seen when they are correctly placed for viewing.

The planets vary in size from Mercury, which is only about a third of the size of the Earth, to Jupiter, which is eleven times bigger than the Earth. Jupiter is more than 300 times as massive as the Earth, but is, itself, only one thousandth of the Sun's mass. This is another difference between stars and planets; stars are much more massive than planets.

Below right: On the left we are shown our Earth and a white dwarf (a hot star) compared with the Sun. On the right our Sun is quite small compared with a red giant (a cool star).

What is the distance to the Moon?

The average distance to the Moon is about 384,000 kilometres. Because the Moon moves round the Earth in an elliptical orbit, its distance varies from about 354,000 kilometres at its closest (*perigee*) to some 404,000 kilometres at its furthest (*apogee*). This distance is roughly equal to travelling ten times round the Earth, and is, so far, the greatest distance away from the Earth that any man has travelled.

A ray of light travels at 300,000 kilometres per second, and so would take about $1\frac{1}{4}$ seconds to cover the distance to the Moon. Radio waves travel at the same speed with the result that if you talk to an astronaut who is standing on the Moon, it will be at least $2\frac{1}{2}$ seconds before you get a reply.

Why does the Moon show phases?

We know that the Moon has no light of its own and shines only by reflecting sunlight. Consequently, only half the Moon's surface is lit up at any one time (the half facing the Sun), while the other half is dark. Now, the Moon travels round the Earth in just under a month, and depending on how much of the sunlit part of the Moon is turned towards us, so we see different phases.

At 'new moon' the Moon lies almost between the Sun and the Earth so that its dark side is turned towards us and we cannot see it. As the Moon continues on its journey round the Earth, it moves away from the Sun in the sky and we begin to see part of the illuminated side. At this stage the Moon appears as a thin, crescent shape. By the time the Moon has completed one quarter of its journey round the Earth, we can see half the illuminated side, and it is then said to be first quarter.

After this we see progressively more and more of the bright Moon until, about two weeks after new moon, the whole visible part of the Moon is lit up at full moon. The Sun and Moon are then opposite each other in the sky, with the Earth lying between the Sun and the Moon. When it is at this stage the Moon rises at about the time of sunset.

As the Moon continues its journey round the Earth, it is now getting closer to the Sun in the sky, so that we begin to see less of it

illuminated. Third quarter occurs when we can see half of the Moon shining in the morning sky, and then finally, twenty-nine days after new moon, the Moon has once more turned its dark side to the Earth.

Left: 1) Newton's original reflector of 1671.

2) A Gregorian telescope made by George Adams in 1740.

3) An early portable telescope, made 1714-1722.

4) A very early telescope of 1673.

Who invented the telescope?

The telescope is usually considered to have been invented by a Dutch spectacle maker called Hans Lippershey, in about 1608. However, nobody is quite certain about this. The real mystery about the invention of the telescope is why it was not invented much earlier!

Glass lenses had been used for hundreds of years before Lippershey's time, and even in the thirteenth century, the English friar, Roger Bacon, is known to have suggested that lenses might be used to make objects appear closer. The true inventor of the telescope may never be known, but as far as astronomy is concerned, it was the work of Lippershey which led the Italian astronomer, Galileo, to make the first recorded astronomical observations with telescopes.

When was the telescope first used in astronomy?

As far as we know, the telescope was first used for astronomical observations in the winter of 1609 by the great Italian astronomer, Galileo Galilei. Once he had heard of Lippershey's work, he decided to design and build his own telescope which consisted of two lenses, one convex, and the other concave. This type of telescope gave an image of distant objects which was erect (the right way up). But the type of telescope that was designed by Kepler the following year (using two convex lenses) gave an inverted (or upside down) image. It did, however, have other definite advantages over Galileo's design.

Although Galileo's telescope was very feeble compared to present-day instruments, he revolutionized people's ideas of the universe with what he could see in the sky. He was able to show that the Sun had spots on its surface (sunspots) and was not a perfectly unblemished disc as had been thought.

Galileo could also see for the first recorded time, that the Moon had a surface covered in mountains, craters, and the dark areas. He took these areas to be seas, although we know today that they are dark plains and that there is no water there. His telescope showed thousands of stars, too faint to be seen by the naked eye, but in many ways, his most interesting observations were of the planet Jupiter.

Galileo saw the shape of the planet and the cloud belts in its atmosphere, but also saw that it had four satellites travelling round it. This led him to believe Copernicus, who said that the Earth and planets go round the Sun.

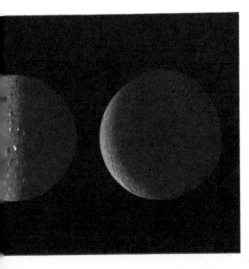

Below left: The Moon is shown here waxing from crescent to full. It can then be seen waning back to crescent. Finally it is 'old moon' which occurs just before 'new moon'.

Who discovered that the Sun sends out different colours of light?

Isaac Newton, in 1666, passed sunlight (which looks white) through a glass prism and saw a rainbow band of colour emerge on the other side. It showed all the colours, red, orange, yellow, green, blue indigo and violet, in that order. He therefore showed that 'white light' from the Sun consists of a mixture of all colours.

Newton went on with his experiments and passed the light through another prism. He found that the colours were spread out into a longer band, but that no new colours appeared. Therefore, these were all the colours in sunlight. He called the band of colour a *spectrum*. His next experiment reversed the second prism and showed that if these colours were combined again, you would find white light once more.

The prism spreads white light out into a spectrum because the different colours are each refracted in varying amounts. In fact, this is just what causes chromatic aberration in a lens, and Newton was then trying to find a way to cure this problem. He did not succeed but went on to develop the reflecting telescope instead.

In fact, the Sun also sends out other types of 'light', or radiation, which we cannot see at all with our eyes. This radiation varies from the short wave-length X-rays (which do not penetrate the atmosphere) to radio waves.

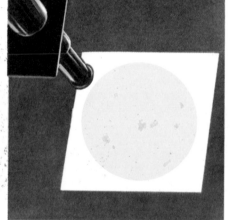

Why is it dangerous to look at the Sun through a telescope?

The Sun sends out large amounts of light and heat, and is really too bright to look at with a telescope. (You should never stare at the Sun without protecting your eyes by means of a thick, dark filter.) However, if you were to look at the Sun through a telescope, which gathers very much more light and heat than your eye, it would bring all of this light and heat to a focus right on your eye, causing a lot of damage, and quite possible blinding you completely. The heat of the Sun can easily be demonstrated by placing a piece of paper at the focus of a lens, such as a magnifying glass. You will soon see it burn. The safe way to observe the Sun is to use a telescope to project it onto a screen (a piece of paper will do). NEVER look at the Sun through a telescope!

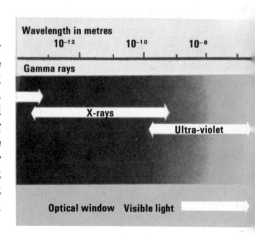

Wavelength in metres
10^{-12} 10^{-10} 10^{-8}

Gamma rays

X-rays

Ultra-violet

Optical window   Visible light

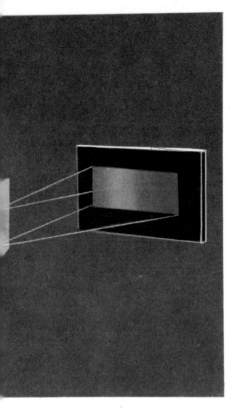

How does a spectroscope work?

A spectroscope is an instrument which splits up light into its various colours in such a way that the astronomer can make precise measurements of the spectrum. It usually consists of a narrow slit, through which light from a telescope is passed, followed by several prisms to split up the light. The spectrum is then viewed through lenses or, alternatively, focussed onto a plate to give a photograph. Very long time exposures are needed with stellar spectra, because the light is so weak. Nearly all the work astronomers carry out with spectroscopes is photographic.

Sometimes, the prism is replaced by a diffraction grating. This is a glass plate on which a series of very fine grooves is ruled, several thousand lines per centimetre! These grooves also split light up into a spectrum, and since the light does not have to pass through the glass, less light is lost.

The spectroscope is a vitally important instrument. When the spectrum of the Sun, or a star or planet, is examined closely, it is found that the bright band of colour also contains many dark lines which occur in definite patterns. These lines are made from light being absorbed by atoms of gas, and each different element of matter gives its own particular patterns of lines. Because of this, the spectroscope gives us a means of finding out what kinds of matter exist elsewhere in the universe.

Above: The principle of the spectroscope.

Far left: The different colours of the spectrum.

Left: Projecting the Sun onto a screen or piece of paper is the only safe way of looking at it.

Below: The electromagnetic spectrum, which ranges from short radiation (gamma rays) to long radio waves.

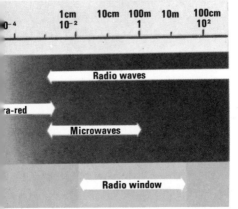

1cm	10cm	100m	10m	100cm
10^{-2}		1		10^2

Radio waves

Infra-red

Microwaves

Radio window

What is the electromagnetic spectrum?

Light is not the only kind of radiation which travels through space. There are others, such as radio waves, and all these different radiations together make up the electromagnetic spectrum. Light is just one kind of electromagnetic radiation, in fact.

Electromagnetic radiation travels through space like a wave, and if we think about visible light, we know it has different colours. Now, like waves on the sea, light waves have wavelength—the distance from crest to crest of two successive waves. Light waves are less than a millionth of a metre in wavelength. The different colours which we see are due simply to light of different wavelengths; blue light has a shorter wavelength than red, for example.

The first invisible electromagnetic radiation to be discovered was infra-red. In 1800, William Herschel conducted an experiment to see which colour in the spectrum of the Sun carried the heat which we feel. He produced a spectrum from sunlight, and placed thermometers at different points in the band of colour. To his great surprise, he found that a thermometer beyond the red end of the spectrum showed the biggest rise in temperature. The rays were therefore called infra-red (longer than red). The following year Johann Ritter discovered rays shorter than visible light and these are known as the ultra-violet rays.

The complete range of the electromagnetic spectrum goes from gamma rays (thousands of times shorter than visible light) to X-rays, ultra-violet, visible light, infra-red, microwave and radio which may be up to millions of times longer than ordinary light. The atmosphere prevents much of this from reaching the ground, and only visible light and certain wavelengths of microwave and radio reach ground level in much quantity.

What is radio astronomy?

Radio astronomy is the study of radio waves coming from space. Our atmosphere will let through radiation of this kind whose wavelength lies between a few millimetres and a few metres, and this range in the electromagnetic spectrum is often called the 'radio window'.

The discovery that radio waves are reaching us from space is fairly recent and dates from the work of the American, Karl Jansky in 1931. He was working on problems of static, the background hissing and crackling that is sometimes heard on radio receivers, and had built an experimental radio aerial for this research. Amongst the radio noise, he found a signal which appeared to be coming from a particular place in the sky, a region which we now know to be the direction of the centre of our galaxy.

Surprisingly little work was done to follow up Jansky's discovery during the following ten years, except for some research carried out by Grote Reber, also in the U.S.A. He found several sources of radio waves in the sky.

Since the last war, progress has been rapid, and radio astronomy has developed to a stage where it is just as important as optical astronomy, and can be used to study the Sun, the galaxy, and some of the most distant objects in the entire universe.

However, since radiation from space is very weak, huge telescopes are needed to gather enough radiation to give a recognizable signal.

Above: The huge telescope at Jodrell Bank in Cheshire. England is more than ten years old.

Above: This diagram shows the reflection of radar pulses.

How does a radio telescope work?

A radio telescope is basically an instrument used to collect radio waves and to focus onto a radio receiver. This receiver then gives out a signal and its strength is indicated on a chart by an automatic pen (the instrument is a chart recorder). You do not look through a radio telescope, and you do not see a picture. All that you receive is a signal, whose strength tells you how much radiation is coming from the direction in which your radio telescope is pointing.

You can, however, draw a map of the object you are looking at by scanning. The telescope is moved at a steady speed in azimuth for a known time. It is then shifted slightly in altitude and moved again in azimuth, so sweeping to and fro across a small patch of sky. The strength of the signal will vary as you scan and this will be shown on the chart recorder. Finally, by analyzing the chart, you can draw a map of the strength of radio signals from different parts of the source. The result looks just like a contour map. Pictures are produced on a television screen in a similar way: a spot scans to and fro, too fast for the eye to see, and as its brightness varies, so a picture is built up for you. The most modern radio telescopes feed their signals directly into a computer, which automatically builds up the relevant picture.

The simplest type of radio telescope to understand is the 'dish' type, such as the eighty metre diameter Jodrell Bank instrument in Cheshire, England. In this, a huge dish reflects radio waves to a focus where the radio receiver is placed. Sometimes, two or more widely separated radio telescopes can be used in conjunction with each other to give a very high resolving power. Such an instrument is called an interferometer.

Does a radio telescope work if it is cloudy?

Yes! This is one great advantage that the radio astronomer has over the optical observer; his instruments are just as effective in daylight or in cloud as they are on a clear night. He can, therefore, continue a programme of observations for twenty-four hours a day, knowing that if a certain special event is going to happen in the sky, then he will definitely be able to observe it (unless his equipment goes wrong!).

The poor optical astronomer, on the other hand, has every chance of being clouded out at the vital moment, and if this happens at some rare event such as a total eclipse of the Sun, then he might not get the chance to try again for years!

Who discovered infra-red radiation?

Infra-red radiation is radiation whose wavelength is longer than that of visible light. It is therefore invisible to our eyes, but can be felt as heat (we feel the infra-red radiation from the Sun). It was first discovered in 1800 by the astronomer William Herschel (the man who discovered the planet Uranus). He carried out an experiment to discover which of the colours of the spectrum of the Sun carried the Sun's heat, producing a spectrum from sunlight and placing thermometers at different points in the band of colour. To his great surprise, he found that a thermometer beyond the red end of the spectrum showed the greatest rise in temperature. Because they were beyond the red end, they must have had wavelengths longer than red light.

Nevertheless, infra-red photographs of the Earth taken from space, have been a great help in identifying diseased vegetation.

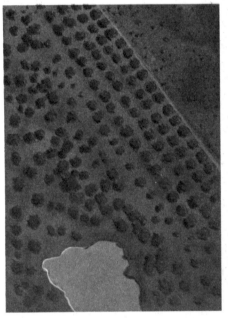

Above: This picture is taken from an infra-red photograph of olive groves.

Left: The picture here is also based on an infra-red photograph. It was taken from Apollo 9 and shows the vegetation areas in the valley as red.

Does the Sun rotate?

Just as the Earth spins round on its axis (once every twenty-four hours) so the Sun rotates, but it takes much longer to do so. We can work out the rotation period of the Sun by watching sunspots. These are carried round on the Sun's surface as it spins and by watching how long it takes particular spots to travel right round (remembering to calculate the Earth's motion round the Sun) we can soon calculate how long the Sun takes to spin.

However, the strange thing is that the Sun does not spin like a solid body. Near the equator, it takes about twenty-five days to rotate, and at about latitude 40 degrees north or south of the equator it takes more than twenty-seven days. Nearer the poles, it is slower still! This helps confirm our view that the Sun is a gaseous body. Although it takes much longer to rotate than the Earth, because it is much bigger, a point on its equator will move at about two kilometres per second.

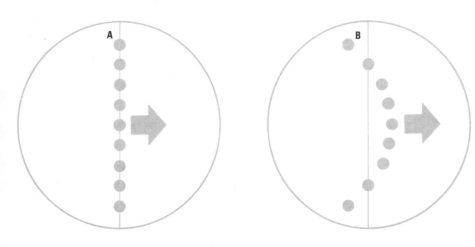

What do we know about the structure of the Sun?

We can think of the Sun as being made of several layers (rather like an onion!). Right in the centre lies the very hot, dense core where the temperature may exceed 14,000,000°C. It is here that the Sun's energy is being produced by the conversion of hydrogen to helium. Outside the core lies a region of hot gas which transmits the radiation from the core to the visible surface. The visible surface is called the photosphere ('sphere of light') and has a temperature of about 6,000°C. This layer has a granular structure which looks rather like porridge because of the rising and falling columns of hot gas. If it were not dangerous to do so, we could see these features through a telescope. Sunspots are found here, too.

Just above the photosphere is a thin layer, possibly only a few tens of thousands of kilometres thick, called the chromosphere. This is cooler, about 4,500°C, and can only be seen with special instruments, except during a total eclipse. The dark lines in the Sun's spectrum are formed here. Above the chromosphere lies the corona, a very rarefied layer of gas spreading out for millions of kilometres. The temperature there is millions of degrees centigrade, but there is so little matter, that the actual amount of heat from the corona is quite negligible.

Corona

Chromosphere

Radiation zone

Prominences

Convective zone

Core

Far left: Imagine that the sunspots at various latitudes are lined up (A). After a spot on the equator has completed one full rotation, a spot at a higher latitude will not have had time to do so, and so will lag behind (B).

Left: A cutout section of the Sun.

Below: The Sun as seen at a total eclipse. The corona is clearly shown, spreading out some distance.

Corona

When can we see the corona?

The corona is very faint, and cannot normally be seen because of the glare from the Sun itself and the brightness of the surrounding sky. However, when a total eclipse of the Sun occurs, and the bright photosphere is hidden by the dark body of the Moon, then the corona leaps into view, looking like a pearly halo round the Sun. In fact it is a layer of very thin gas.

It is possible to see the inner corona at other times by using an instrument called the coronagraph, but this is only effective if used in very clear skies with a telescope thousands of metres up a mountain. Now, however, that men can go into space and so be free of the effects of the atmosphere, it is possible to make an artificial eclipse (you might do this by holding a coin of the right size in front of the Sun!) and see the corona at any time. For the rest of us, though, an eclipse is our only chance.

The appearance of the corona varies, depending upon the sunspot cycle. Near sunspot maximum, it is more or less symmetrical round the Sun, while near minimum, it tends to have a less regular shape.

Why do eclipses occur?

An eclipse of the Sun occurs when the Moon passes between the Sun and the Earth, blocking out the Sun's light, and an eclipse of the Moon occurs when the Moon passes into the shadow of the Earth, so that its supply of sunlight is cut off. It is a strange coincidence that the Sun and the Moon should look the same size in the sky. In fact, the diameter of the Sun is four hundred times greater than that of the Moon, but the Sun is also four hundred times further away. Because they appear the same size in the sky, it occasionally happens that the Moon completely blocks out the visible surface of the Sun, and we say that a total eclipse has occured.

During an eclipse, the shadow of the Moon falls on the Earth, and consists of two parts, the dark central umbra, and the lighter penumbra. The umbra covers a very small area on the Earth, and only inside this area will a total eclipse be seen. A partial eclipse will be seen in the much larger penumbra, which means that only part of the Sun will be covered by the Moon. Because the Moon moves round the Earth in an elliptical path it is sometimes further away than others, and because of this, its apparent size in the sky varies. Should an eclipse occur when the Moon is at its greatest distance, then it may not be able to cover the whole Sun. In this case, observers in the centre of the Moon's shadow will see a thin ring of sunlight round the dark body of the Moon; this is known as an annular eclipse.

As the Moon moves in front of the Sun, its shadow races across the surface of the Earth. This means that if you are standing at a particular point you will not be able to see a total eclipse for more than seven minutes. (The 1971 total eclipse was just about the longest possible.)

During eclipses of the Moon, the shadow of the Earth falls on its surface, and, since the Earth (and thus its shadow) is much bigger than the Moon, the chance of a total eclipse of the Moon happening is greater than that of a total eclipse of the Sun.

Above: If the Earth (A), Moon (B) and Sun (C) move into a direct line as they have here, a total eclipse will occur. The Moon is in the middle, blocking out the Sun's light. Eclipses rarely last more than 8 minutes.

Below: When there is solar flare, emitted particles (A) enter the outer zone of charged particles (B). Somehow these are pushed down in the upper atmosphere. producing the aurora.

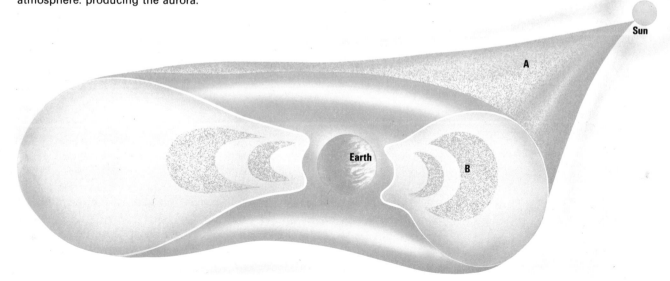

What is the solar wind?

The solar wind is a term used to describe the stream of atomic particles emitted by the Sun. These particles are mostly electrons and protons, the basic building blocks of atoms, and because they are electrically charged, they interact with the magnetic field of the Earth when they meet it.

The solar wind varies in strength, although sometimes great outbursts (flares) on the Sun cause an excessive number of particles to be emitted. These particles have been measured by satellites and space probes, and particularly, were investigated by the Apollo 11 astronauts on the surface of the Moon. An aluminium screen is used to collect the particles. Another effect of the solar wind is to help drive the tails of comets away from the Sun.

What causes the aurora?

The aurora is a fascinating sight, best seen from about the latitudes of the arctic (or antarctic) circle. It simply looks like coloured glows in the sky. The aurora is caused by electrons spiralling along the lines of force of the Earth's magnetic field, entering the atmosphere, and causing the thin gases high in the atmosphere to glow rather like a fluorescent strip light.

These electrons originally have come mostly from the Sun, and the number of electrons depends upon the activity of the Sun itself. Near sunspot maximum, when the surface of the Sun is very active, we tend to see many more displays of the aurora than near sunspot minimum, when the Sun is much quieter.

The aurora can take many different forms, sometimes looking like hanging curtains, or moving bands, rays or arcs of light. The colour varies, too, but most auroral displays have a greenish or pink shade.

Above: The aurora, or Polar Lights, are a truly wonderful sight.

How much of the Moon can we see from the Earth?

From the Earth we can see just over half of the Moon's surface. We cannot see all of its surface at some time or another because the Moon rotates on its axis (or spins round) in exactly the same time as it takes to make a complete orbit round the Earth (27·3 days). This means that, because the Moon spins on its axis and revolves round the Earth in the same direction, it must keep the same face turned towards the Earth all the time. Perhaps a practical experiment would help to make this clear.

Set a chair, or some similar object, in the middle of a room. Face the chair and walk round it so that you keep facing the chair. You will have looked in every direction in the room as you moved round. In other words, while you walked a full circle round the chair, you have also turned round your own axis by one complete revolution.

Because the Moon moves in an elliptical orbit, its speed varies (depending on how far it is from the Earth), and so the rotation of the Moon gets out of step with its motion round the Earth. So we can see a little way round to the far side of the Moon depending on its position in its orbit. As a result, if you watch carefully for a long time, you will see a total of 59 per cent of the surface of the Moon.

Above: The Moon as seen at full moon.

What is the barycentre?

We usually think of the Moon as going round the Earth, but this is not quite true. In fact, both the Earth and the Moon really move round a point which lies somewhere between their two centres. This point is called the barycentre and this motion takes place because the Earth and Moon are exerting gravitational pulls on each other.

The barycentre is therefore the balance point between the Earth and Moon; the centre of mass (or sometimes called the centre of gravity). If you had two equal weights joined by a bar, then you could balance this by holding it in the middle. If the Earth and Moon were equal, then the barycentre would likewise lie mid-way between them. However, because the Earth is eighty-one times as massive as the Moon, the barycentre lies eighty-one times nearer the centre of the Earth than the centre of the Moon. In fact it lies 4,700 kilometres from the centre of the Earth.

Above: The barycentre lies inside the Earth's globe at A.

Why do we have tides?

The tides in the sea are caused by the gravitational pull of the Moon and Sun on the water. Because the Moon is much nearer to us than the Sun, it plays the larger part in raising the tides. The Moon exerts a gravitational pull on the Earth which is slightly stronger on the side facing the Moon than on the side facing away from it. This causes the solid surface of the Earth to move up and down very slightly as the Moon passes overhead.

The effect of this is too small to be noticed. However, the oceans on the side facing the Moon are also raised up as it tries to pull them away from the Earth, and since water is a liquid, it flows in the direction of the Moon's pull, so building up a hump of water on that side of the Earth.

On the opposite side, where the Moon's pull is weaker, the effect is to pull the Earth away from the water, so that the oceans tend to fall away from us. Again, the water flows into a hump, on that side of the Earth's globe.

As the Earth rotates on its axis, the Moon seems to cross the sky, and the humps of water try to keep pace with it. As the hump passes by a particular place, the sea level rises, and we have 'high tide', after which the water level drops to 'low tide'. Since there are two humps, we have two high tides in a day. (In fact, because of the motion of the Moon in its orbit, we have two high tides in about twenty-five hours rather than twenty-four hours). Incidentally, the rise and fall of water in the oceans caused by the Moon's pull is quite small, less than a metre. The much greater rise and fall in sea level round our coasts is a result of the build-up of water in the coastal shallows as the tidal hump passes by. Local conditions make a big difference. For example, very much higher tides will occur in river estuaries which rapidly get narrow, because of the funnelling of water from the sea.

The tidal forces caused by the Sun are less than half as strong as those of the Moon. However, when Sun and Moon both lie in a straight line, their pulls add together to give very high tides (called 'spring tides'). On the other hand, when they are at right angles their pulls tend to cancel out, and so a low tide range will be seen. (These are 'neap tides'.)

Below: If the Earth, the Moon and the Sun are in line, the ocean bulge is big. If the Moon and Sun pull at right angles to each other, the bulge is smaller.

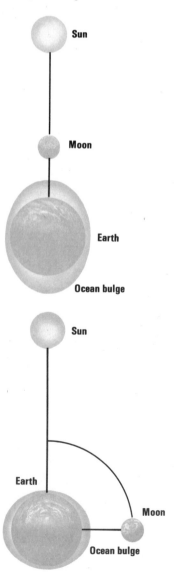

Sun

Moon

Earth

Ocean bulge

Sun

Earth

Moon

Ocean bulge

Which was the first space probe to pass behind the Moon?

The Russian space probe, Luna 3, which was launched on 4 October 1959, passed behind the Moon on 6 October of that year. It photographed the far side of the Moon (which is never seen from Earth) from a range of about 60,000 kilometres. Later it transmitted the pictures back to Earth, showing us for the first time what that side of the Moon looks like. Luna 3 then continued to move round the Earth in a very elongated path until it was burned up in its atmosphere the following year.

The photographs revealed that the far side of the Moon had hardly any of the dark plains which cover much of the visible surface. Instead it had more mountains and craters. This seemed to suggest that the Earth had some influence on shaping the Moon's surface.

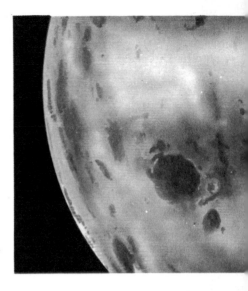

What is the surface of the Moon like?

Since the manned landings of the Apollo programme, we know a great deal more about the surface of the Moon than we did a few years ago. However, the Apollo results have not changed our basic ideas of what it looks like. Looking at the Moon through a telescope, we can see many different types of features; mountains, dark plains, craters and valleys. There is little colour, because the surface is entirely rocky. There is no vegetation, no seas, and the surface seems very unfriendly. The early astronomers (such as Galileo) thought that the dark plains were seas, and labelled these areas 'seas' on their maps (for example, the 'Sea of Tranquillity', the site of the first Moon landing of Apollo 11). The seas, however, are no more than relatively flat plains covered with a thin layer of dust, and strewn with craters and boulders. There is no water on the Moon's surface.

The craters are basically saucer-shaped depressions in the surface of the Moon. They range in size from giant features such as the crater Clavius (240 kilometres in diameter) or Bailly (nearly 290 kilometres across) down to tiny pits and hollows less than a metre across. The very large ones tend to have quite flat floors, complicated mountainous walls (only a few thousand metres high at most) and, often, mountain peaks at their centres. There are, however, tremendous variations in the types of craters seen.

Mountains seem to occur either as isolated peaks (such as the great mountain Piton in the Sea of Rains) or as long ranges curving round the edges of the great plains. Two of the most striking ranges visible in small telescopes are the Alps and the Apennines, both on the edge of the same Sea of Rains. The highest mountains, such as the Doerfel range near the Moon's south pole, are nearly 10,000 metres high. By and large, though, photographs sent back by orbiting space probes and the manned expeditions show that the mountains are not sharp and jagged, but rounded.

The valleys on the Moon range from broad, deep chasms, such as the Alpine Valley which runs for two hundred kilometres, to narrow twisting features, usually known to astronomers as 'rilles'. One of these, Hadley rille, was visited by the astronauts of Apollo 15 when the lunar rover was driven to the edge of the valley and rock samples were collected.

What is the Moon made of?

Well, we can safely say nowadays that it is NOT made of green cheese. In fact, Apollo expeditions have shown us that it is made up of rocks quite similar to those found on the surface of the Earth. One of these is basalt, the basic material making up the surface layers of our planet.

One interesting clue to the composition of the Moon is the fact that the density of lunar surface rocks is about three times that of water–very similar, in fact to rocks on Earth. However, the density of the Moon as a whole is about 3·3 times water, while the density of the Earth's globe is about 5·5 times water. This means that the Moon does not grow much denser towards the centre, quite unlike our planet which has a dense metallic core. We can safely conclude that the Moon does not have such a core.

Analysis of the moonrock samples has shown that the Moon never had seas in the past, and there is no evidence of the existence of living matter at present or in the past. There is no atmosphere, but there is some evidence of occasional mild volcanic activity. For example, the scientific equipment of Apollo 14 detected emission of gas from beneath the surface. The seismometers have detected 'moonquakes'. The Moon is therefore not completely inert.

Above: A typical crater.

Below: A crater forming:

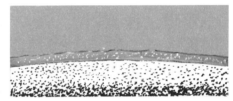

Hot magma below crust

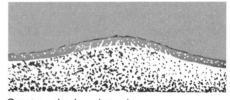

Crust pushed up into dome

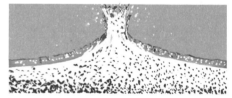

Crust ruptures

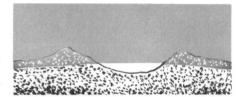

Collapsed dome melts back into magma

Final crater

If the Earth were put on a pair of scales, you would need 81 Moons to balance it!

Is there any air on the Moon?

It has been known for a long time that there is no air on the Moon. Measurements made from the Earth show that if the Moon had an atmosphere, then it must be less than one hundred thousandth of the density of the Earth's. It is not difficult to check for yourself that the Moon has not got a thick atmosphere. As the Moon moves round the Earth it quite frequently passes in front of stars (astronomers call these events 'occultations'). If you watch one of these stars through a telescope as the Moon approaches, then the star disappears in an instant as the Moon passes in front of it. If the Moon had a dense atmosphere, the star would fade out more slowly as its light passed through the layers of air. Measurements made from the surface confirm the lack of air on the Moon which means that it is unprotected from radiation and meteorites.

How were the Moon's craters formed?

This question has been argued by astronomers for generations, and even now, after the Moon landings, the answer is still not clear. The two basic theories are (a) that they were caused by the impact of meteorites, and (b) that volcanic action of some kind in the Moon itself was responsible. Supporters of either theory can produce evidence to support their case. In recent years it has been shown that the planet Mars is also covered in craters, and observations made by radar seem to indicate the existence of craters on Venus as well. Does this mean that the craters on these bodies were formed by the same process that made the lunar ones?

The Earth has craters, too, but very few compared with the Moon. In the Arizona desert in the U.S.A. lies the Barringer crater some 1,300 metres in diameter and 200 metres deep. It is thought to have been caused by the impact of a giant meteorite some 50,000 years ago. (A meteorite is a lump of rocky or metallic matter which pursues its own orbit in space and which may collide with the Earth, the Moon or some other body.) There are other examples of meteorite craters on Earth, but none of them seems to be very large. There are volcanic craters on Earth, too, in Iceland, for example, and Hawaii. There is also another type of crater called a caldera. This occurs usually where internal forces in the Earth cause hot material to swell up into a dome-shaped feature. As time passes and the matter cools down, the centre of the dome collapses, leaving a crater. Some of these can be very large.

It now seems likely that both meteorite craters and volcanic or caldera type craters exist on the Moon. But we are still uncertain about which process was responsible for most of the craters. Many astronomers think that meteorites were mainly responsible, but not everyone agrees about this. Meteorites can explain the 'rays' of bright material spreading out from some craters as being matter thrown out in the impact. On the other hand, it is difficult on this theory to account for the lack of dark plains on the far side of our Moon. No doubt the answer will come soon.

How was the Moon itself formed?

There have been many theories to explain the origin of the Moon. Earlier this century a popular idea was that the Moon was once part of the Earth and that it broke off for some reason, leaving the wide ocean of the Pacific. Thanks to the analysis of moonrock samples it is now clear that the Moon never was part of the Earth. The surface rocks of the Moon have been closely studied, and the oldest ones are known to be more than 4,000 million years old. In fact, the oldest rocks are about the same age as the Earth itself; our planet is thought to have been formed between 4,500 million and 4,700 million years ago, which seems to suggest that the Earth and the Moon were formed independently at about the same time.

The question which remains to be decided is whether the Moon was formed close to the Earth, and so has always been with us, forced by the Earth's greater gravitational attraction to orbit round us, or whether it was formed somewhere else and captured later by the Earth. If the Moon's orbit passed too close to us, then the Earth's gravity could have captured it.

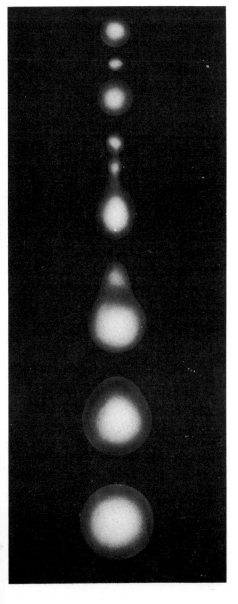

Below: It was once believed that Mars and the Moon were part of the Earth. When Mars separated and went into its own orbit, the Moon was left behind as 'debris'.

Which is the nearest planet to the Sun?

The nearest planet to the Sun is Mercury which moves in an elliptical orbit round it at an average distance of sixty million kilometres. Being so close to the Sun, Mercury moves very fast, taking only eighty-eight days to make one lap round the Sun. It is quite a small body, more like the Moon than the Earth, with a diameter of only approximately 4,800 kilometres. It is a solid body and seems to have no detectable atmosphere. From the Earth we can see some dark markings on its surface and there is little doubt that these will turn out to be dark plains like those of the Moon. Mercury is a very unfriendly world – the temperature on the sunward side may be greater than 400°C, while at night on the other side, temperatures may drop to –100°C.

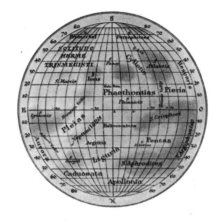

Above: A map of Mercury.

Why is Mercury hard to see?

Below: The size of Mercury compared with Earth.

Mercury is difficult to see because it is very close to the Sun. Its orbit is much smaller than the orbit of the Earth and so the planet can never be seen in the sky very far from the Sun. This means that Mercury either sets very soon after the Sun or rises just before it, depending on which side of the Sun it happens to be. Thus it can never be well seen against a dark sky.

Mercury can only be observed in a satisfactory way in daylight. To do this you need a telescope which can be accurately pointed to the right position in the sky. Because of these difficulties, astronomers who observed the planet came to the conclusion that Mercury keeps the same face turned towards the Sun all the time. It was only when radar was used in 1965 that astronomers found out that it rotates on its axis in fifty-nine days instead of eighty-eight. The difficulties of observations had misled earlier astronomers.

Below: Artist's impression of the surface of Mercury.

Which planet do we sometimes call 'the morning star' and at other times 'the evening star'?

The planet Venus is sometimes known by these names because, like Mercury, it is seen either in the evening sky just after sunset or in the morning sky, just before sunrise. The ancient astronomers at first thought that these 'stars' were two different objects, but as time went by it became clear that they were one and the same planet. Venus moves round the Sun in an orbit whose radius is 105 million kilometres, about 70 per cent of the Earth's distance from the Sun. It is bigger than Mercury and reflects more light, so appearing very much brighter in the sky. In fact, when it is at its brightest, Venus is by far the brightest object in the sky apart from the Sun and the Moon. Furthermore, since its orbit is larger than Mercury's, it can be seen further from the Sun in the sky. This, combined with its brightness, makes it very easy to see.

What do we know about Venus?

Until a few years ago the answer to that question would have been 'very little'! Since the development of space probes, however, we have learned a lot about our 'twin planet'. Venus is regarded in some ways as the Earth's twin because it is almost exactly the same size (a diameter of just over 12,000 kilometres, only a few hundred less than the Earth) and has a similar mass (89 per cent of that of the Earth). It can come closer to us than any other planet, but despite this, it is very difficult to observe. This is partly because it is closer to the Sun than we are.

Venus therefore shows phases like the Moon, and when it is at its closest, it lies between us and the Sun so that the planet's dark side is turned towards us. We only see it fully lit up (like full moon) when Venus is on the opposite side of the Sun to the Earth. It is then at its furthest from us (about 250 million kilometres) and too close to the Sun in the sky to be safely observed. In between these two positions it takes phases ranging from a thin crescent to nearly full.

To make matters worse, we cannot see the planet's surface, because it is permanently covered by a dense, cloudy atmosphere. When you look through a telescope all you can see is a bright featureless disc, and possibly a few faint shadings in the clouds, but nothing more. However, in 1962, the American space probe Mariner 2 flew close by the planet, sending back information which suggested that Venus was a very unpleasant world indeed.

In 1967 the American Mariner 5 flew past at the same time as the Russian Venus 4 crashed through the planet's atmosphere, and later Russian Venus probes have successfully landed there. Their results show that the atmosphere of Venus contains almost 90 per cent carbon dioxide (a heavier than air gas, which only makes up 0.03 of the Earth's atmosphere). It would therefore be impossible to breathe there. The atmosphere is very dense, so that the pressure it exerts at the surface is one hundred times greater than the pressure of the Earth's atmosphere; (if you stood on Venus, you would be squashed by a pressure of about one hundred kilograms on each square centimetre of your body!). The temperature, too, is very high, about 500°C in places. This is because the Sun's heat is trapped by the atmosphere. Altogether, Venus is quite uninhabitable!

Above: Five phases of Venus.

What is meant by a transit of Mercury or Venus?

Mercury or Venus are said to be in transit when they are seen to pass directly in front of the Sun. When this happens they look like small dots (quite a large dot in the case of Venus) crossing the visible face of the Sun. Now, because both Mercury and Venus are closer to the Sun than we are, they both move faster than the Earth. (Mercury takes eighty-eight days to orbit the Sun, Venus two hundred and twenty-five days and the Earth three hundred and sixty-five days). They can therefore catch up with the Earth at regular intervals (every one hundred and eighteen days in the case of Mercury, five hundred and eighty-four days in the case of Venus). Since they are closer to the Sun than the Earth, why don't we see a transit every time they catch up with us? The reason is that the orbits of Mercury and Venus do not lie quite in the same plane as the orbit of the Earth. Usually these planets pass either just above or just below the Sun.

Transits are quite rare events, in fact. The last transit of Mercury was in November 1973; the next one will be in 1986. The last transit of Venus was in 1882; the next one won't occur until 2004! Transit of Venus used to be important because measurements made could then be used to calculate its distance. Nowadays this can be done directly by radar.

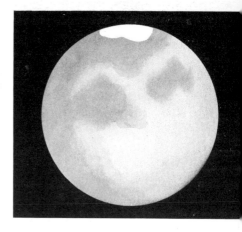

Above: The south polar cap of Mars changes with the seasons

Left: Transits of Mercury (A) can only occur during two months of the year; May (X) and November (Y). The Earth is shown as B.

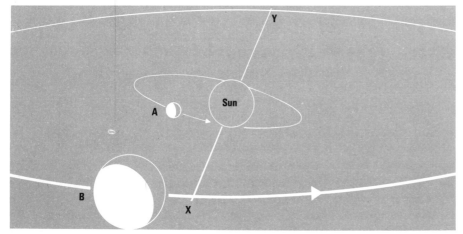

What is unusual about the Earth as a planet?

The unusual thing about the Earth is that two thirds of its surface is covered in water. No other planet in the solar system seems to have any surface water at all; Mercury is airless and barren, Venus too hot, and so on. Another feature of the Earth is that so far as we know (and we cannot be at all certain about this) it is the only planet in the solar system on which life (or at least advanced form of life) exists.

The Earth is the third planet away from the Sun, and is a solid body some 12,700 kilometres in diameter travelling round the Sun in an orbit whose average radius is 150 million kilometres, in a period of $365\frac{1}{4}$ days (a period we call the year). The Earth spins on its axis in twenty-three hours fifty-six minutes, so that the stars seem to us to rotate round the Earth in this period of time. As the Earth moves round the Sun so the Sun appears to move round the sky, so that in a year it traces out a circle in the sky which we call the ecliptic.

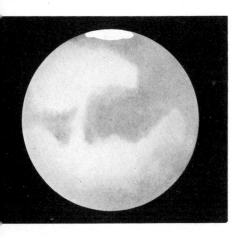

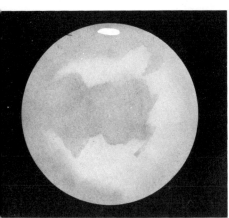

We know more about the structure of the Earth than any other planet. It has a dense iron core some 3,400 kilometres in radius on top of which is the rocky mantle 2,900 kilometres thick. The outer shell of the Earth is the crust, only 50 kilometres thick, on which we live. Our atmosphere contains 78 per cent nitrogen gas and 21 per cent oxygen which is essential for us to breathe.

Which planet is named after the god of war?

Mars was the Roman god of war, and the planet was so named because of its colour which some people describe as 'blood red', although it never seems so particularly striking to me! Mars is further from the Sun than we are, at an average distance of 228 million kilometres and so takes six hundred and eighty-seven days to travel round the Sun. It can, at its closest, approach to within 56 million kilometres of Earth at the time of opposition. However, its orbit is quite elliptical so that its opposition distance varies from year to year up to a maximum of 96 million kilometres. The Earth catches up with Mars every seven hundred and eighty days or so, so that oppositions occur only every second year.

Although Mars is smaller than the Earth (its diameter is 6,700 kilometres), we can observe it quite well when it is at opposition and we already know a great deal more about it than we did about Venus, even before the era of space probes.

What are the Martian canals?

In the year 1877, the Italian astronomer, Schiaparelli, observed some thin straight, dark markings on the surface of Mars. He called these 'canali' which in English means 'channels'. However, they were called 'canals' instead and very soon afterwards the idea grew up that these features were indeed canals constructed by an imagined advanced race of intelligent creatures. It was believed that they were used to supply water to the arid deserts on the planet's surface. The source of the water was thought to be the polar ice caps of Mars (which can be seen in quite small telescopes). Thanks to space probes we now know that these polar caps are made of frozen carbon dioxide, not water ice at all, but this was not known at that time. An American astronomer, Percival Lowell, built an observatory specially to study these canals, and drew maps showing dozens of them. It now seems that most of these were optical illusions, but some of them may be related to mountain chains and valleys on the planet's surface.

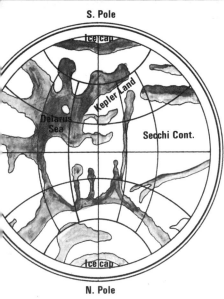

Above: This is based on a nineteenth century map of Mars, actually drawn in the 1870s.

Right: Pictures produced by astronomers, showing the 'canals' of Mars.

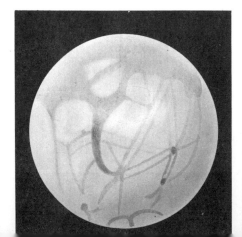

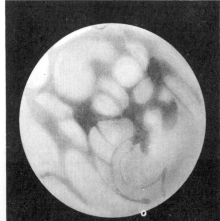

What is the surface of Mars like?

Looking at Mars through a telescope you can see that the surface is mainly red in colour and that there are many well defined dark markings which can be mapped. You should also be able to see either the north or the south polar cap, or possibly both. The markings may change slightly in intensity and shape, but they are pretty constant things. One of the most prominent of the markings is a wedge-shaped area called Syrtis Major. This was first recorded as long ago as 1659 by the Dutch astronomer, Christian Huyghens. By comparing his drawing with later ones it was possible to work out very accurately, the rotation period of Mars on its axis. In fact, Mars has a 'day' of twenty-four hours thirty-seven minutes, very similar in length to our own.

The craters of Mars are similar to those of the Moon and range in size from over a hundred kilometres across, down to the smallest detectable features. Mars has many impressive volcanic peaks, such as Nix Olympica. This is a giant volcano measuring five hundred kilometres across the base rising in a conical shape to a height of twenty-five kilometres above the surrounding countryside. At its summit is a sixty-five kilometre volcanic structure. It seems very likely that some volcanic activity still occurs on Mars. There are numerous valleys, too, ranging in size from narrow twisting features that look just like dried-up river beds to the vast rift valley in the south west of Mars. It runs for about five thousand kilometres reaching widths of four hundred kilometres and depths of as much as seven kilometres. From the appearance of these features there is not much doubt that there must have been water on the surface of Mars within the last few hundred thousand years. The reddish areas do seem to be made up of a type of sand, so that 'desert' is a good word to use when describing them. Temperatures at the equator can reach almost 20°C, but at night the temperatures quickly fall to below −70°C. Nevertheless, the surface of Mars is not nearly as unfriendly as that of Venus.

Above: Artist's impression of the surface of Mars showing a vast canyon.

Below: This is a cross-section of part of the surface of Mars, in its northern hemisphere, showing that it is quite a rugged world. This was based on measurements carried out by radar methods.

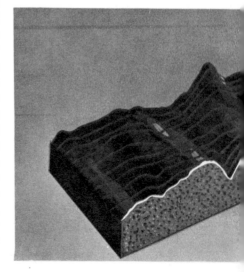

Above: Mars has two small Moons. Phobos is shown to the right of the planet and Deimos to the left. The inset shows the appearance of Phobos as seen by the American space probe, Mariner 9, in 1971.

Can we breathe the air on Mars?

The answer here is definitely 'no'. The atmosphere of Mars is very thin indeed and the pressure of the atmosphere is less than 1 per cent of that on Earth. In fact, the Martian surface air is about as thin as our atmosphere at a height of fifty kilometres! The main gas is carbon dioxide; other gases, such as water vapour are present only in very small quantities. The atmosphere provides very little protection against radiation or meteorites and it is unlikely than any earthly form of life could exist if taken there (this does not exclude the possibility that some different form of life which might have formed on Mars may exist). Nevertheless, strong winds do blow on Mars and these can whip up tremendous dust storms, such as the one which obscured nearly all of the surface of the planet during the approach of Mariner 9 in 1971.

Will men land on Mars this century?

In theory, it would certainly be possible. To save fuel, it would be best to pick a year when Mars was going to make one of its closest approaches, and the next really suitable occasion would be 1986. Outline plans for such a mission exist. One possibility would be to send nine men in three spacecraft which would go into orbit round the planet before dispatching expeditions to the surface in a similar way to the Apollo missions. However, there are many difficulties. For one thing, existing rockets are not powerful enough to take a direct path, and so the spacecraft would have to follow a long curving path, taking perhaps eight months to get there. They would then have to wait more than a year for a favourable opportunity to come home, taking eight months for the return trip. Altogether more than two and a half years would be required! The main problem would be the cost which would be truly colossal, and for this reason, a manned mission may not take place before the end of the century.

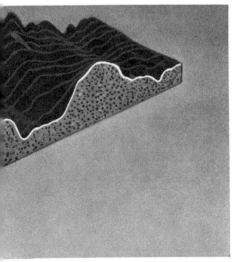

What can we see on Jupiter with a telescope?

Jupiter is an interesting sight through even quite a small telescope. The most obvious features are the cloud belts which run parallel to the planet's equator. There are many of these, and their appearance is always changing, but usually the most obvious ones are the North Equatorial Belt and the South Equatorial Belt, located on either side of the equator.

A closer look will show that Jupiter is not perfectly round. It is flattened at the poles and bulges out at the equator so that its shape is elliptical. This shape is due to the high rotation speed of Jupiter; it spins on its axis in less than ten hours, despite the fact that it has a diameter eleven times greater than the Earth. The material at its equator is moving round at a speed of nearly 50,000 kilometres per hour, and this causes the equator to bulge out. By watching features on the cloud belts we find that the planet does not rotate uniformly; the equator rotates in nine hours fifty minutes but further north or south the rotation period increases to nine hours fifty-five minutes. This shows that the planet is not a solid body.

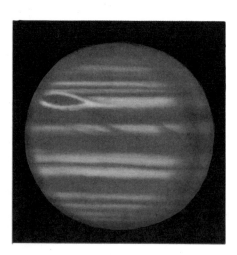 

Above: The planet Saturn is certainly one of the most beautiful things in the sky. Here it is shown with its three rings. Two of them are very bright (they are separated by a gap). The third, the Crêpe Ring, is transparent.

Left: Different pictures of Jupiter show that the Great Red Spot moves in its atmosphere.

What is the Great Red Spot?

The Great Red Spot is the only feature of Jupiter that is semi-permanent. The appearance of the cloud belts is always changing, and many spots appear, develop and then disappear on its cloudy disc. But the red spot was first seen as a really clear feature of the planet in 1878, although it had been seen before that in 1831. There is some evidence, too, to show that it was observed as far back as 1664. This spot looks oval in appearance and although its appearance and colour varies, it is generally a brick-red colour. It is very large, measuring nearly 50,000 kilometres long by 11,000 kilometres wide, and so has a surface area slightly greater than that of the Earth!

No one knows exactly what it is. One theory, the raft theory, suggests that the spot may be a solid or partly solid body, actually floating in the atmosphere. The other idea is that it may be the top of a column of stagnant gas, rising above some obstruction deeper down, known as a Taylor column. Neither theory is completely convincing, and for the time being we must admit that the red spot is something of a mystery.

Right: The changing aspects of Saturn's rings. We can see how, like the Earth, Saturn's axis is tilted, although this time it is at an angle of 26·7 degrees.

What are Saturn's rings made of?

The rings round Saturn cannot be solid. If they were, they would be torn apart by Saturn's gravitational pull, which would be much stronger on the inside of the ring than on the outside edge. In fact, astronomers can tell quite readily that they are not solid simply by looking at the spectrum of sunlight reflected from the rings. Analysis of this shows that each part of the ring moves at a different speed, the inside edge much faster than the outside edge. This is just what we would expect if the rings were made up of millions upon millions of tiny particles, each orbiting round Saturn like a tiny moon.

By looking at the rings' spectrum, astronomers have deduced that the rings are mostly made up of ice of various kinds. Recently, in 1973, the giant Golstone radio telescope has been used to study the rings by radar. The results show that the rings contain many large, rocky fragments (these may, however, be covered in ice). It is not known where the rings came from, but is it possible that they are the fragments of a former moon which strayed too near Saturn and was torn apart by gravitational forces.

Why does the appearance of the rings change from year to year?

The angle from which we see the rings is continually changing because of the relative motion of the Earth and Saturn. Sometimes we see the rings quite well displayed so that we can see part of the ring system sticking up above and below the body of the planet. However, at other times the rings are edge-on to us and can hardly be seen at all.

The tilt of Saturn's axis of rotation is mainly responsible for the changing appearance of the rings. Just as the axis of the Earth is not perpendicular to the Earth's orbit, but tilted over at an angle of $23\frac{1}{2}$ degrees, so Saturn's axis is inclined at an angle of 26·7 degrees. As Saturn moves round its orbit, taking twenty-nine and a half years to complete one lap of the Sun, so our view of the planet will change. For example, at one point its north pole will be tilted towards us, then, after nearly fifteen years Saturn will have moved half-way round its orbit and the south pole will be tilted towards us.

Now, since the rings lie in the same plane as the planet's equator it stands to reason that when the north pole of the planet is tilted towards us, we will be looking down on the north face of the rings, and when the south pole is towards us we will see the south face of the rings. Halfway between these two extremes, the rings will be turned edge-on to us.

The rings were edge-on in 1966; then the south face began to become visible, reaching a maximum angle of viewing in 1973–74. They then gradually became narrower from our point of view until they were edge-on again in 1979–80. The north face is now becoming visible.

When the rings appear edge-on to us, they disappear completely if viewed through small telescopes because they are so thin. Although the system is more than 270,000 kilometres in diameter, it is only about ten kilometres thick. The rings are a wonderful sight through the telescope, and their changing angles only add to the fascination.

Which planet was discovered in 1781?

The planet Uranus was discovered in 1781 by the astronomer William Herschel. He was a musician from Hanover who settled in England and then developed a strong interest in astronomy, using telescopes he constructed himself. His main astronomical work was in mapping the distribution of stars in our galaxy, and his discovery of Uranus was accidental. Through his telescope, it appeared as a star which changed its position from night to night. This was the first planet to be discovered with the aid of a telescope.

Uranus is a giant planet. With a diameter of nearly 50,000 kilometres, it is four times larger than the Earth. Like Jupiter, it is a gaseous body without a solid surface; all we can see is the top of its cloudy atmosphere. It rotates on its axis in ten hours fifty minutes. It is very far from the Sun, lying at an average distance of 19·2 A.U. (2,800 million kilometres) and so takes eighty-four years to complete an orbit of the Sun. An odd thing about the planet is the fact that its axis is tilted by 98 degrees so that its pole is almost parallel to its orbit. This means that during its eighty-four year orbit we, from the Earth, can see successively, its north pole, the equator, the south pole, then the equator again.

Above: Sir William Herschel (1738-1822). He discovered the planet Uranus.

Below: Urbain le Verrier, the great French astronomer. His calculations led to the discovery of Neptune.

How was Neptune discovered?

After the discovery of Uranus, its positions were carefully mapped and its orbit round the Sun calculated. After a time though, it became clear that Uranus was not moving quite as it should have been. Up until 1822 it seemed to move rather too fast, while afterwards it seemed to lag behind its proper position. It seemed as if some unknown body was exerting a gravitational pull on Uranus, speeding it up before 1822 and holding it back after this. Perhaps this was another planet beyond Uranus and therefore moving more slowly, so that Uranus overtook it in 1822.

In 1843, a young English mathematician, John Couch Adams, began to work on the problem of the unknown planet, and by 1845 he had worked out the mass and position of it. He sent his results to the Astronomer Royal of the time, George Airy, who did nothing about it. Meantime, in France, the mathematician, Urbain le Verrier, had independently arrived at almost the same conclusions as Adams, and a copy of his results reached Airy who decided that, after all, perhaps he should start a search for the unknown body.

However, because of a series of misfortunes, le Verrier's action was too late. Two observers, Galle and d'Arrest began a search from the Berlin observatory and on 25 September 1846 found the planet within a degree in the sky of the predicted position. The new planet came to be called Neptune.

Neptune is very similar in size and mass to Uranus. But Neptune is a good deal less flattened than Uranus, and is more dense. It is also a gaseous planet, spinning quickly on its axis in a period of about fourteen hours. Its average distance from the Sun is 4,500 million kilometres, and so it takes nearly 165 years to travel once round the Sun. If you could visit Neptune, the Sun would appear only one thirtieth of its size as seen from the Earth, and you would only just be able to see it as a disc. It would have only one thousandth of the brightness, too.

What is strange about Pluto?

Pluto is in many ways a very odd world. It was discovered in 1930 and seems to be a small, solid body, much more like the terrestrial planets than the Jovian ones, and may be about mid-way in size between Mercury and Mars. Because of its great distance of 39·5 A.U. (5,800 million kilometres) it is too small to be seen as a disc except in very large telescopes, and then only if conditions are very good indeed.

The possible existence of a planet beyond Neptune was suspected after observations seemed to indicate that the discovery of Neptune did not completely account for the motion of Uranus. Percival Lowell, best known for his observations of Martian 'canals', attempted to calculate where the ninth planet might be and started a search in 1905. It was not until 1930 that Pluto was discovered by Clyde Tombaugh, then a young observer working at Lowell's observatory. It soon became clear that Pluto was much smaller than planet X predicted by Lowell. In order to produce measurable effects on Uranus or Neptune, Pluto should have a mass much greater than that of the Earth, but if it is as small as it seems, then it would only have a tiny fraction of the Earth's mass. This prompted some astronomers to suggest that perhaps Pluto has a completely frozen surface and that all we see is the reflection of the Sun from this surface, not the whole planet itself! However, it is now fairly certain that Pluto really is very small.

Another odd thing is that Pluto's orbit is so elliptical that for part of its 247 year path round the Sun it actually comes closer in than Neptune (in fact it is in this position at present). Because of this it has been suggested that Pluto may be an escaped moon of Neptune, and not a proper planet at all. Finally, it is quite possible that another planet exists further out than Pluto, but only time will tell whether or not this is so.

Above: Uranus with its five moons. Three of them are about 2,500 kilometres in diameter while the others are somewhat smaller.

Right: These two pictures are based on photographs taken in March 1930, showing the discovery of Pluto. The top picture is from 2 March and the bottom from 5 March, indicating how Pluto moved. On the left is the over-exposed image of a third magnitude star.

Left: The planet Neptune. The faint points of light are its moons.

What are comets?

Comets, or at least bright ones, look far more impressive objects than they really are. A bright comet has a head, from which luminous tails stretch out, and in some cases we can see a brighter central nucleus in the head, surrounded by a more diffuse region called the coma. Comets seem to be just rather loose collections of solid matter, mostly ice (the ice is contaminated with various impurities according to the 'dirty ice' theory), gas and dust.

They move mostly in very elongated orbits approaching close to the Sun, then receding to the depths of the solar system. Some comets have orbit periods of only a few years, but mostly they are longer than this, thousands of years in some cases. There are some comets (such as Kohoutek, a new comet discovered in 1973, and named after its discoverer) which may never return again to the vicinity of the Sun.

Most comets are very faint objects and many of them never develop tails at all. However, really bright comets look most impressive, and were regarded in early civilizations as omens of future disasters. For example, a bright comet was seen just before the Battle of Hastings, and another (in fact the same one) about the time of the death of Julius Caesar.

Above: Donati's Comet of 1858, as shown in an old woodcut. This comet was very brilliant indeed and could be seen with the naked eye.

Far left: Morehouse 1908 III. Although this was not so very bright, its complicated tail structure was particularly interesting.

Left: Comet 1948 I. This comet was quite bright. It had a very long, gaseous tail which can be seen here.

Right: These pictures show the development of the tail of Halley's Comet. They are based on photographs taken when the Comet last appeared, in 1910.

Why do comets' tails always point away from the Sun?

When a comet is far from the Sun it doesn't have a tail at all, but as it gets closer, radiation from the Sun heats the matter in the comet and causes gas to be given off. The comet expands, and material is driven away by the solar wind, the stream of charged particles being constantly emitted by the Sun.

It is this material which forms the tail of the comet, and because the wind is 'blowing' directly away from the Sun, the comet's tail must likewise always point directly away from it. Thus, as the comet approaches the Sun, its tail will be behind it, but as it swings round and begins to recede again, its tail will precede it! Because of this, too, a comet looses material each time it passes close to the Sun, and this explains why short period comets (those orbiting the Sun in a few years or even a matter of tens of years) are usually particularly faint. They have lost too much matter ever to be really bright again. Really bright comets make very rare visits to the Sun, or may even pay only one visit.

Normally, a comet has only one or two tails, but in 1744 Cheseaux' Comet at one point actually developed seven tails. The great comet of 1843 had a tail which was twice as long as the distance from the Earth to the Sun!

Above: Solar wind affets the small particles in the tail of a comet and they are blown away from the Sun.

Who was Edmond Halley?

Edmond Halley was a great astronomer and close friend of Newton who lived in the latter part of the seventeenth century and the early part of the eighteenth. He is best known for his work which showed that the orbits of the comets of 1682, 1607 and 1531 were very similar. He suggested that these comets were not different objects but the same one returning to the vicinity of the Sun at intervals of about seventy-five years. He predicted that the comet would return again in late 1758 or early 1759.

Halley himself died in 1742, but his comet returned right on time, early in 1759, so confirming his theory that comets move round the Sun just as planets do (although usually in more elongated orbits). Halley's Comet last appeared in 1910 (when the Earth actually passed through its tail) and is due back in 1986.

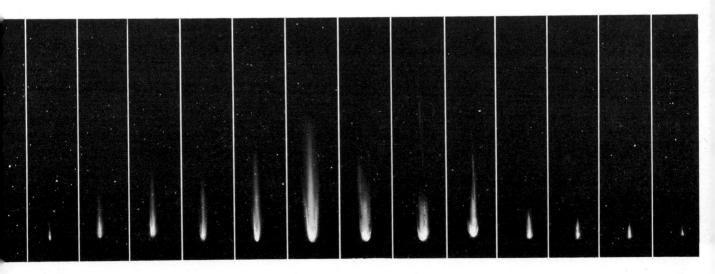

What is the difference between comets and meteors?

A comet is a large object moving round the Sun in the same sort of way that a planet moves. However, a meteor is merely a tiny particle, like a grain of sand, which also orbits the Sun, only becoming visible when it hurtles into the Earth's atmosphere and burns up in a flash of light caused by friction with the air. The Apollo astronauts, entering the Earth's atmosphere at a speed of eleven kilometres per second, burn off a protective covering on the spacecraft created by the tremendous heat generated, while some meteors can enter the atmosphere at speeds as high as seventy kilometres per second! Comets can be seen at distances of hundreds of millions of kilometres, but meteors may be only a hundred kilometres up in the air. There is evidence, though, that some meteors are debris left over from former comets, so there is nevertheless a connection between the two types of object.

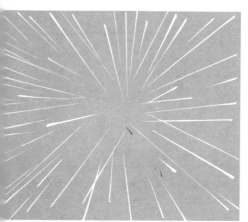

Left: Because of the effects of perspective, meteor showers appear to come from one particular point. This is known as the meteor radiant.

Right: An exploding meteor.

What is a meteor radiant?

There are two types of meteor: sporadic ones, which can appear at any time, moving in any direction, and shower meteors, which come from particular directions at special times of the year. These meteors move in a stream along an orbit round the Sun and if the Earth crosses this stream, a large number of meteors, a meteor shower, will be seen. Because all these meteors are coming from the same direction their paths in the sky will seem to diverge from a particular point, known as the meteor radiant. This appearance is due to the effects of perspective. If, for example, you look along straight railway tracks or the lanes of a motorway, then it looks as if the lines or the lanes converge at some point in the distance. Of course, you know that the lines remain the same distance apart all the way, it just looks as if they converge. Likewise, the meteors approaching us along parallel paths look as if they are coming from one point.

There are many well known meteor showers, but the most famous is the Leonid shower, whose radiant is in the direction of the constellation Leo. It appears in mid-November each year. In 1833 and 1866 tremendous showers of Leonids were seen, thousands of meteors per hour raining across the sky. Since then, though, the orbit of the meteor shower has altered, and such great numbers have not been seen since.

Above: An artist's impression of the Leonid Shower of 1833. This meteor was last seen in 1966.

222

Right: The Arizona meteor crater. It is approximately one kilometre in diameter and it is also very deep. It was caused by a prehistoric meteorite which must have weighed about 50,000 tonnes.

Above: A meteorite found in Greenland, weighing 36 tonnes.

Are meteorites different from meteors?

Meteorites are much larger lumps of material than the meteors which we can see on an ordinary night, and are much less common. (In fact, all in all, something like one hundred million tiny meteors enter the Earth's atmosphere every day, but only a few meteorites are found each year.) Because they are much larger they can pass right through the atmosphere and reach ground level. Quite often, the meteorite may explode before reaching ground level and scatter its fragments over a wide area. The passage of a meteorite through the atmosphere can often be quite spectacular; it can look as though it is a fireball sometimes throwing off fragments and moving at quite high speed.

There are two basic types of meteorite; stony meteorites, composed mainly of rock and known as aerolites, and nickel-iron ones, called siderites. Most of the meteorites which have been found on Earth have been iron ones, but on the other hand, it is much more difficult to distinguish the stony ones from ordinary bits of rock, so that this probably does not indicate their true proportions. There are other types of meteorite, too, and there was a suggestion a few years ago, that some meteorite fragments had been found to contain organic matter, the basic building blocks of life. There is some doubt about this, but the possibility is interesting enough. Study of meteorites is vitally important in helping to understand how the solar system was formed in the first place. After all, they are free rock samples from space!

The largest meteorites which have been found are the Hoba West meteorite (sixty tonnes) in South Africa, and one discovered in Greenland, weighing thirty-six tonnes. However, it is known that larger ones have fallen in the past. The meteorite crater in Arizona is thought to have been caused by a 50,000 tonne lump of material. A curious case is the Siberian 'meteorite' of 1908. Something fell through the sky onto Siberia in that year, causing a tremendous explosion which blew trees flat for one hundred kilometres around and was heard one thousand kilometres away. No fragments have been found. It may have been a giant meteorite, or the nucleus of a small comet, but nobody really knows.

Why do stars have different colours?

The different colours of the stars are an indication of their different surface temperatures. If you take a piece of iron and heat it (for example by putting a poker in a fire) it will begin to glow dull red. If it is heated further, it will become bright red, then yellow, then white. Thus red stars are fairly cool, having surface temperatures of about 3,000°C (3,000°C is quite cool by stellar standards!), yellow stars, such as the Sun, have temperatures of about 6,000°C, white stars about 10,000°C and blue stars are hotter still.

Next time you look at the stars on a clear night try to pick out their colours and work out which are really hot and which are really rather cool stars. Two examples of stars that are easy to see are Rigel and Betelgeuse in the constellation of Orion. Rigel is a blue-white star with a surface temperature of 11,000°C, while Betelgeuse is red, and 3,000°C at its surface.

Of course, stars do not only give out visible light, they emit all kinds of electromagnetic radiation from X-rays to radio waves as well. However, most stars give out most of their radiation in the form of visible light. Nevertheless, some extremely hot stars radiate large quantities of ultra-violet radiation, whereas very cool ones give out mostly infra-red radiation. In fact, some 'stars' are so cool that we can't see them at all except by detecting their infra-red rays.

How many stars can you see on a clear night?

On a good, clear night, with no Moon in the sky to hide faint stars with its glare, you can see about 2,000 stars. Altogether, over the entire sky there are nearly 6,000 stars which are bright enough to be seen with the naked eye if conditions are just as they should be. But at any one particular time, of course you can only see half of the complete sky, and stars near the horizon are not as clearly visible as those near overhead (because of their light being absorbed in our atmosphere). With binoculars, thousands more are easily seen, and reasonable telescopes will reveal millions.

How can we tell what stars are made of?

Astronomers can tell quite a lot about the composition of stars by using the spectroscope. Usually, the spectrum of a star looks like a rainbow band of colour on which dark lines can also be seen. The German scientist, Fraunhofer, first noticed these lines in the spectrum of the Sun in 1814, but the first person to explain why these lines appear was Kirchhoff, in 1859.

Kirchhoff proposed three laws of spectroscopy. The first one stated that hot, luminous solids, or gases under high pressure, emit a continuous spectrum (a complete rainbow band of colour when seen through a spectroscope). The second law said that a luminous gas under low pressure will give out an emission spectrum consisting only of bright lines of certain wavelengths. The third law showed that if you pass a continuous spectrum through a rarefied gas, then dark lines (absorption lines) will appear in the spectrum. They will appear at the same wavelengths at which the rarefied gas would emit light if it were heated up.

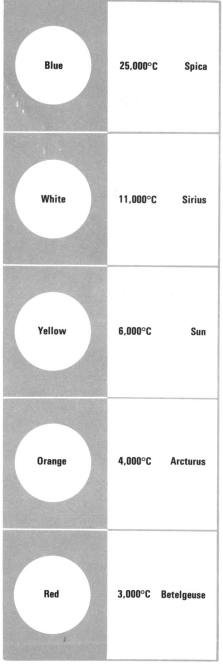

Blue	25,000°C Spica
White	11,000°C Sirius
Yellow	6,000°C Sun
Orange	4,000°C Arcturus
Red	3,000°C Betelgeuse

Above: The different kinds and temperatures of stars.

Now a star is made up in the same way as the Sun. The visible surface we see is hot and luminous, and so gives out a continuous spectrum. Above the visible surface (the photosphere) lies the cooler and thinner layer called the chromosphere. As light from the photosphere passes through this layer, some of it is absorbed at particular wavelengths. The dark lines in the spectrum are the result of the light being absorbed.

Now, all the matter in the universe seems to be made up of 92 basic elements, and each element gives rise to its own particular series of absorption lines in the spectrum of a star. By looking at these lines, the astronomer can tell which elements were responsible for causing them, and can therefore work out the composition of the outer part of the star. Observations of the Sun, stars, and clouds of gas in space show that hydrogen is by far the most common element in the universe. They also show that most stars are basically globes of hydrogen gas.

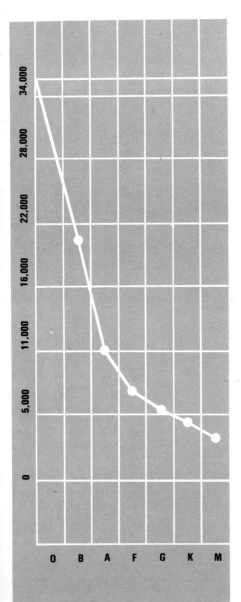

Below: The diagram shows the relationship between the temperature of a star and its spectral class. The scale begins at zero degrees and goes up to 34,000°C, so it is easily seen that stars of type O and B are very much hotter than stars of types K and M.

What is spectral class?

Stars can be classified according to their spectra depending on which lines are present, how intense they are and so on. The appearance of a spectrum depends on how hot the star is. Each star has a particular wavelength of its own at which it gives out the greatest amount of light, blue for very hot stars, and red for relatively cool ones. Furthermore, the lines which appear in the spectrum also depend on temperature. For example, in very hot stars the dark lines caused by hydrogen are extremely prominent, while in stars like the Sun, lines caused by various metals can be seen. In very cool, red stars, broader dark bands caused by molecules (combinations of atoms) appear.

The spectral class system in use today is based on a scheme that was developed in 1890 by the astronomer, E. C. Pickering, at Harvard in the U.S.A. A star is placed in a class denoted by one of the following letters: W, O, B, A, F, G, K, M, R, N, S and this corresponds to the temperature of the star. W, O, B stars are very hot and M, R, N, S are very cool. A useful way to remember the order of the classes is to recall the following unforgettable sentence: 'Wow, Oh Be A Fine Girl, Kiss Me Right Now, Sweetie', where the first letter of each word gives a spectral class! Nearly all the visible stars lie in the classes O to M; W stars are exceptionally hot (called Wolf-Rayet, after their discoverers). These are stars whose spectra show emission lines, while R, N, S are cool, red stars which have certain particular properties.

The classes are each divided into ten subsections, numbered from 0 to 9. Thus the Sun, for example, is of spectral type G2, while the much cooler Betelgeuse is of type M2. The properties of stars of some different classes are shown below:

Type	Colour	Surface Temp.	Prominent lines in spectrum
B	blue-white	21,000°C	helium
A	white	10,000°C	hydrogen
G	yellow	6,000°C	calcium and other metals
M	red	3,000°C	bands due to molecules

How are stars formed?

Stars are thought to form out of clouds of gas and dust in space. If a dense region forms in a gas cloud, it may begin to contract because of the gravitational pull of each gas particle on every other one. As it gets smaller and smaller, its density and temperature increase until the pressure and temperature in the centre of the object become so great that nuclear reactions begin, changing hydrogen to helium and giving out enormous amounts of energy. When this happens (the temperature inside the new star is greater than 10 million degrees centigrade) the star stops shrinking. In fact, the pressure of the very hot gas balances out the effect of gravity, trying to make it contract. The star can then remain stable for long periods of time, and is said to be a main sequence star.

The Sun itself is a main sequence star and has been in existence for over 5,000 million years. It has sufficient hydrogen 'fuel' in its central core to keep it shining in a stable sort of way for another 5,000 million or so! The Sun and all the stars we can see are part of a huge star system, which is our galaxy. In the past our galaxy must have consisted mostly of hydrogen gas from which the stars then formed. Even now, however, new stars are constantly forming from the remaining gas.

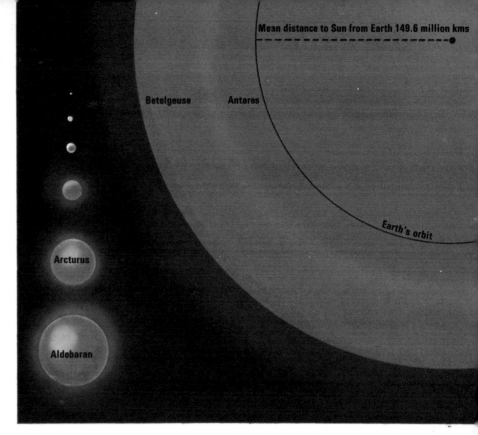

Mean distance to Sun from Earth 149.6 million kms

Betelgeuse   Antares

Earth's orbit

Arcturus

Aldebaran

Left: The development of a massive star. After the red giant stage, the star may suffer a supernova explosion. Much of its material will be sent into space and a neutron star will be left. This will be of high density and low luminosity.

Right: Some giant stars compared in size with the Earth's orbit round the Sun. The red giants Antares and Betelgeuse are so big they could contain the Earth's orbit.

Below: The possible stages of a star. Rotating gas and dust clouds condense into a globe and nuclear reactions form a star. This then expands into a red giant and then a pulsating star. Finally it becomes a white dwarf.

Why are red giants so called?

Red giants are cool stars of very large size, such as Betelgeuse whose surface temperature is 3,000°C and whose diameter is about 400,000,000 kilometres. They are very much brighter than main sequence red stars (which are much fainter than the Sun, such as Proxima Centauri) yet, because of their colour, must be of the same temperature.

If you have two stars of the same temperature, but one is brighter than the other, this can usually only mean that the brighter one is larger than the fainter. Thus compared to main sequence stars of the same temperature, such stars truly are giants. Red giants are stars which have left the main sequence because they have used up the hydrogen fuel in their central cores. They are rapidly consuming their remaining fuel resources and are getting into 'old age' as far as stars' lifetimes are concerned. The Sun is expected to become one in about 5,000 million years time.

What is a white dwarf?

A white dwarf is a very hot, but nevertheless, extremely faint star. It may have a similar colour and temperature to, say, Sirius (10,000°C) but will be thousands of times fainter. It must, therefore, be very much smaller, and so merit the term 'white dwarf'. White dwarfs may be only about the size of the Earth, and some are even smaller. They represent almost the final stage in the life of a star like the Sun. When a star finally runs out of fuel, gravity causes it to collapse into a very dense object. A matchbox full of white dwarf matter might weigh several tonnes. This collapse makes it very hot for a while, but eventually white dwarfs cool down and may end up as cold, solid bodies.

What is a nova?

A nova is a star which suddenly flares up to thousands of times its original brightness, then usually fading away to insignificance once more. It is called a 'nova' because the early astronomers thought such things were new stars. Novae are relatively rare, and no two novae ever behave in exactly the same way.

For example, in 1967, the English amateur astronomer, George Alcock, discovered a nova in the little constellation of Delphinus which reached magnitude four at its brightest. It then remained fluctuating at about magnitude five for five months, and faded very slowly, still being of magnitude eight two years later. On the other hand, Nova Aquilae, which was discovered in 1918, reached magnitude −1·4 (as bright as Sirius) in a few days, then faded to fifth magnitude within four months.

What causes a nova is not certain, but it certainly seems to involve a violent eruption in the outer layers of a star, causing it to flare up and hurl a shell of gas from its surface into space. These shells of gas have been observed directly in some cases. Sometimes a star is affected several times in this way, in which case it is known as a recurrent nova.

How does a supernova occur?

A supernova is a much more violent event than a nova. In a nova the outer layers of a star may be hurled into space, but if our ideas are right about supernovae, then a supernova is a star literally blowing itself apart. When this happens (which is very rarely indeed) the star involved may flare up so brightly that for a short time it may radiate many thousands of millions of times more light than the Sun! Very few supernovae have been seen in our galaxy; the last one was observed by Kepler in 1604! In fact only four have been recorded in our galaxy (all of them becoming naked eye objects), in 1006, 1054, 1572 (observed by Tycho Brahe) and 1604, so that none of them could be studied at the time by modern instruments! All the supernovae which have been observed in recent years have occurred in other galaxies beyond our own star system.

The best known example of the remnant of a supernova is the Crab Nebula, a turbulent cloud of luminous gas which is visible in telescopes in the constellation of Taurus (the Bull). This is in the position in the sky where the Chinese astronomers saw a supernova in the year 1054, a 'new star' which became bright enough to be seen in daylight. It soon faded away, though, and vanished completely from view to the naked eye. However, the Crab Nebula is still rapidly expanding (at a rate of well over 1,000 kilometres per second) and sending out all kinds of radiation, and there can be little doubt that this is matter from the star that was seen to shatter itself so violently in 1054.

It seems likely that only stars a great deal more massive than the Sun can become supernovae. The more massive a star is, the brighter and hotter it is (for example, a star ten times as massive as the Sun would shine more than a thousand times brighter than the Sun), and therefore the quicker it uses up its nuclear fuel. Finally, the processes inside the star become completely out of control, and this shattering explosion occurs.

Above: Nova Aquilae as it looked in 1931. It was the brightest of all modern novae and was brighter than any star, even Sirius. However, after 1941 it had faded so much it could no longer be seen.

Below: The Crab Nebula.

What are pulsars?

Pulsars, or 'pulsating radio sources' were first discovered in 1967 by Jocelyn Bell (now Burnell) working with Professor Anthony Hewish at Cambridge; and many more have been found since. The first one was an unidentified radio source which gave a pulse of radio signal every 1·3 seconds, as regular as clockwork and others have periods between a tenth of a second and a few seconds. Astronomers were at first baffled by these strange objects, and some went so far as to suggest the signals were artificial; in other words, they were suggesting that the radio pulses were signals being transmitted to us by other civilizations in our galaxy. (This has come, unkindly, to be known as the LGM, the 'Little Green Men' theory!) However, it was soon shown that this could not be so.

Several theories have been proposed to account for pulsars, but it now seems fairly certain that the objects responsible for the signals are neutron stars, which are far more dense than white dwarfs, spinning round on their axes once every second or so. A neutron star is thought to form when a star (at least one and a half times as massive as the Sun) runs out of fuel and collapses on itself because of its own gravity. When this happens, the forces are so great that atomic particles are squashed together to incredible densities, and a star originally bigger than the Sun, is compressed into a globe only about ten kilometres across. A thimble full of such matter might weigh about a hundred thousand million tonnes! The strong magnetic field of such a star causes a beam of radiation to be emitted, rather like the beam from a lighthouse, and each time the star spins round, we pick up the beam as a radio pulse.

It is thought that the central remnant of a supernova could collapse down to form such a neutron star (if the remnant were massive enough), and this idea is supported by the identification of a pulsar in the middle of the Crab Nebula (itself the remnants of a supernova). A pulsar, then, may represent the final stages of a dying, massive star.

What do astronomers mean by a black hole?

If a star, or the central remnant of a supernova, is more than about twice the Sun's mass, and collapses under its own gravitational forces, then nothing can halt this collapse. Even the incredible density of a neutron star is not enough to stop gravity crushing the star's matter to denser and denser states. Now, as a body is compressed into a smaller volume, the force of gravity at its surface becomes stronger and it becomes harder for anything to escape from the surface. Nothing in the universe can travel faster than light, but if the collapsing star becomes dense enough, then not even light or radiation can escape from it, the body becomes invisible, and we say it has formed a black hole.

The size of a black hole depends on how much matter is inside it; once the collapsing star forms a black hole, the star's matter may continue to grow denser and denser, but the size of the actual black hole remains the same. No one has yet discovered one for certain, and we cannot be sure that any exist, but it does seem possible that very massive stars may end their days by collapsing into black holes, and disappearing forever from view!

Above: A supernova in a distant galaxy is indicated by the arrow.

What is the Milky Way?

The Milky Way looks like a faint band of light across the sky, passing through such constellations as Cassiopeia, Cygnus, Sagittarius, and Centaurus. It can be seen with the naked eye on a really clear, moonless night. With a telescope, it is seen to consist of millions upon millions of stars, which seem to be very closely packed together. This is not so, however; they seem close together only because they happen to lie in the same direction in space.

When we look at the Milky Way, we are in fact looking at the part of the galaxy which can be seen from the Sun. If you think about the Sun in this disc, then it is clear that if we look anywhere in the direction of the disc, we will see very large numbers of stars but, since the disc is thin, if we look in a direction away from it, we will see far fewer stars. Mostly when we glance up at the sky, we look away from the plane of the disc, but when we do look in the right direction, we see the Milky Way.

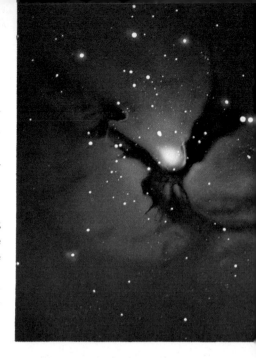

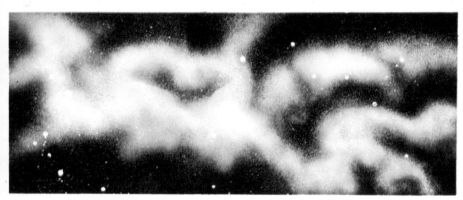

What is a nebula?

A nebula is a cloud of gas and dust in space. The easiest ones to see are the bright emission nebulae such as the Great Nebula in Orion, which can just be seen with the naked eye as a small, fuzzy patch of light. The Orion Nebula is a luminous gas cloud some 1,500 light years away and more than thirty light years across. The spectrum of a nebula such as this consists of emission lines showing that the light is given out by rarefied gas and, in fact, the density of the Orion Nebula is only one thousand million millionth that of the air we breathe! The reason that the nebula is shining is that the gas absorbs energy emitted from very hot W, O, or B type stars in the vicinity, and re-emits this in the form of light. If there is no suitable hot star nearby, then a gas cloud will not shine. The visible size of a nebula does not necessarily indicate the full extent of the gas cloud; only the region of gas which is excited by the hot star will shine, the rest will remain invisible. Regions such as this are called HII regions because they consist of hydrogen gas, where the atoms have been stripped of their electrons by radiation.

There are many beautiful nebulae to be seen in the sky, but long exposure photographs are needed to bring out their full details. Some of them are illustrated here. These nebulae are located in the spiral arms of our galaxy, and in some of these (particularly the Orion Nebula), it is thought that new stars are forming at this moment.

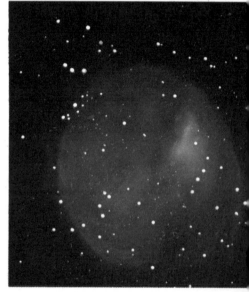

230

Why do dark nebulae exist?

Dark nebulae appear as dark patches against the background stars. For example, in the Milky Way we see millions upon millions of stars, seemingly packed closely together. Now and then, however, we come across regions where the stars seem to be missing; these are dark nebulae.

These nebulae are clouds of gas and dust which are denser than the thin spread of matter between the stars, and lie between us and background stars. As the light from distant stars passes through one of these clouds it is scattered and faded out by the tiny dust particles, so that very little gets right through. The background stars are thus hidden from our view.

Above: The Trifid Nebula in Sagittarius. The Trifid contains hot, early-type stars. Its distance is 2,300 light years.

Far left: The Milky Way.

Left: The Dumbell Nebula.

Right: The Horse's Head Nebula.

Below left: The Great Nebula in Orion. Its distance is 1,500 light years.

Below: Planetary Nebula NGC 7293. This nebula is easy to see with a small telescope and is the brightest of all planetaries.

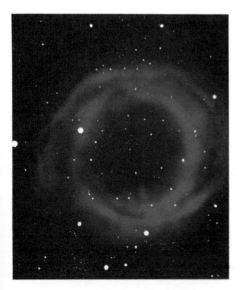

What is a planetary nebula?

Planetary nebulae are small nebulae which look rather like planetary discs when seen through small telescopes. The name was chosen by William Herschel, who was the first astronomer to pay attention to these objects. In fact a planetary nebula has nothing whatever to do with a planet; it is an expanding shell of gas surrounding a faint central star. It seems very likely that the shell of gas was ejected from the central star in a tremendous eruption, and many astronomers think that a planetary nebula is the remnant of a nova. Certainly, there is evidence to suggest that the stars inside some planetary nebulae are very old, and may be approaching the white dwarf stage.

The best-known planetary nebula is the Ring Nebula in the constellation Lyra. It looks just like a ring, and is located between the stars Beta and Gamma Lyrae, not far from the very bright star Vega. It can be seen with the use of small telescopes, but the central star needs telescopes bigger than 50 centimetre aperture. It lies at a distance of 1,400 light years.

Is space empty?

Space is not truly empty at all. Between the stars lie very thin gas and dust which cannot be seen directly, except in the case of bright or dark nebulae. In any case, most nebulae are much denser than the very thin gas between the stars, where only one or two atoms exist on average per cubic centimetre (ordinary air contains about 10,000,000,000,000,000,000 molecules per cubic centimetre!). How can we tell that this gas exists?

The gas was first detected by observing spectroscopic binaries (pairs of stars too close together to be seen as separate objects in a telescope). Astronomers found some spectral lines which could not belong to the stars and so must have been produced as the light passed through space on its way to us. Interstellar gas had to be responsible. Interstellar dust, which is made of small, solid particles, can be detected by its effect on starlight. The dust fades out short wave light such as blue, much more than longer wave light such as red. Careful examination of the spectra of stars shows this effect, which is known as interstellar reddening.

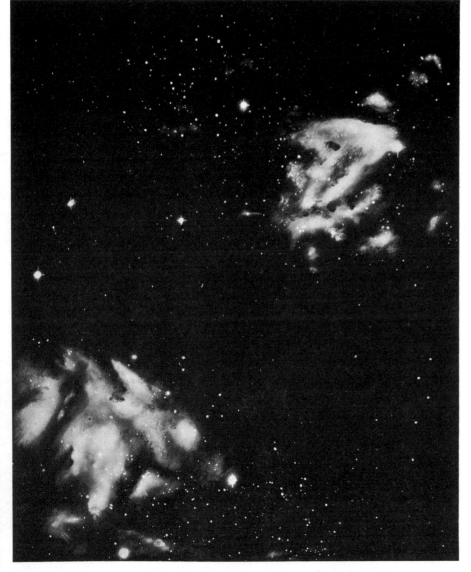

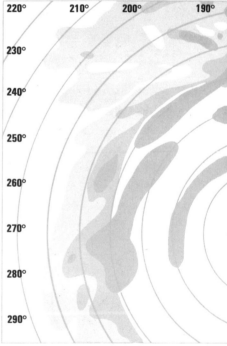

Left: This picture shows dark and light nebulosity near Gamma Cygni. It is based on a photograph taken with a 48-in Schmidt telescope.

Can we see the centre of our galaxy?

We cannot see the centre of our galaxy with optical telescopes because the interstellar dust fades out of starlight as it passes through the galaxy disc. Some astronomers have estimated that if a star existed at the centre of the galaxy, its light would be reduced by hundreds of magnitudes by the time it got here! There does seem to be a lot of dust, in fact, close to the galaxy centre, but this dust was not known to earlier astronomers, such as William Herschel. Because of this, they came to the wrong conclusion, thinking that the galaxy was smaller than it really is. In fact, the diameter of the system is about 100,000 light years; its central nucleus is about 20,000 light years, while the disc is only about 1,000 to 1,500 light years.

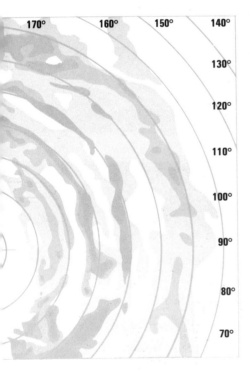

Above: The arrow showing the position of the solar system in our galaxy shows that we are not at the centre.

Above: A radio map of our galaxy. Clouds of neutral hydrogen are shown distributed in the plane of the galaxy.

How does radio astronomy help us find out about our galaxy?

Radio waves are much longer than light waves and so are not affected by the tiny particles of interstellar dust. Therefore, radio sources can be picked up in any part of our galaxy. However, a very important prediction was made in 1945 by the Dutch astronomer, H. C. van de Hulst. He said that ordinary hydrogen gas floating around in space should give out radio waves with a wavelength of twenty-one centimetres (a frequency of 1,420 MHz), and this wavelength could be detected from ground level on Earth. This radiation was first successfully detected in 1951, and since then the hydrogen gas in our galaxy has been mapped in detail.

Because the radio emission is a line of twenty-one centimetre wavelength (not a continuous spectrum), radio astronomers can measure the Doppler effect, the change in wavelength of the line due to the motion of the gas. Using this effect combined with measurements of the strength of the radio signals from different directions in space, they have been able to show that nearly all the hydrogen gas in our galaxy lies in spiral arms in the galaxy disc, and practically none in the centre. There are other sources of radio emission in the galaxy too; continuous, or line emissions which have helped to build up a picture of what the galaxy is really like. In recent years, radio astronomers have discovered radio emission from molecules (groups of atoms joined together) in space. More than two dozen different molecules have now been identified, some of which are the basic building blocks for living matter!

Does our galaxy rotate?

Our galaxy does rotate round an axis perpendicular to the disc and passing through the centre. Stars and matter nearer the centre rotate in shorter periods than stars and matter further out. The Sun and nearby stars move in nearly circular paths round the galaxy centre, taking 225 million years to complete one revolution (this period is sometimes called the Cosmic Year). It means that the Sun is moving round the galaxy at a speed of some 250 kilometres per second. All the other stars nearby are being carried round at more or less the same speed, too. Globular clusters rotate round the galaxy centre in elliptical paths, tilted to the galaxy plane.

233

What are the Magellanic Clouds?

The Magellanic Clouds are two small galaxies which are satellites of our one, just as the Moon is a satellite of the Earth. They were first recorded by the navigator and explorer, Ferdinand Magellan, during his circumnavigation of the world in 1519. They are clearly visible to the naked eye in the southern hemisphere, and look rather like detached bits of the Milky Way, but in fact they are too far south to be seen from Europe or North America. There are two of these 'clouds'; the Large Magellanic Cloud measures about eight degrees across as seen in the sky, and the Small Magellanic Cloud is about half that size. They are about 160,000 light years away, and they are also much smaller than our galaxy, some 25,000 and 10,000 light years across, respectively.

Both are rather irregular in shape, though the Large Cloud shows some signs of being a type of galaxy known as a barred spiral. The Large Cloud is a fascinating object as it contains many very bright Population I stars (very hot, bright blue stars), galactic clusters, gas, dust and bright nebulae.

The largest emission nebula known, the Tarantula Nebula, lies within the Large Cloud, and the extremely luminous star S Doradus (which is a million times as bright as our Sun) is also there. There are also globular clusters in the Large Cloud, but unlike the globulars round our galaxy, these contain very young, bright blue stars. It looks as though the stars in the cloud are, on average, younger than those in our galaxy.

It was by studying Cepheid variables in the Small Magellanic Cloud that Henrietta Leavitt was able to show that there was a relationship between the periods and the brightness of these stars. This enabled them to be used to help find out all kinds of distances in the universe.

Above: The Large Magellanic Cloud. It is about 25,000 light years in extent and it is classified as a satellite galaxy of our own.

Are there other galaxies beyond our own?

With present day telescopes, thousands of millions of galaxies can be seen beyond our own. It was only in 1923 that it was finally proved that other galaxies do lie beyond our system, for in that year the distance of the Andromeda galaxy was measured and shown to be far beyond the edge of our galaxy. William Herschel, in the eighteenth century, suggested that some of the objects which were called nebulae might in fact be 'island universes' like our galaxy, but until the distance to one of these things could be discovered there was no definite proof, and many astronomers believed that our galaxy contained all the stars in the universe.

The galaxies take all sorts of shapes and forms. Some are spiral, like our own (the Andromeda Galaxy is of this kind), others are elliptical (oval) in shape, while some are irregular, with no particular shape at all (like the Small Magellanic Cloud). They are generally smaller and fainter than our galaxy which seems to be a rather bright one. The Andromeda galaxy is thought to be slightly bigger than our own. We see galaxies in every direction in space, except in the plane of the Milky Way where they are hidden by interstellar dust, and the further we look into space, the more galaxies we see. The most distant galaxies we can see so far are more than 5,000 million light years away.

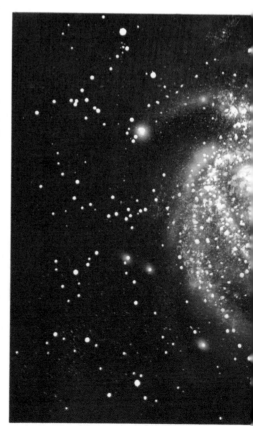

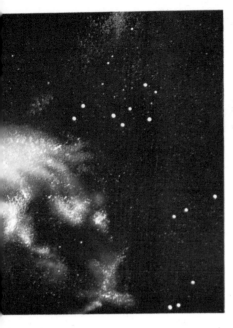

Above right: The galaxy in Sculptor. This is situated millions of times farther away then the most distant star we can see!

Below: NGC 6946. This is an example of a regular galaxy, or loose spiral.

How many planets are in a galaxy?

Nobody knows the answer to this question. The only planets we know much about are the nine making up the solar system. However, present theories on how the solar system was formed suggest that planets may be very common indeed, and that most stars may have them. There are a number of reasons for thinking that very hot stars (of types O, B, A) will not have planets, but stars of types F, G, and K are quite likely to have some, and possibly main sequence red dwarf stars may have them too. If these ideas are true, then there are thousands of millions of stars of the right type in our galaxy and there may well be many thousands of millions of planets!

The trouble is that we cannot see planets of other stars; they are too tiny, too faint, and too far away to be seen with any telescope yet built. However, for nearby stars there is a way to detect massive planets. A star and a massive planet will revolve round their centre of mass, so that if we observe the way the star moves through space then it should just be possible to see the star wobbling from side to side and to work out the size of planet responsible. This has been done for several nearby stars and in one case, Barnard's star, two planets have been found.

How can we tell a galaxy from a nebula?

Many nebulae and galaxies look very similar when seen through a telescope, so astronomers were not sure for a long time that William Herschel was right when he suggested that other galaxies existed. One way to tell them apart is to take photographs with very large telescopes which will be able to show individual stars in nearby galaxies. But another way is to use a spectroscope. Since nebulae are luminous gas clouds they have a spectrum consisting of bright lines. The spectrum of a galaxy will be a continuous one with dark lines (because it combines the spectra of thousands of millions of stars), and so will look quite different from that of a nebula.

Do all the galaxies look the same as ours?

Each galaxy is different in appearance, but it is possible to pick out basic types of galaxy and so classify them. Hubble divided galaxies into three main types; elliptical, spiral, and irregular. Elliptical galaxies look in some ways rather like overgrown globular clusters, and Hubble classed these according to how elliptical (how flattened) they were. Spherical galaxies he called EO, galaxies which bulged out a little at their 'equators' were E1, and very squashed galaxies were labelled E7.

There are two types of spiral galaxies; normal spirals like our own (where the spiral arms spread out from a central nucleus), and barred spirals (where the arms spread out from what looks like a bar of stars and matter running through the nucleus). No one knows why this bar shape arises. Hubble split up the normal spirals into Sa, where the arms are tightly wound round the nucleus, Sb where they are more open, and Sc where the arms are spread out wide and loose. Our galaxy is of type Sb. The barred spirals are classed SBa, SBb, SBc in the same way.

Irregular galaxies have no particular shape, no nucleus and no spiral arms. An example of this kind of galaxy is the Magellanic Clouds. They are usually quite small and faint. There are, too, dwarf galaxies, which are the most common of all but difficult to detect because they are so faint (often less than one per cent of the mass of our galaxy) and a number of special types, such as Seyfert galaxies which have very bright compact centres.

Right: An example of possible colliding galaxies.

Left: The Whirlpool Galaxy is an example of a spiral galaxy. This was the first to be identified as a spiral and is at a distance of 37 million light years.

Below left: NGC 3034 in Ursa Major is an irregular galaxy. It is 10 million light years away and is a strong radio source.

Below: A diagram to show how Hubble classified the galaxies. Sa, Sb and Sc are spirals; SBa, SBb and SBc are barred spirals.

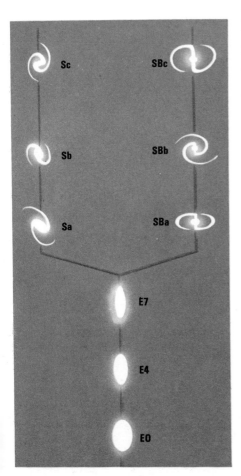

Do all galaxies contain the same number of stars as ours?

It is difficult to tell how many stars there are in a galaxy. Ours is thought to contain at least 100,000 million. Some galaxies contain more. For example, the giant elliptical galaxy M87 contains nearly a million million. At the other end of the scale there are dwarf galaxies containing only a few million. Some galaxies contain a higher proportion of stars than others. In our galaxy, 80 to 90 per cent of the mass is made up of stars, the rest of gas and dust. Many of the elliptical galaxies contain little or no gas, and are made up almost entirely of old stars of Population II. This also applies to some irregulars but there are some galaxies where there is more gas than stars.

Are all the galaxies the same age?

The galaxies seem to be of different ages, although we cannot be certain about this. It seems likely that galaxies with a great deal of gas and few stars are fairly young, while stars with no gas and lots of stars are probably older. Giant elliptical galaxies with no gas must be in a state where all the original gas has been converted into stars, and the lack of bright blue O,B stars implies that all the massive stars have already gone through their life cycles and ended up as white dwarfs, neutron stars or whatever.

However, the picture may not be as simple as this. It is quite possible that stars may have formed at a faster rate in elliptical galaxies than they have done in spirals such as our own, so that the lack of gas may not necessarily mean that they are actually older in terms of years. Much work remains to be done, but it does seem as if our own galaxy is about 10,000 million years old, roughly twice the age of the Sun.

Do we know how the universe began?

This is still one of the greatest mysteries in astronomy, but astronomers do have some theories to try and explain how the universe began, how it developed, and what is likely to happen in the future. (The branch of astronomy which deals with these problems is called cosmology.) Since the galaxies are rushing away from each other, it seems quite obvious that they must have been closer together, and if we go far enough back in the past, the galaxies may have been lumped together in one place. In the 1930s a Belgian, George Lemaître, suggested that all the matter in the universe was originally (perhaps more than 20,000 million years ago) contained in one tiny, incredibly dense lump which he called the 'primeval atom'. There would have been enough matter, he thought, to make up a hundred, thousand million galaxies. This, he thought, must have exploded, scattering in all directions, eventually forming the galaxies we now see.

Most astronomers at present believe that something similar to this must have happened; that the universe was formed in a 'Big-Bang' many thousands of millions of years ago. When all the matter in the universe was packed together it must have been in the form of an unbelievably hot fireball containing a lot of radiation and matter. After the explosion, as matter hurtled outwards and cooled down, galaxies began to form, then stars and planets formed in the galaxies. The radiation from the fireball, if this theory is right, should also have spread through the universe and should still be seen today as very weak microwave radiation. In recent years, this radiation seems to have been discovered by several groups of astronomers.

If the universe is expanding, then because of gravity the galaxies must be slowing down. It is possible that they may eventually stop, in which case gravity will cause them to rush together until they are all lumped together again. Some astronomers believe that another big bang will then occur and the universe will expand once more. This idea is called the oscillating universe theory.

Another theory suggested about 25 years ago by Bondi, Gold, and Hoyle, was the Steady-State theory. They said it was possible that the universe never had a beginning, and will never have an end. As the galaxies moved apart, new galaxies were created to take their place, so that, although individual galaxies changed, the appearance of the universe always remained the same. If this theory were correct, then new matter must be continously created in space. (However, the amount necessary is far too small to be measured.) Nowadays, very few astronomers think this idea is the right one, but we cannot be sure that the Big-Bang theory is right either.

Right: The theory of the origin of the universe according to Bondi, Hoyle and Gold in the 1940s. The Steady-State Theory suggests that there never was a beginning and that matter is being constantly created. Although galaxies do move away from each other as time goes by, new galaxies form in the space between them, so that generally the distance between galaxies remains about the same. In other words, the overall appearance of the universe does not change.

How old is the universe?

If, as many people believe, the universe began as a Big-Bang, we can work out when this happened. If we know how fast galaxies are moving, and how far away they are, all we need to do is divide their distances by their speeds, and we will know how long it is since they were all lumped together. If the value of Hubble's constant, $H = 100$ km/sec/Mpc, is right, then the age of the universe is about 10,000 million years. Some recent measurements make it a little older than that, but it certainly *seems* to be between ten and twenty thousand million years old.

Right: The distances (R) of galaxies are measured by the scale along the bottom of the diagram, where each unit equals 1,000 million light years. The red shift (Z), which galaxies at these distances may have, is shown by the vertical scale. For example, a galaxy 5,000 million light years away will have Z which equals 0.75, while a galaxy 8,000 million light years away will have Z equal to about 2.2.

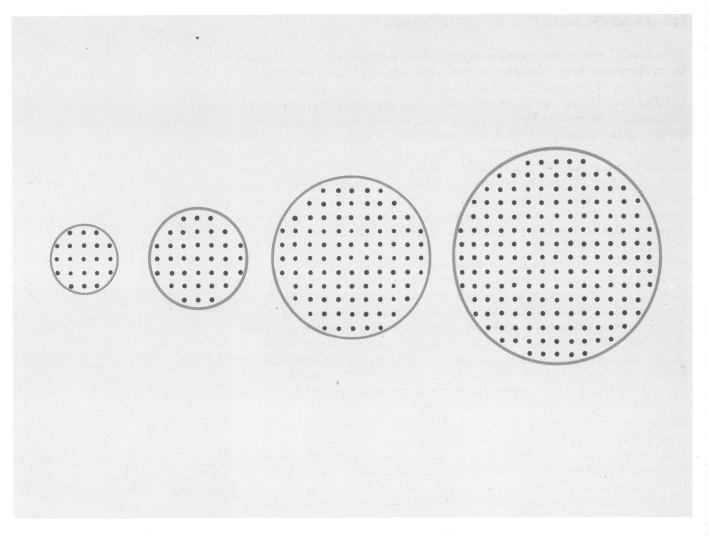

How big is the universe?

Ideas on the size of the universe have changed a great deal since the days of the early civilizations, when the Earth was thought to lie at the centre of the universe. Thomas Digges suggested, as far back as the seventeenth century, that the universe was infinite; that it continued in every direction forever. William Herschel's measurements showed that the galaxy was at least 7,500 light years in extent, but more recent results show it is nearly 100,000 light years in diameter.

The distance to another galaxy, M31 in Andromeda, was measured in 1923, and we now know it is 2,200,000 light years from us. Nowadays we can see galaxies which we think are more than 5,000 million light years away, and radio telescopes show objects which seem to be even further away.

Measuring distances like these is very difficult indeed. One way is to measure a galaxy's red-shift and use Hubble's law to say how far it must be to be moving as fast as it is. In this way astronomers have shown that certain objects (quasars) may be more than 8,000 million light years distant. If the Big-Bang theory is right, the universe may not be much more than 10,000 million light years in radius. However, we still of course cannot be sure that it does not continue forever in all directions.

What are quasars?

Quasars are most mysterious objects. Their name stands for 'quasi-stellar radio sources'; in other words, sources of radio waves which look rather like stars. They are extremely powerful sources of infra-red, light and radio radiation. Quasars were discovered in 1960 when a radio source measured at Cambridge and known as 3C48 was shown to coincide in position with what looked like a faint blue star. The spectrum of this 'star' turned out to be very odd. In 1963, Martin Schmidt studied the quasar 3C273, which again looked like a peculiar blue star, and carefully analyzed its spectrum. He found that the spectral lines had very large red-shifts which explained their peculiar appearance. If this red-shift was caused by the expansion of the universe, then 3C273 must be very far away indeed and certainly could not be an ordinary star.

Since that time, hundreds of quasars have been studied and some of them seem to be moving very fast indeed, nearly 90 per cent of the speed of light in some cases. Using the accepted value of Hubble's constant, this means that the quasars with the biggest red-shifts are nearly 9,000 million light years away. The most baffling thing about quasars is that if they are as far away as this, they must be emitting a hundred times as much energy as our galaxy. They are tremendously bright, yet seem to be very small. For one thing they look like stars, and furthermore many of them vary in brightness in periods of less than a year (a few weeks in some cases). An object cannot vary in brightness in a period much less than the time taken for a ray of light to travel across it. This means that some quasars are less than a light year across, yet they still emit more light than a hundred galaxies! Astronomers have still not been able to explain how quasars could be such powerful objects.

Some astronomers have suggested that they are not at vast distances at all, but that they are quite near our galaxy. It has also been suggested that they may be material hurled at very high speed from our galaxy in the past. However, this seems fairly unlikely, and no other nearby galaxies have objects flying out of them in this way. It is possible, though, that not all of the red-shift in a quasar's spectrum is caused by its speed. Recently the American astronomer, Arp, has observed a few examples of quasars apparently attached to normal galaxies by bridges of matter. Although this suggests that the quasar and the galaxy are at the same distance from us, their red-shifts are different. One explanation could be that part of the red-shift is due to strong gravitational fields.

What is the most distant 'galaxy' known?

It is difficult to answer a question like this and be sure that one is really being accurate, because new discoveries are continually being made. Certainly one of the most distant galaxies is 3C295 (in the constellation Boötes), rather more than 5,000 million light years away. At the time of writing the most distant quasar is 0Q172, whose red-shift is 3·5. This means that spectral lines will be seen to have wavelengths 4·5 times longer than they would have if the object were standing still. This indicates a speed of recession of 91 per cent of the speed of light and a distance of over 9,000 million light years (using the normal value of H).

Above: Quasar 3C273 studied in 1963 by Martin Schmidt. It is well known as an X-ray source as well as a source of radio radiation.

Right: Red shifts on this graph (Z) are shown against the apparent magnitude of quasars. The shape of the line drawn should help us to decide which of the three main theories of the origin of the universe is correct. A represents the Oscillating Universe Theory, B the Big-Bang Theory and C the Steady-State Theory. It has already been suggested, however, that more information is needed before we know the correct answer.

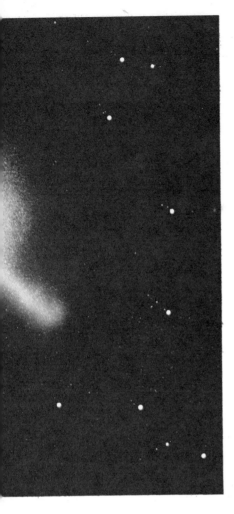

Will the universe expand forever?

If the 'Steady-State' theory were right, then we should expect the universe to continue to expand forever as individual galaxies move apart and new ones form. On the 'Big-Bang' theory, there are two possibilities; either the expansion continues forever, or it eventually stops, and the universe then contracts as the Oscillating Universe idea suggests. The expansion of the universe must slow down because of the gravitational effect of each galaxy on every other one, but it will only stop if the amount of matter in the universe is greater than a certain limit.

The problem is that we do not know how much matter there is in the universe. We can see the galaxies, and can estimate approximately how much matter there is, provided that all the matter in the universe is in the form of galaxies. However, recent observations suggest that there may be a lot of invisible matter between the galaxies. For example, clusters of galaxies exist whose members are moving too fast for the cluster to be stable, unless hidden matter also exists in these clusters. More observations will be required before this question can be answered.

How can we tell which theory of the universe is correct?

The Steady-State theory says a) that the numbers of galaxies in a given volume of space (the density of galaxies) is the same everywhere in the universe, b) that the rate at which galaxies are moving should increase steadily with distance (double the distance and you double the speed) and c) that we should see old and young galaxies in every part of the universe.

On the other hand, both the Big-Bang and the Oscillating Universe theories require a) that galaxies were closer together in the past and so, since we see distant galaxies as they used to be thousands of millions of years ago, distant galaxies should be packed closer together than nearby ones; b) that distant galaxies should be moving apart faster than nearby ones (again because they would have been moving faster in the past) and c) that we should see more young galaxies at very large distances than nearby, because all the galaxies would have been younger in the past.

It should be easy to show which theory is wrong by making the right kinds of observations of distant galaxies. However, these observations are extremely difficult to make. Careful counts of the numbers of radio galaxies and quasars of different brightnesses and the numbers of galaxies with different red-shifts show that the universe was different in the past from its appearance today. This means that the Steady-State idea cannot be right.

The observations which really well and truly sealed the fate of the Steady-State theory were those of the so-called microwave background radiation. If the universe began in a big bang, then even today, we should be able to pick up faint traces of the radiation that was left over from the original fireball. The first observations of this were made in 1965 by Penzias and Wilson, and later observations seem to agree.

Whether or not the Big-Bang theory or the Oscillating Universe idea is correct we cannot yet tell. The future may yet show that none of our theories is right!

Above: Sputnik 1 from Russia, the world's first artificial satellite, launched in 1957.

When was the first artificial Satellite launched?

The first artificial satellite was the Russian Sputnik 1, which was launched 4 October 1957. It weighed eighty-four kilos and was a spherical object sixty centimetres in diameter, with four aerials sticking out, and it carried a radio transmitter. Its orbit round the Earth was an ellipse with a maximum height above ground level of 946 kilometres (this point in its orbit is called apogee) and a minimum height of 229 kilometres (perigee). Moving along at nearly eight kilometres per second (almost 29,000 kilometres per hour) it travelled round the Earth in a period of ninety-six minutes. It was not high enough to be completely free of the thinnest traces of the Earth's atmosphere and so was affected by friction with the air as it moved along. As a result of this it spiralled into the atmosphere and was burned up on 4 January 1958.

Who was the first man in space?

The first man to go into space was the Russian, Major Yuri Gagarin. On 12 April 1961 he made one complete orbit of the Earth in the spacecraft Vostok 1, then returning to Earth and landing by parachute 108 minutes after take off. The maximum height above ground reached in this flight was 327 kilometres. The rocket for this first manned spaceflight weighed about 400 tonnes at launch and Vostok 1 itself nearly five tonnes. During his orbit of the Earth, Gagarin became the first man to experience weightlessness for any length of time and he suffered no ill-effects. (Weightlessness can be experienced for short periods in aircraft if they are made to fly on a precisely curved path). Tragically, he was killed in a plane crash in 1969.

The following month, on 5 May 1961, the American Alan Shepard made an 'up and down' flight to an altitude of 185 kilometres in a spacecraft of the Mercury type called 'Freedom 7'. It was not until 20 February 1962 that an American, John Glenn, made a true orbital flight round the Earth in the spacecraft 'Friendship 7'. He made three orbits, taking four hours fifty-five minutes in all. Meantime, the Russian craft Vostok 2 had been launched on 8 August 1961. With Herman Titov as pilot, it made a total of seventeen revolutions of the Earth, reaching a maximum height of 257 kilometres, and taking twenty-five hours eighteen minutes in all. The first woman astronaut was Valentina Tereshkova, who piloted Vostok 6 in 1963.

Above: Major Yuri Gagarin, the first man to go into space.

Right: This diagram shows how an artificial satellite must be launched. Even if a tower could be built so big that it rose above the Earth's atmosphere the satellite's orbit would depend on the initial speed. If this were too slow (A or B), then the vehicle would soon hit the ground. At its correct speed (C), of 8 kilometres per second, it would stay in its orbital path.

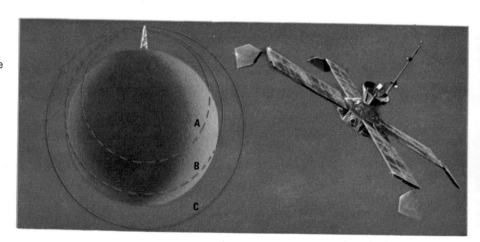

Above: An astronaut floating in space.

Above right: This was one of the most exciting moments in space exploration; Edwin Aldrin walks off across the Moon for the first time. The small picture on the right (*inset*) shows the special camera the astronauts used.

Who was the first man on the Moon?

The first man to set foot on the Moon was the American astronaut, Neil Armstrong, who did so at 2.56 GMT on 21 July 1969. He was joined later by Colonel Edwin Aldrin. They had landed in a fairly smooth part of the Moon on one of the dark plains called the Sea of Tranquillity, in a spidery-looking craft called a lunar module and named 'Eagle'. The preparations for the landing had taken many years from the Mercury and Gemini Earth orbit missions to the Apollo programme. In December 1968 Apollo 8 had gone into orbit around the Moon at an altitude of 110 kilometres with Frank Borman, James Lovell and William Anders as crew. However, they were not equipped for a landing, and after ten orbits fired their rocket motors to take them out of lunar orbit and they returned safely to Earth.

Apollo 9 tested the lunar module in Earth's orbit, then in May 1969, Apollo 10, crewed by Tom Stafford, Eugene Cernan and John Young went into orbit round the Moon. Stafford and Cernan then took the lunar module down to within sixteen kilometres of the Moon's surface, taking close-up photographs and testing out the systems of the lunar module. They then rejoined Young, who was orbiting 110 kilometres up in the command module, and returned to Earth. It was only after all these tests that Apollo 11 was able to go ahead for a landing. (Michael Collins remained in orbit with the command module while Armstrong and Aldrin carried out the landing.)

The Apollo programme continued until 1972, when the last one, Apollo 17, successfully completed its mission. Only Apollo 13 failed to land because of an explosion on board on the outward flight.

How does a satellite stay in orbit round the Earth?

The explanation of this goes back to Newton. In his great book, the *Principia* (where he explained his theory of gravity), he pointed out that if you could build a high enough tower, and throw something fast enough parallel to the horizon from the top of it, then that object would travel right round the Earth, and would continue to do so forever, unless something stopped it.

Imagine you are standing on top of such a tower. If you throw a stone parallel to the horizon, it will fall to the ground, but because of the speed at which you threw it, it will land some distance from the foot of the tower. If you throw another one faster it will land further away, and if you could throw an object at exactly eight kilometres per second, it would never reach the ground but travel round the Earth in a circular orbit. All the time, the Earth's gravity is attracting a satellite and making it fall towards the Earth but, because of its high speed parallel to the horizon, the satellite never gets nearer the surface. Instead its path is bent into a circle round the Earth. If the Earth's gravity did not exist, the satellite would simply fly off into space in a straight line.

The speed that a satellite needs to stay in orbit depends on its distance from the Earth. Close to the surface, a satellite must travel at eight kilometres per second, while at a distance of 25,000 kilometres from the centre of the Earth (nearly 19,000 kilometres above the surface) only half that speed is needed. The Moon, at a distance of 384,000 kilometres only needs to move at about one kilometre per second in its orbit. The further away the satellite, the longer it will take to complete an orbit.

For example, a satellite close to the Earth's surface will take about ninety minutes to complete its orbit, while the Moon takes 27·3 days. A satellite moving in a circular orbit 42,000 kilometres from the centre of the Earth will take twenty-four hours to revolve round the Earth, exactly the same time as the Earth requires to spin on its axis. Therefore the satellite will appear to stand still in the sky when seen from the Earth. This distance is used by communications satellites so that transmissions can be sent at any time.

What is escape velocity?

Escape velocity is the minimum speed that a spacecraft needs if it is to continue to travel away from the Earth, and never return. Again, think about throwing things from a tall tower. We know that a stone thrown parallel to the horizon at eight kilometres per second will travel right round the Earth in a circular orbit. If we throw the stone faster than this, it will move in an ellipse, reaching a maximum distance from the Earth (apogee) and with a minimum distance (perigee) equal to the height of the tower. It will then continue to orbit the Earth in this elliptical path. The faster we throw the stone the greater will be the apogee distance until, if we throw it at eleven kilometres per second, it will move outwards, and never return. This speed is called escape velocity. Because of the Earth's gravitational pull, the spacecraft will slow down as it moves away, but it will never fall back again. In order to get anywhere in a reasonable length of time, interplanetary probes are fired rather faster than this (at hyperbolic velocity).

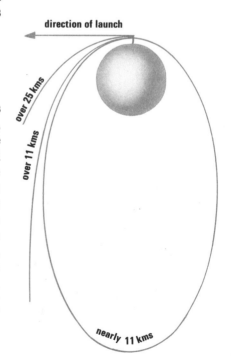

Below: A space vehicle moves round the Earth in an elliptical orbit if it moves at 8 to 11 kilometres per second. If the speed exceeds 11 kilometres per second, the vehicle will leave the Earth and enter into an orbit round the Sun.

direction of launch

over 25 kms

over 11 kms

nearly 11 kms

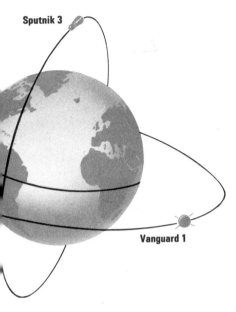

Vanguard 1

What is a transfer orbit?

A transfer orbit is the path taken by a spacecraft to go from one body to another; for example, from the Earth to Mars. If rockets had unlimited power, and could keep their engines running continuously, they would be able to travel very quickly on straight paths to their targets. However, this is not so. Present-day rockets use up almost all their fuel in a few minutes, and must build up enough speed in that time to let them coast along without power for the rest of the journey. They therefore have to follow paths which take longer and use as little fuel as possible.

In order to reach Mars, for example, a spacecraft must be fired in the same direction as the Earth itself is moving round the Sun. The speed of the spacecraft (after 'escape' from the Earth) is then added to the speed of the Earth and so the spacecraft moves round the Sun on an elliptical orbit which takes it further out from the Sun. If the sums have been correctly done, it will cross the orbit of Mars just when Mars reaches the crossing point!

Above: The orbit of the U.S. Vanguard was near the equator, while the larger Russian Sputnik 3 entered a polar orbit.

Right: It is not economical to send a rocket on its shortest route to a target, for this uses up too much fuel. To reach Mars a probe is speeded up so that it swings out in an elliptical orbit in the same direction as the Earth is moving round the Sun. A represents the transfer orbit which is longer, but most economical. B is the quicker, direct, but most expensive route.

Below: A Mariner space probe.

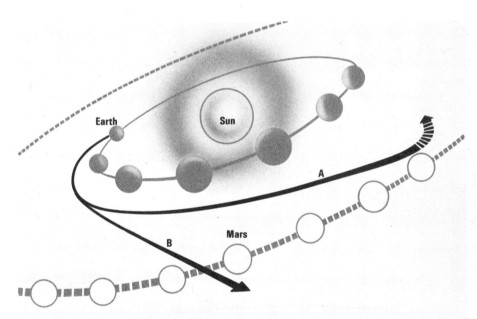

Earth
Sun
A
B
Mars

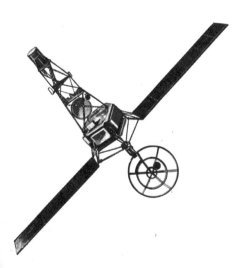

Which was the first successful interplanetary space probe?

The first successful interplanetary probe (excluding Moon probes) was the American craft, Mariner 2. Launched on 17 August 1962, it passed within 35,000 kilometres of the planet Venus on 14 December of that year, sending back detailed information about conditions there. The results came as a surprise to most astronomers who had not expected that the surface temperature would be about 450°C. On the other hand, many astronomers had expected that Venus would have a strong magnetic field, but Mariner showed this was not so. In order to reach Venus, Mariner had to be fired in the opposite direction to the Earth's motion so that it ended up moving slower than the Earth. This caused it to move in closer to the Sun on an elliptical path which intercepted Venus four months later.

Index